EDUCATIONAL LEAVES FOR EMPLOYEES

*European Experience
for American Consideration*

A REPORT FOR THE CARNEGIE COUNCIL
ON POLICY STUDIES IN HIGHER EDUCATION

Konrad von Moltke
Norbert Schneevoigt

EDUCATIONAL LEAVES
FOR EMPLOYEES

European Experience
for American Consideration

Jossey-Bass Publishers
San Francisco • Washington • London • 1977

EDUCATIONAL LEAVES FOR EMPLOYEES
European Experience for American Consideration
The Carnegie Council on Policy Studies in Higher Education

The Carnegie Council on Policy Studies in Higher Education,
2150 Shattuck Avenue, Berkeley, California 94704, has sponsored
preparation of this report as part of a continuing effort to
obtain and present significant information for public discussion.
The views expressed are those of the authors.

Copies are available from Jossey-Bass, San Francisco,
for the United States, and Possessions, and for Canada,
Australia, New Zealand, and Japan.
Copies for the rest of the world are available from
Jossey-Bass, London.
Library of Congress Catalogue Card Number LC 76-50725

International Standard Book Number ISBN 0-87589-316-3

Manufactured in the United States of America

DESIGN BY WILLI BAUM

FIRST EDITION

Code 7712

The Carnegie Council Series

The Federal Role in Postsecondary
Education: Unfinished Business,
1975-1980
*The Carnegie Council on Policy
Studies in Higher Education*

More than Survival: Prospects
for Higher Education in a
Period of Uncertainty
*The Carnegie Foundation for
the Advancement of Teaching*

Making Affirmative Action Work
in Higher Education: An Analysis
of Institutional and Federal
Policies with Recommendations
*The Carnegie Council on Policy
Studies in Higher Education*

Presidents Confront Reality:
From Edifice Complex to
University Without Walls
*Lyman A. Glenny, John R. Shea,
Janet H. Ruyle, Kathryn H. Freschi*

Progress and Problems in Medical
and Dental Education: Federal
Support Versus Federal Control
*The Carnegie Council on Policy
Studies in Higher Education*

Low or No Tuition: The Feasibility
of a National Policy for the
First Two Years of College
*The Carnegie Council on Policy
Studies in Higher Education*

Managing Multicampus Systems:
Effective Administration in an
Unsteady State
Eugene C. Lee, Frank M. Bowen

Challenges Past, Challenges
Present: An Analysis of
American Higher Education
Since 1930
David D. Henry

The States and Higher
Education: A Proud Past
and a Vital Future
*The Carnegie Foundation for
the Advancement of Teaching*

Educational Leaves for Employees:
European Experience for American
Consideration
*Konrad von Moltke
Norbert Schneevoigt*

Contents

Foreword

Lifelong learning is a growing aspect of all advanced industrial nations, and the prospect is that it will keep on growing indefinitely into the future. The United States historically has led in provision of classroom opportunities for recurrent education for adults, but it has recently fallen behind in the financing of leaves to take advantage of these opportunities. Several nations have now moved out in front and they are the new pioneers. What have they done? What can we learn from them?

The opening of Britain's Open University in the fall of 1971 aroused widespread interest in the United States and led to the development of a variety of nontraditional study programs, such as Empire State College in New York, which have been extensively studied and evaluated. Another significant development of the 1970s has been a succession of proposals for financing lifelong learning—some sweeping in their scope and others much more limited and narrowly defined—from the Carnegie Commission's tentative suggestion for "two years in the bank" in its 1971 report, *Less Time, More Options,* to the modest proposal recently introduced in the Massachusetts legislature for a voucher system to provide tuition costs for low-income adults with relatively little previous education. Also modest, but perhaps opening the door to eventual involvement of the federal government on a more extensive scale, was the lifelong learning bill introduced by Senator (now Vice President) Walter Mondale in the fall of 1975. Enacted as part of the Education Amendments of 1976, it provides $10 million to states to encourage use of existing facilities for lifelong learning programs.

The present volume is concerned with a different, though clearly related, series of developments—the evolution of paid educational leave programs for workers in Western Europe. Among these, and by far the best known in this country, is the French scheme, which was enacted into law in July 1971, and which is extensively analyzed here along with paid educational leave provisions in three other countries. These other countries are West Germany, where there are provisions for paid educational leave in four of the *Länder* (states); Italy, where the provisions have been developed under collective bargaining agreements negotiated by some of the stronger unions; and Sweden, where the provisions for paid educational leave are embodied in a group of three interrelated laws enacted in 1974 and 1975. Examined more briefly are similar developments in Austria, Belgium, the Netherlands, Norway, and the United Kingdom.

This is not the first extensive study of European paid educational leave programs, but we believe it is the first to place its primary emphasis on the *effects* of these schemes, rather than on a discussion of their provisions. What are the characteristics of the workers who participate? Are their leaves short-term or long-term in duration? Is the education or training they receive predominantly vocational, or does the scheme encourage enrollment in general education or culturally oriented courses? Do workers enjoy considerable freedom of choice in the selection of types of education or training, or do employers dominate the workers' choices?

The authors show that the development of paid educational leave programs in Western Europe was more in the nature of a "next step" in the evolution of postwar labor market policy than a radical departure from previous policy. The schemes must be viewed, moreover, in the context of labor market and social policy and not primarily "as an educational venture." For the most part, they have had little or no effect on educational institutions, with the possible exception of some impact on the lower secondary schools in Italy. Workers' educational leaves have been predominantly very short-term in duration and have been very largely oriented toward participation in vocational courses closely related to the individual worker's occupation. Employers have had considerable influence on who gets leave and what kinds of courses are pursued, although here again Italy constitutes something of an exception.

Probably one of the study's most important conclusions—and the one most relevant to the American scene—is that, in the absence of strong trade union pressure, paid educational leave programs would not have been adopted in Western Europe. In fact, say the authors, "employers' organizations and trade unions throughout Europe have steadily developed their arguments for and against educational leave over the last ten years."

This type of debate has been notably absent from the American scene, at least as a national phenomenon, although a few unions have negotiated provisions for paid educational leave in their collective bargaining contracts. Employer-sponsored programs that provide tuition assistance are also widespread, especially in the larger companies, but for the most part these do not provide for paid leave during working hours except for technical, professional, or managerial personnel who are taking work-related courses not available outside working hours.

Why has there been no national labor union drive for paid educational leave along European lines? The answer, I believe, is that the American labor movement has had other priorities. In contrast with virtually every other industrial country, the United States does not have a comprehensive national health insurance system, and this has been high on labor's list of priorities for some time. Under conditions prevailing in the fall of 1976, moreover, a more effective program to combat unemployment takes precedence over other objectives. This is also largely true at present for the union movement in Western Europe, where unemployment is a serious problem for the first time in many years.

We can surely anticipate a gradual spread of collectively bargained provisions for paid educational leave, but the launching of a sustained national union drive for either collectively bargained or federally legislated provisions of this type may be some years away. And other initiatives toward increasing opportunity for recurrent education could well turn out to be more important. The paths to increased opportunity are many, and they are not mutually exclusive. They can take the form of a limited voucher proposal, as proposed in Massachusetts, a more comprehensive federal scheme of lifelong drawing rights (the "two years in the bank" type of proposal), or extension of nontraditional study programs. The Carnegie Council will be developing a report on these options in the near future.

The most difficult challenge is how to overcome the problem inherent in all adult education programs—that those with the most limited earlier education are least likely to participate in adult education. As the present work makes clear, European paid educational leave programs have not made much progress toward combating this problem as yet, although the Swedish program holds out considerable promise in this respect for the future.

This study was conducted for the Carnegie Council by the Institute of Education of the European Cultural Foundation, with its headquarters in Paris. We are most grateful for the cooperation of the Institute and also for the cooperation of several other organizations in individual countries that aided the principal investigator by providing expert knowledge and assistance in conducting the necessary interviews. Especially fortunate was the central involvement of Konrad von Moltke at all stages of the study, and of his able co-author, Norbert Schneevoigt, in the preparation of the final manuscript. Currently director of the Institute for European Environmental Policy of the European Cultural Foundation, located in Bonn, von Moltke not only is a leading European expert on higher education but also has an exceptional command of languages—clearly a special asset for the present comparative study.

CLARK KERR
Chairman
Carnegie Council on Policy
Studies in Higher Education

The Authors

Since 1976 Konrad von Moltke has been director of the Institute for European Environmental Policy in Bonn, which provides assistance to parliaments in Europe in matters of environmental policy. He has been associated with the Education Institute of the European Foundation since its founding in 1974. In the United States, he was a staff member of the Assembly on University Goals and Governance of the American Academy of Arts and Sciences in 1969–70. Between 1972 and 1974 he was a consultant to the Organization for Economic Cooperation and Development (OECD) on educational policy and planning: he was an examiner in the OECD reviews of national educational policy for Norway (as rapporteur) and Austria.

Von Moltke received a BA in mathematics from Dartmouth College in 1964 and a Ph.D. in medieval history from the University of Göttingen in 1970. The most important influence on his work was exerted by Eugen Rosenstock-Huessy. From 1968 to 1972 he was an assistant professor of history at the State University of New York (SUNY) at Buffalo. During 1970 to 1972 he was the first director of the collegiate system at SUNY/Buffalo. Through this experience he became actively involved in educational reform and the processes of curriculum development. As an associate professor of History, he left SUNY/Buffalo on leave in 1972. From 1973 to 1976 he was director of the Curriculum-Gruppe Amerikakunde in der Amerikagesellschaft in Hamburg, an innovative approach to teacher-based curriculum development in Germany.

In areas other than educational policy, von Moltke has published historical works (*Siegmund von Dietrichstein,* 1970, and *Leopold Ranke: The Theory and Practice of History,* 1972, the latter with Georg G. Iggers) and works on American Studies for German high schools (*Arbeitsbuch Amerikakunde,* 1976 and *Bausteincurriculum Amerikakunde,* 1976).

Since returning to Europe in 1972, von Moltke has been actively involved in the analysis of European cultural policies and the development of nongovernmental European institutions.

Norbert Schneevoigt, born in 1945, studied economics and sociology at Johann Wolfgang Goethe University in Frankfurt am Main, Germany, from which he graduated in 1971 as "Diplom-Volkswirt." His special interests center on the history of social philosophy and the conditioning factors of modern consciousness, both from a social and individual point of view. He is engaged in a dissertation on innovation and education. In 1974 he participated in a technology study investigating possibilities to enhance the innovative potential of enterprises; his field of research concerned individuals as members of enterprises in the light of motivation-for-achievement theory.

Schneevoigt has gained educational experience as tutor in municipal adult education and at the University of Frankfurt. He pursued nondegree studies in his preferred subject areas at Stanford, California, in 1972–73. Working for the Paris Institute of Education of the European Cultural Foundation, he is presently involved in a comparative study on the employment problems of underqualified school-leavers.

EDUCATIONAL LEAVES
FOR EMPLOYEES

*European Experience
for American Consideration*

A REPORT FOR THE CARNEGIE COUNCIL
ON POLICY STUDIES IN HIGHER EDUCATION

1

Introduction: Educational Leaves for Employees

The research design employed for this study departs from previous practice in institutional investigations in comparative education. Three basic approaches become accepted practice in this field. The first, the international conference on a given topic, depends on prepared papers and the subsequent publication of the conference proceedings. The approach assumes that a major gathering of experts is a better means of crystallizing issues than is the simple process of collecting and editing papers. Often, however, the papers presented at the conference will still vary so much in both goals and quality that the investigation of central issues is frustrated.

The formation of an international working group, consisting of a number of experts adequate to cover all pertinent topical and regional variations is a second approach. Inherent problems are the amount of time required to integrate a diverse group into a working unit, the cost of travel, and the need for more time together than such a group of knowledgeable people can usually spare for the venture. Moreover, the approach requires a full-time coordinating staff if it is to produce results.

The subcontracting approach utilizes a number of decentralized, partially coordinated groups who receive subcontracts on a given problem. The resulting work is then edited or rewritten to produce a unified report. The problems here are the difficulty

in achieving uniformity among diverse groups and the wide variation in the quality of the reports produced. As a rule, it is extremely
difficult to ensure that the products of subcontracted work are
commensurate to the problem concerned; thus those responsible
for the synthesis may be forced to prepare it on a tenuous basis.

Various combinations of these three basic styles have been
tried in an attempt to eliminate their defects. An additional approach assigns the entire research task to one or more staff members, who must acquire the necessary information and expertise
by developing contacts in the various countries concerned. It is,
however, virtually impossible to acquire the requisite sources of
information and to assimilate large quantities of formal material
reflecting specific and different cultural and social backgrounds.

The approach we have adopted to the basic problems of gathering, analyzing, and synthesizing information from diverse countries is essentially a mixture of institutional and individual styles.
All the evidence indicates that the ultimate responsibility for the
synthesis of the information must lie with an individual or with a
very small group able to work continuously and closely together:
consequently, the research design must provide them with accurate
information and appropriate analyses of the situation in individual
countries and assist them in developing an adequate understanding of this information; for while the data may be accurate, it may
not necessarily be meaningful. This can be viewed as a learning
situation for those ultimately responsible for the synthesis. Such
assistance as can be acquired in the respective countries must provide those producing the synthesis with the necessary insight into
the national situation—information must be interpreted in national
context. The basic relationship should be one of teaching and learning rather than one construed in terms of providing a product or
information.

For the present study, the Institute of Education of the European Foundation contracted with an individual or group in each
of the four countries that were being given detailed attention—
France, Germany, Sweden, and Italy. The people chosen, it was
assumed, possessed a comprehensive and critical knowledge of
the issues involved. They were not expected to provide a specific
product, but they offered to introduce members of the institute's

staff to the issues relating to educational leave in their countries, to provide access to relevant research documents, and to evaluate and establish contacts with other institutions and individuals. Not the least of their contributions was to provide the institute's staff with an environment in which the issues of educational leave were being actively and critically discussed in the context of the individual countries among a working group of researchers. The absence of such an environment is one of the critical problems of comparative research in general; most research of this type tends to be undertaken in isolation from any such ongoing policy and research debate.

The institute's staff has benefited in this manner from the assistance of *Peuple et culture* in Paris, the *Arbeitsgruppe für empirische Bildungsforschung* in Heidelberg, the Institute of Sociology of the University of Milan (in particular, Danilo Giori and Carla Facchini), and Folke Albinson in Sweden. The fact that an individual rather than an institution was employed in Sweden is a first indication of the diversity of the four countries: in Sweden, it was impossible to identify a research institution that was not so intimately associated with the preparation of government policy during the period of the institute's study (February to October 1975) as to call into question its ability for independent critical evaluation of this policy. While Swedish policy initiatives are probably more carefully researched before implementation than those of any other country, parallel independent and follow-up research is surprisingly weak, often occurring only in the context of preparations for the next reform.

Representatives of these institutions and a number of other experts attended a seminar organized by the institute in early October 1975 to discuss a draft of the report. While we have shamelessly absorbed and incorporated the advice of these experts, as well as that of the more than one hundred other people we have consulted in the course of our work, we assume full responsibility for what we have made of their assistance.

2

What Is Educational Leave?

Comparing educational systems of different countries can be a tantalizing undertaking. Educational institutions reflect the history and the social and economic characteristics of a country. While it is true, sociologically speaking, that their functions are essentially comparable, and that solutions to particular problems tend to have a similar basic structure, the operation of these systems and their relative effectiveness depend at least as much on the national conditions under which they exist as on intrinsic characteristics, and they are therefore quite incomparable to one another.

The virtue of comparing educational systems is that such comparisons can reveal basic common factors in educational policy and can identify factors in individual national conditions that may be counteracting the expressed intent of policy makers. To do so, however, requires finding a solution to the problem of basic incomparability. Where national characteristics are particularly evident, or where developments are fragmentary, it may be impossible to undertake a direct comparison; one must resort to a theoretical construct, a *tertium comparationis* that may not correspond to conditions in any one country, as an analytical tool for understanding the general characteristics of national experience.

In recent years, the problem of comparability has come much

closer to resolution in what one might term the major fields of education, the initial "front-load" phases of primary, secondary, and higher education. Through a long series of studies, a reasonable understanding of the structure of systems of initial education in the developed countries has been achieved, together with an awareness of the main national factors influencing this structure in various countries. Accepted conventions of what is to be included under the terms *primary, secondary, tertiary,* and *higher* education by now exist, as well as reasonable guidelines for the preparation of statistical material—although smaller countries are more apt to adhere to them than larger ones because small countries tend to use international organizations as a source of expertise not available nationally and because they are more dependent on cooperation in general (OECD, 1972a; UNESCO, 1972).

No conventional definitions or guidelines exist, however, for the more "peripheral" areas of education—preschool education; to some extent, vocational education; and particularly adult, continuing, or permanent education. In these areas international comparisons are problematic not only because the applicable definitions have not yet been agreed on internationally but also because national policy often is neither systematic nor consistent. Therefore variations dependent on national and even regional characteristics can be very substantial.

Unfortunately, there has been a tendency in international comparative studies to disregard these definitional problems. The relevance of comparison is simply assumed without explicit regard to the fact that simple description or comparison that ignores national characteristics may not prove relevant at all. This is particularly so in the case of the complex of questions surrounding policy making in the areas of adult education. Two recent publications on educational leave reflect this tendency particularly vividly (OECD, 1975; European Bureau of Adult Education, 1975). It is true that definitional problems are an unsatisfactory research topic in themselves: they are only implicitly substantive and thus tend to circumscribe the validity of research conclusions in an oblique fashion. They can be considered a sign of immaturity; but the area of educational leave, in spite of much recent work, remains very immature.

Definitions of Educational Leave

There is no generally accepted international definition at present as to what constitutes educational leave. In its most simplistic meaning, an educational leave is that which is called an educational leave by the policy makers of a country. Thus France, Sweden, and four of the *Länder* of the German Federal Republic (Hamburg, Bremen, Niedersachsen, and Hessen) have forms of educational leave at present. Such an approach assumes, however, that the terms which translate into English as *educational leave* have comparable meanings in the contexts of different countries. The French have several terms (*congé éducatif, congé ouvrier, congé de formation, autorisation d'absence*) which must be translated as educational leave; the German word *Bildungsurlaub,* while a reasonable rendering, has several meanings depending on whether it is used legally, politically, or in research; in Swedish, *ledighet vid studier* has primarily a legal, and no pedagogic, meaning; the term *educational leave* has no current equivalent in Italian (see also Charnley, 1975, pp. 20–23). The definitional problem can be transformed into a fruitless linguistic exercise.

A more generally applicable definition underlies the resolutions adopted by the International Labor Organization (ILO) in 1974: educational leave is defined as "leave granted to a worker for educational purposes for a specified period during normal working hours with adequate financial entitlements."

Either the ILO definition or the simplistic equation of name with content is most likely to underlie discussion of educational leave in Europe.

In its work on educational leave, the Organization for Economic Cooperation and Development (OECD) fails to spell out which definition of educational leave it is basing its analyses on. The working documents are, however, visibly influenced by the organization's program area on recurrent education, the context in which educational leave is being considered (OECD, 1975). There is a strong emphasis on educational leave as an *individual* right of adults, whereas the ILO resolution restricts this right to educational leave to workers—that is, persons in dependent employment or seeking such employment—and thereby excludes housewives and the independently employed. The distinction is an important one: it can be viewed as separating an educational leave policy from a broader policy of recurrent education.

A further definition that incorporates certain programmatic elements is widely used in research in Germany: only education of political and social relevance to the participant, and not job-related or employer-initiated educational experiences, can be considered as educational leave (Görs, 1974, p. 154). This definition tends to include training of trade union representatives and to exclude all forms of in-service or vocational training.

For the purpose of this study, we will adopt a definition derived from the ILO definition. We will consider as educational leave the opportunity for dependent employees to participate in education or training during working hours without complete loss of pay and without loss of employment rights. We will study opportunities for educational leave in Europe without regard to the legal basis on which they exist.

A number of important considerations have entered into this definition. We have essentially accepted the ILO restriction to workers but have preferred the broader English rendering of the all-embracing French term *employé*. It seems unrealistic to speak of "leave" in connection with any other group. We have also altered the financial conditions proposed by the ILO. "With adequate financial entitlements" was adopted by the ILO drafting committee in preference to the more embracing "without loss of earnings or other benefits," the latter being effectively impossible to sustain in view of the complexity of pay structures in most countries. The new ILO definition, however, begs the question of what constitutes "adequate financial entitlements" and consequently fails to provide a criterion for deciding what might constitute educational leave. Like the ILO, we consider it immaterial whether remuneration of the worker on educational leave is on the basis of laws, labor contracts, or voluntary payments by the employer.

By referring specifically to education and training, we wish to ensure that considerations of program content—vocational or academic—do not enter into determining whether opportunities for educational leave exist. While we recognize that the nature of the educational experience depends to a significant extent on content, we do not believe that a satisfactory distinction can be made between vocational and other forms of education. Too often, the distinction lies not in the content but in the motivation of the participant (see Chapter 9). This does not obviate the necessity of identifying the intention of any given measure, for which the distinction between functional and emancipatory objectives is important.

Our definition does not refer to educational leave policies. We are convinced that (with the possible exception of those of Sweden) no policies presently exist in Europe that meet all the criteria of educational leave as we define it here, if one understands *policy* to be a concerted approach to the attainment of an identifiable goal by explicitly defined means. Elements of educational leave policies exist in all countries, and in some they are more advanced than in others; but in no country has the question of educational leave been considered in all its aspects at a policy-making level—primarily because there has been no urgent need to do so. As a matter of fact, it is still questionable whether a comprehensive policy of educational leave should be formulated in any country (see Chapter 9).

A great deal of attention has been given to the stipulation that educational leave requires continuation of pay; not nearly as much has been devoted to the question of job security. From an educational viewpoint this is, however, a very material problem: in most instances, the necessity of job security will imply a limit to the duration of educational leave, one that is often shorter than may be educationally desirable (see Chapter 9). Job security is inherent in any definition of educational leave, but we have included in our overall consideration those programs that provide educational opportunities for the unemployed and those that are available only to persons who have resigned their previous position. In Europe, these programs have been discussed in terms of two aspects: in the context of *countercyclical* educational policy (the provision of more education as an investment in times of recession) and of *alternation* policies (alternating periods of work and education). These concepts and programs are closely related to educational leave. In societies with strong programs of social security (for example, Sweden and Germany), it may indeed be argued that while security in a specific job cannot be guaranteed, all the social and economic effects of continued employment can be safeguarded—thus ful-filling the intention behind the requirement for employment se-curity in educational leave. This concept of providing job security through social programs rather than through a specific place of employment is known as *social salary*.

Educational Leave Effects

Discussions of educational leave in all European countries have usually covered only certain portions of the basic issue, namely, those aspects of educational leave policy that appeared most read-ily soluble or most urgently in need of attention within the context of national educational, social, and economic policy at a particular time. The comparative approach to the issue of educational leave policy reveals quite clearly that what is considered educational leave in any given country is in fact only part of a much more com-plex issue.

To achieve a better understanding of the interplay of various policies in the area of educational leave, it is useful to consider not so much educational leave *policies* as the educational leave *effects* of a variety of educational, social, or economic policies. Thus far, no systematic attempt has been made to identify all the elements of educational leave as they appear in various countries and to assess their relative importance. This task would appear to be an important one to undertake before attempting to identify the means of defining policies for educational leave.

Our approach to the question of educational leave disregards the basis on which an employee is able to leave his place of work: it simply asks what opportunities actually exist that have the *effect*, whether originally intended or not, of enabling employees to pursue study during working hours without full loss of pay. This approach involves not only the study of the scope of adult educa-tion; it also involves the study of a number of measures undertaken in most countries by public and private groups that have not tradi-tionally been viewed as part of the complex of adult education but that certainly need to be included in any study of educational leave. A basic difficulty of a survey of all measures producing educa-tional leave effects is that comprehensive or reliable information on the entire area of adult education, even as traditionally defined, is unavailable in any country (OECD, 1975b). This state of affairs makes it necessary to piece together information on educational leave from diverse sources, often differing from country to country. Six important areas will be considered in the four principal countries studied.

Voluntary Adult Education

Obviously, the greater part of ongoing voluntary adult education activities in most countries fails to qualify as educational leave because it takes place outside company time and has no assured effect, either positive or negative, on an employee's status. Nevertheless, certain groups of employees, in particular salaried employees, can often take adult education courses on company time if this is seen to be of benefit to the company: consequently, a de facto educational leave is already achieved. Moreover, the introduction of any educational leave policy will tend substantially to affect the present adult education sector. We can assume that a significant number of those presently engaged in adult education will tend to pursue their studies within the framework of an educational leave policy if this is possible. Furthermore, the social composition of participants in voluntary adult education approximately reflects the groups at present most strongly motivated for further education.

Training Financed by Industry

This is probably the area in which the greatest number of educational leave effects are presently being felt. In most industrialized countries between 5 percent and 10 percent of the work force are currently exposed every year to some kind of vocationally related training provided at the expense and request of their employer. At the same time this is also the area about which the least is reliably known. Many discussions of educational leave exclude it, arguing that this form of education constitutes a right of the employer rather than of the employee and that it is exclusively vocation-oriented. The latter claim is probably not completely accurate, but it does reflect the predominant trend. The former identifies one of the critical issues in discussions about educational leave, namely, the relative rights of employer and employee in determining the conditions of leave for education. It is not advisable to exclude this area of present practice from the discussion by postulating a particular solution to the larger problem of the relationship of the employer and employee within educational leave programs. Moreover, from the point of view of the economy as a whole, the resources being devoted to education within industry for purposes of industry are an important factor in determining the total resources that can be made available for educational leave. Certainly, a transfer of activities in this sector to educational leave as defined by the relevant laws is to be expected wherever this is possible. Consequently, this area requires our careful attention.

Trade Union Training

Nearly all countries by now have policies providing for training of trade union officials on company time, with the cost of courses borne by the trade unions or even by public funds. This, in effect, constitutes a right to educational leave for a selected group of workers.

In-Service Training for Civil Servants

Previous studies of educational leave disregard to a surprising extent the very substantial rights to educational leave that have already been realized in the public sector. These rights are in some ways comparable to those granted by industry to its employees, in so far as programs are nominally restricted to topics of vocational relevance. In the case of academically trained public employees, however, this can very often be interpreted to cover almost any kind of educational experience.

In attempting to project a reasonably complete picture of educational leave effects in European countries this element of present policy must also be considered.

Labor Market Training Schemes

There are generally two types of policy for labor market intervention: those designed to adapt the employed to new or changing conditions or to provide protection against unemployment (adaptation, job instruction, upgrading, refresher, and certain types of retraining programs) and those designed to assist the unemployed in finding new positions or to facilitate greater job mobility in the labor force. The former are essentially an extension of in-service training, except that individual or public interests are given greater emphasis. Where individual or public interests coincide with those of the employer, these programs are indistinguishable from in-service training.

In terms of educational leave, the latter programs do not fulfill the requirement that job security be maintained. Nevertheless, in some countries present practice has led to the creation of educational leave effects through these programs. They are all geared to facilitating the return of unemployed persons to the work force; hence a significant number of the participants are able to engage in these programs while receiving remuneration from public authorities, with assurance of further employment. In most cases, however, job security is achieved in general terms, not in regard to a specific position. The effects of these programs are comparable to those of many educational leave programs, and, as with general adult education, it must be assumed that a more general right to educational leave will ultimately also affect the character and scope of labor market training schemes. Consequently, these existing measures need to be considered prior to any discussion of possible educational leave policies.

Educational Leave Effects Within the Military

For a variety of reasons, military establishments in most Western countries have developed very extensive educational programs for their personnel. These programs are used both as an inducement and to provide continuous training and upgrading. In terms of educational leave policies this area should be considered along with on-the-job training financed by industry and in-service training for civil servants. These programs in the military service have much the longest tradition of any systematic program of in-service training or educational leave. Ever since the French Revolution introduced conscripted armies, the military has also been seen as an instrument for civic training. After World War I, this aspect of the military became increasingly suspect; in recent years, however, there has been a reemphasis on the opportunity to learn special skills in the military as a means of recruitment, and as a result this sector needs to be considered more carefully than would have been the case a few years ago—although information is very sparse indeed.

From this diversity of sources it transpires that it is probably premature to talk of educational leave policies in Europe in any but the most restricted and nationally circumscribed contexts. The notion of educational leave effects nevertheless provides a useful analytical tool since it defines the entire complex of formal education available to those who have left the system of initial education. This is an area of major concern to policy makers in all countries, although it will probably remain true for the foreseeable future that only elements of an educational leave policy will be implemented in individual countries, rather than an all-embracing policy consonant with any one definition of educational leave.

3

The European Debate on Educational Leave

Common Elements in the Educational Leave Debate

Elements of an educational leave policy have been the subject of public debate in recent years in every country in Western Europe. Although these debates have been conducted in the context of national policy making, a number of common features emerge quite clearly. There appears to be a common denominator, deriving both from similarity of issues and positions and from increasing awareness of the interrelatedness of developments in the various countries of Europe. As the charge to the Russell Committee studying adult education in the United Kingdom put it: employers and trade unions should study the question of educational leave "to take action to ensure that we do not lag behind" other European countries (Department of Education and Science, 1973, p. 91, s. 273)

Common features involve a number of issues, from attitudes toward policies for intervention in the labor market to the critical issue of the relationship between vocational and general education. They can be discussed here in general terms without reference to any particular country since they recur in one form or another in each of the countries we have considered.

Labor Market Policies and In-Service Training in Industry

There is virtually unanimous agreement in all countries on the need for an active labor market policy that includes the possibility of retraining grants to individuals or to industry. This is no longer viewed as a controversial measure but simply as part of the normal policy of social support that a modern industrial society must offer its citizens. These labor market policies provide a large proportion of presently identifiable educational leave effects in European countries. Common to all countries is the priority attached to maintaining an adequate program of labor market interventions. These policies are considered as educational policies only in a secondary sense, a fact reflected in the administrative responsibility and in the allocation of resources: as a rule, the ministry of labor or of social affairs or a branch of these ministries, such as the unemployment insurance agency, is responsible for the program. The principal exception is Italy, where regional educational authorities have recently taken over this responsibility from the Ministry of Labor; Italy is, however, the one country without a policy of further training oriented toward the labor market. In other countries, the ministries of education play a fairly marginal role, even more marginal than in the initial phase of vocational training. While the institutions of initial vocational education (which reflect some measure of influence on the part of the educational authorities) are normally also involved in retraining, special arrangements exist in most countries which allow the creation of retraining institutions or the use of industry facilities not subject to the control of the ministry of education.

Similarly, industry in Europe has accepted the fact that in-service training programs are a necessary part of normal operations. The justifications for these programs vary, depending on whether they are part of medium- and long-term personnel planning, under the authority of the operational divisions, or viewed as staff benefits needed to retain qualified employees. Form and content vary, depending on whether courses are contracted for outside the firm or carried out by an internal education department at the place of work or in training centers. In all industries, however, in-service training has become an accepted fact.

The existence of labor market policies—which may vary in detail from country to country—and the reality of in-service training must be taken into account in any discussion of educational leave policies. These conditions initially had led to suggestions that

any further educational leave policies should be designed specifically to exclude vocational elements, but this has proved imprac-
ticable since it is impossible legally to define the dividing line
between vocational and general education (see Chapter 9).

Labor market policies, together with the in-service training
programs of industry—which are in turn often partially subsidized
through the labor market policies—provide a broad base of intervention relative to changing conditions of work. It is not too much
to say that there exists a full range of programs with educational
leave effects outside the purview of the traditional institutions of
education and beyond the ken of most educational authorities.
In discussing educational leave programs, employers and trade
unions have tended to view these activities as privileged and not
subject to reconsideration in the light of a more comprehensive
policy of educational leave.

Employer and Trade Union Arguments

Employers' organizations and trade unions throughout Europe
have steadily developed their arguments for and against educational leave over the last ten years. While details of national policy
making vary, there is virtually no variation from country to country in the attitudes and arguments of principle of the employers
and trade unions. This congruence extends even to certain points
of detail and nuances of emphasis, and it appears not to be influenced even by differences in the political situations of such countries as Austria, Germany, Sweden, France, or Italy. While a certain congruence is to be expected, its extent is nevertheless surprising. The arguments of principle from both employers and
trade unions are largely interchangeable between countries, and
it is consequently unnecessary to study them country by country.

Employers' organizations will typically be in favor of educational leave in principle, but they distinguish between leave benefiting the enterprise and leave benefiting the individual. The enterprise is to be responsible for the former, while the individual must
develop the resources and motivation for the latter. Typically, at
this point in the argument, reference is made to the responsibilities of the individual in a democratic society and to the principles
of liberal policies in a free market. Such a view is based on an analysis

of the role of industry in modern societies that differs fundamentally from that used by the trade unions. The neat compartmentalization assumes a much less pervasive influence by industry on the lives of its employees and on the development of society than the employees themselves feel. The employees' subjective sense of dependence is, however, of fundamental importance to the prospects for educational leave policies since it will tend to play a major role in the individual motivation of workers when they are engaged in educational experiences on the fringe of their working life (Kern and Schumann, 1970).

Almost inevitably, employers' organizations tend to emphasize the cost factor and the limited ability of the economy in general and of industry in particular to carry the burden of additional expenses for social or educational policies. This is the case regardless of the current proportion of GNP being devoted to such purposes, which varies greatly between countries (see Table 1). In the Common Market countries there has been an effort to equalize these burdens, since they are viewed as factors in the relative competitive position of enterprises. Nevertheless, national differences in the distribution of resources do exist that are too great to be explained by variations in national systems of accounting. The problem is that the allocation of available resources appears as a stable balance and that reallocation would cause comparable social and political difficulties, even if it could be shown to be economically feasible.

Thus far it has proved impossible to develop satisfactory instruments to determine the financial parameters of educational expenditures relative to GNP. There is some evidence to suggest that the larger the per capita GNP, the greater is the proportion that can be devoted to social and educational policies (*Economist*, *256* (6891), pp. 46–51). At any rate, the employers' emphasis on the lack of economic resources is generally viewed by the trade unions as self-serving, and thus far no adequate analysis exists that could counter this political response and provide a basis for reaching a defensible description of the actual possibilities.

Employers frequently develop "full-cost" analyses of the expense of establishing educational leave policies; these will tend to include three elements: direct costs of instruction (administra-

Table 1. Population, Gross National Product, Social Security, and Educational Expenditures for Twelve Selected Countries, 1966, 1968, 1970

Countries	Population (Millions) 1973	1966 GNP $ billions	1966 % Social Security Expenditures	1966 % Public Education Expenditures	1968 GNP $ billions	1968 % Social Security Expenditures	1968 % Public Education Expenditures	1970 GNP $ billions	1970 % Social Security Expenditures	1970 % Public Education Expenditures
Belgium	9.7	17.8	15.1	5.7	20.4	16.5	*	25.2	16.0	*
Denmark	5.0	11.1	*	5.0	12.3	*	6.4	15.6	19.4	6.9
France	52.1	104.9	15.5	4.5	124.8	15.9	4.5	141.0	15.9	4.9
Germany	61.9	121.7	16.0	3.0	133.7	17.2	3.1	185.5	17.0	3.5
Italy	54.9	63.2	15.9	4.8	75.1	16.4	4.8	92.7	16.5	*
Netherlands	13.4	20.4	16.5	6.7	24.8	17.5	7.1	31.6	18.6	7.5
Sweden	8.1	23.8	15.6	*	27.3	*	7.7	33.0	*	7.7
Switzerland	6.3	15.2	8.9	3.6	17.4	*	3.9	20.6	*	4.2
United Kingdom	56.0	105.6	*	5.2	103.2	*	5.4	120.6	13.7	5.7
United States	210.0	758.6	7.2	5.1	874.8	*	5.7	983.2	*	*
Austria	7.5	10.6	18.5	3.8	12.0	*	4.3	14.7	*	*
Norway	3.8	7.6	7.9	*	9.1	*	*	10.1	*	*

*Comparable figures not available

Sources: Population, GNP and Social Security Expenditures: Eurostat, 1974; Education Expenditures: CME, 1975b, p. 43, table 2.

tion, instructors' salaries, and materials), cost of continuing to pay beneficiaries' salaries, and investment costs (particularly for instructional facilities). In some instances, production loss has been included as a factor, but this assumes a complete inelasticity of production, as well as of the labor market (Zekorn, 1967).

In response, the trade unions have compiled alternative calculations which vary from those of the employers by as high a factor as seven. The variations in such projections reflect the extremely haphazard systems of accounting still in use in most of the educational institutions of Europe, and in adult education in particular. It is in fact virtually impossible to project the cost of policy initiatives in adult education in Europe.

The arguments put forward by the trade unions, across national boundaries, represent the obverse of the reasoning adopted by the employers. Taking the nature of the work place as their point of departure, they will emphasize the need for collective action to overcome the isolation and alienation of the worker; they will stress the desirability of having articulate citizens in a democratic society, of making adult education available to underprivileged groups, and of maintaining the work force at a high level of mobility. These trade union arguments must be seen in the context of a strong class consciousness, often combined with an ideological view of society and the intention of initiating fundamental change.

The area of agreement between employers and trade unions is clearly restricted to the complex of established measures oriented toward the labor market—state intervention and the inservice training of industry. The common ground on all other issues is so minimal that agreement can be reached only through political decision making or through the victory of one point of view over the other in contract negotiations.

In all European countries, the educational authorities have been less involved in the educational leave debate than might have been expected. Their coinage is still the relatively much more vague concept of recurrent education, and they have yet to realize the significance of institutionalized education that exists beyond the institutions under their control—in the form of the internal training of industry and the activities of the labor market authorities. Insofar as educationalists have been involved in the debate on educational leave to date, that involvement has mostly occurred within the framework of adult education rather than with reference to vocational training or the institutions of front-load education.

Education or Training

One of the central issues in the debate on educational leave in all European countries is the relationship between vocational and general education. The issue is posed differently in different countries and the terms vary, but fundamentally the same questions are under discussion. In France, the issue is posed in terms of "culture," that is, the degree to which "cultural" education also receives support under the available policies. In Italy, the trade unions opted for courses allowing workers to complete compulsory education—explicitly a decision against vocational courses. In Germany, a sharp distinction is made between labor market intervention and educational leave. Nevertheless, there is debate concerning the extent to which vocationally oriented courses are to be supported through educational leaves and as to whether existing vocationally oriented programs are to be extended to include nonvocational education. In Sweden, important elements of general education are integrated into the courses for vocational training.

This debate on education versus training is central to any educational leave policy, since it implies a number of subsidiary conclusions concerning finance and control of such policies. Insofar as educational leave is vocationally oriented, employers are significantly more willing to provide special financial support directly or indirectly, through payroll levies or special tax funds; other cases, so they argue, are primarily social, and should be considered the responsibility of the community at large, that is, funded from general taxation. Control of courses is, moreover, vested to a varying degree in various interested bodies (ministries of labor, education, social affairs; the employers and trade unions; voluntary organizations), depending on how the basic balance between vocational and general education is struck. The issues involved are, consequently, not only theoretical but imply a distribution of influence and control which can determine the future course of educational leave in the countries concerned.

It does not diminish the importance of the issues involved to point out that they replicate the continuing debate in two other areas of educational policy making. First, virtually the same questions are being disputed in attempts to reformulate policies for initial vocational education. The central issue here is not vocational versus general education but how much general education vocational education requires. The arguments in favor of extending the general education elements of vocational education are identical with those generally adduced in favor of educational leave policies; thus the parallelism of issues is not really surprising. In terms of critical policy issues, the major questions in this version of the debate are the "scholarization" of vocational education and the development of comprehensive schools. For the purpose of our discussion of educational leave policies, it follows that it cannot simply be a matter of deciding for or against vocational or general education programs—the two are linked in some way which nobody has yet been able to define satisfactorily. Second, the debate on general and vocational education is replicated at an even more comprehensive level in the developing dispute on the relationship between education and working life. Basically, the question is no longer simply the significance of general education as a supplement to vocational education but the vocational, and even social and economic, significance of formal education, irrespective of its source or label.

Viewing the vocational versus general education debate in educational leave policies in this broader context indicates that it deals with issues which are irresolvable in general terms: a satisfactory distinction between vocational and general education is not possible in abstract terms. One of the major conclusions of the extended research related to the above two areas of dispute is that it is impossible to define the effect of a course in terms of its content alone: context is equally determinant in relation both to what is learned and to how it affects the participant's working life. Context encompasses all the elements of time, place, and group that characterize a given educational experience. In other words, a course which is clearly vocational in content (computer programing, automobile mechanics) can prove to be recreational or general in practice, while courses of "general" content (languages, social sciences, history—that of the labor movement in Italy, for example) have vocational applicability.

That the proper relationship between vocational and general education is irresolvable in theory does not mean that the related issues of influence and control must remain unresolved; it means that these issues are resolved not in terms of educational theory but in terms of the relative ability of the interested parties to influence them economically and politically—a situation not uncommon in educational policy making. Consequently, some of the variations in educational leave arrangements in the various countries of Europe can be viewed as a reflection of political conditions rather than as examples of differing approaches to educational problems.

As in the case of many other such debates of principle, there are underlying features of the controversy over vocational and general education that are not spelled out in public. The opposition, for example, of most employers' associations to "general" education in educational leave programs stems from a fear that it may involve the teaching of political, economic, social, or philosophical views inimical to them; here too, the underlying issue is often a political one.

Education does not exist in a vacuum. Initial education must deal with the emotional development of children and young people and with the social and economic situation of their families. Adult education must do so no less. In addition to the social and economic situation of participants and their families, educational leave must take into account work conditions, for these are likely to be the strongest motivating force—positively and negatively—in any program so explicitly linked to employment through the continued payment of salary and the guarantee of job security. Under these circumstances, one must assume that it is impossible to exclude vocational motivations in educational leave programs; even where employees can opt for nonvocational topics, conditions may in fact make it exceedingly difficult to exercise this right. For this reason, proponents of emancipatory educational leave programs seek to provide safeguards against these impediments, or even to change the conditioning influences themselves.

The Right to Education

The constitutions of continental European nations all include reference to education, in the sense that the citizen has the right to full development of his personality and the state has the responsibility of providing equal access to education. Traditionally, this constitutional obligation has been interpreted as applying only to the institutions of initial schooling. Increasingly, however, the question being raised is whether it does not extend to all forms of education, including adult education in general and educational leave in particular. At the 1974 meeting of the ILO, this question was debated for three days; after a vigorous debate in the drafting committee, the decision was taken to delete the phrase asserting that educational leave was "a new labor right meeting the real needs of the individual in a modern society." It was replaced by the more general assertion that "paid educational leave should be regarded as one means of meeting the real needs of individual workers in a modern society" (ILO, 1974a, p. 17A/2; ILO, 1974, p. 35).

The arguments in favor of considering educational leave in the light of constitutional guarantees have not, however, changed the basic frame of reference of the debate in the countries involved. Reinterpretation of the constitution in so fundamental a manner is not merely a matter of legal logic; it involves political decision making and involvement as much as does any other approach to educational leave. Such arguments must consequently be viewed as further justification of educational leave, but certainly not as a conclusive case in its favor (Gurrieri, 1975).

The Debate in the International Organizations

Since World War II, Europe has experienced a burgeoning of international institutions, both European and those broader in scope. The many different groupings by now represent a complex level of debate in their own right, even though most of them have no executive responsibility in the field of education. This constitutes a uniquely European phenomenon, insofar as these international institutions contribute toward establishing a number of major issues as items for discussion beyond the borders of any one country.

For several years now, educational leave and related topics

have been the subject of lively debate in these international organizations. The origins of the concept are by now obscure, but the adoption by the International Labor Organization (ILO) of a resolution in favor of paid educational leave as early as 1965 (ILO, 1972, p. 55) indicates that it must already have had a certain currency by then. Between 1965 and 1968, the Council of Europe undertook a first international study of the issues involved (Council of Europe, 1969). This was followed by work by the OECD and UNESCO, and culminated in the 1974 session of the International Labor Organization, which adopted a resolution and a recommendation on educational leave (ILO, 1974a). In 1975 the biannual conference of European ministers of education (covering the member states of the Council of Europe) in Stockholm devoted itself to questions of implementing recurrent education in the member states. In addition, the last two years have seen a number of international studies on educational leave. Besides the published work of the OECD and the Adult Education Institute in London (OECD, 1975; Charnley, 1975), unpublished studies have been undertaken by the Commission of the European Communities and by research institutes in Germany and France.

It is interesting to compare the debate in individual countries with that in international organizations. What is most noticeable in the international sphere is the virtual absence of negative opinions on educational leave such as those that employers' organizations or financial experts tend to represent in the national context. A similar, but rather more general, phenomenon is the absence of intersectoral negotiations within the international organizations. Documents are, as a rule, prepared by and for specialists in one area, and insofar as the concerns of other areas are attended to, they are considered, not in the negotiating stance typical of national policy making, but in an informative sense—the reason being the continued absence of policy making and, more important, of executive responsibility in the international organizations. Their publications and resolutions tend to be consultative in character and to reflect academic points of view more strongly than do executive documents of national governments. This is also true of the Commission of the European Communities with regard to educational and social policy. The commission normally prepares directives and guidelines which, after consultation with the European Parliament and the Economic and Social Council, are presented to the appropriate group of ministers of the nine member states and, if necessary, ultimately to the European Council, an organization composed of the heads of the executive branches of the countries. The commission is then charged with assuring implementation. In the fields of education and social policy, however, this process has not proven effective. A good example of the divergence between the commission's views and those of the national ministers of education is a document on "the first principles of educational policy at community level" (Commission of the European Communities, 1973, p. 5.) This document emphasized permanent education as a priority field for community intervention. But in response to an enquiry from a member of the European Parliament, the commission had to concede that the ministers of education did not include permanent education among the priority items for action, thereby limiting the commission's scope for intervention (European Parliament, Written Enquiry no. 19-75).

International Labor Organization

The International Labor Organization is the oldest of all international agencies. National delegations are composed of representatives of government as well as representatives of employers and trade unions. The ILO can issue recommendations and propose formal conventions dealing with problems of labor relations; to take effect, labor conventions must be ratified by the appropriate national authorities. Consequently, the ILO can make a direct impact on national policy making.

On the initiative of the trade union representatives, the ILO considered the issue of educational leave at the fifty-ninth session of the International Labor Conference in 1974. Preparations for the debate on educational leave took several years and included a survey of national practices and a consultation process in the course of which several countries were forced to declare an official position on educational leave for the first time (ILO, 1972; 1973; 1973a; 1974). The tendency throughout this process was skepticism on the part of the employer representatives from the developed countries, caution on the part of the government representatives, and pressure on the part of trade union representatives. The fact that the conference voted not only a recommendation but also a convention reflects the strength of the worker representatives. On the other hand, the government representatives were able to force a reformulation of the definition of educational leave and the deletion of some of the more controversial phrases.

These last changes reflect the somewhat pragmatic stance of the International Labor Conference. The impact of the proposed convention is nevertheless likely to be marginal; the problem is that nobody can say with conviction what an educational leave policy is (see Chapter 2), and consequently, even if the convention is ratified, it will most likely be ratified under the impression that an educational leave policy already exists in the country concerned or to avoid the stigma of nonratification, without intent to act on the convention(N.N., 1974, p. 2). The distribution of political forces is, moreover, different within the individual countries from that existing in the ILO. The trade union and government delegates of the European countries covered by our study all voted for both the convention and the recommendation; the employer representatives of Austria, Germany, Switzerland, and the United Kingdom voted against the convention, while the employer representative of Italy abstained; the employer representatives of Austria, Germany, and Switzerland even abstained on the recommendation (ILO, 1974a, pp. 32/11 and 32/13). The ILO has undertaken no research or systematic analysis of available information on educational leave thus far.

OECD, Council of Europe, UNESCO

The OECD, the Council of Europe, and UNESCO have all engaged in studies on educational leave or related topics during the last few years. These three organizations have, in fact, been the source of by far the greatest volume of comprehensive studies on the subject, having produced even more than most countries have internally. National studies have tended to deal with various aspects of educational leave rather than with the entire issue, thus reflecting the pragmatic, step-by-step approach of national policy making.

The three organizations have in common the fact that they bear no administrative responsibilities in the field of educational or labor policy. Their primary role is the exchange of information between countries and the stimulation of studies leading to greater coordination of national policies. Since they are all intergovernmental agencies, their primary audience consists of the relevant national authorities, which derive a substantial part of their knowledge of developments in other countries from the work of these bodies. It is difficult, however, to assess the possible impact of such information on national policy-making debates, since many of the other interested parties—employers' organizations, trade unions, and the interested public—do not yet view developments in other European countries as a legitimate point of reference.

Through the efforts of the OECD and UNESCO, frames of reference have been created for a comparative understanding of the basic elements of educational policy. Their work on adult education in recent years has begun to identify the parameters of comparison, but it has not yet progressed to the point where useful results have emerged. The difficulties of these programs reflect the fact that ultimately the international organizations cannot by their own efforts advance beyond the stage member states have reached.

The work of the three organizations overlaps, but each has nonetheless developed a distinctive style and approach. The OECD is the most effective in its capability to sustain extensive discussion of major issues over long periods of time. Through its Manpower, Social Affairs, and Educational Directorate and the Center for Educational Research and Innovation (CERI), the OECD has been working on problems of adult education and recurrent education. Since problems of educational leave are considered in the context of its program on recurrent education, there is a resulting tendency to view educational leave in this light, as well as a strong emphasis on educational leave as an individual right. While the work of the OECD is based on individual reports of experience with educational leave in various countries, there is also a strong undercurrent of advocacy involved. The OECD tends to represent educational leave as a policy that member states should develop more vigorously, just as it is strongly committed to the identification of strategies to implement recurrent education.

The Council of Europe's publications on educational leave

are much more eclectic. After the first report on educational leave in Europe (Council of Europe, 1969), further publications have dealt with permanent education (Council of Europe, 1970) and adult education (Simpson, 1972). The compilers show a strong tendency to be inward-looking, making the resultant publications less relevant to an outsider than they might be. Both the OECD and the Council of Europe experience substantial delays between the compilation of a report and its publication, so that information is often much older than the date of publication suggests.

UNESCO is a world organization that must take the needs of a much greater variety of member states into account. Educational leave thus tends to be viewed in its relationship to adult education—one of UNESCO's main areas of concern (UNESCO, 1972)—and at a fairly broad level of generalization that is often of little relevance to the specific conditions of European countries.

The work of these organizations on recurrent education was the main topic of the ninth session of the European Council of Ministers of Education (CME)—a body under the umbrella of the Council of Europe but with ties to the OECD and the Common Market, as well as to UNESCO—in Stockholm in June 1975. Documentation was prepared by the Council of Europe and the OECD (CME, 1975a; 1975b). The reaction of the ministers of education was reserved. The prepared statements of most countries expressed a strong sentiment that recurrent education should not jeopardize what was viewed as the achievements of the last fifteen years in the development of initial education. The joint communiqué went somewhat further in its commitment to recurrent education, but with the important restriction that it be viewed as a long-term planning strategy particularly suited to postcompulsory education.

The ministers committed themselves actively to promote four short- and medium-term measures (based on the German version of the final communiqué): (1) educational opportunity for those sixteen to nineteen years old, (2) adaptation of postcompulsory education to the diverse needs of individuals, (3) reform of access to higher education so as to give more positive recognition to prior work experience, and (4) restructuring of the postcompulsory education system into a modular form, allowing more alternation between work and education. Educational leave was mentioned only among measures of interest that might prove useful depending on national conditions—a clear indication that in the eyes of the ministers of education it has an extremely low priority at present, since a number of the measures referred to include items of great generality on which many of the signatories will not be able to take specific action in the foreseeable future.

This attitude reflects two important facts. First, ministers of education have little or no commitment to educational leave. Institutionally, they are tied to the system of initial education; often they have no authority over adult education and vocational training, or must share it with other ministries. Politically, they view their role as defending the expansion achieved in the last fifteen years against competing public expenditures, and they will consequently resist policies which may weaken their position in this regard, or at least try to harness new policy initiatives to this overriding objective, even though it may negate the effect of the initiative. Second, a significant number of topics of importance in the debates of international institutions are viewed as not being directly relevant to individual national situations.

Permanent Education, Recurrent Education, Educational Leave

Permanent education and recurrent education have become accepted and reasonably well-defined concepts in the educational debate in Europe since they first obtained currency in the late sixties (Bengtsson and Bengtsson, 1975, is the latest bibliography on the subject of recurrent education). Strikingly, however, they are more important in the debate on educational affairs at the international level than in national policy making. Perhaps this is an indication of their value as instruments for conceiving policy initiatives. Apparently they represent a level of generality that is helpful in developing a frame of reference for understanding comparable policies and problems developed under diverse circumstances but one that is inadequate to the more specific needs of policy formation in the restricted circumstances of politics, parliament, and administration. Whether such generalizations are useful in describing the processes of education itself, the relationship between teachers and learners, is another question altogether. When national policy makers refer to "permanent education" or "recurrent

education" one may certainly question whether they are not using
these terms more as a smoke screen than as substantive concepts
(see Chapter 4).

In spite of their lack of specificity, the concepts of recurrent or
permanent education are helpful in describing what appear to
be common problems of educational systems in the developed
countries. Educational leave would seem to be one of the major
policy initiatives aimed at realizing the ideas behind the postulate
of recurrent education. We will not attempt to distinguish between
permanent education and recurrent education; we are convinced
that both draw on the same analysis of educational institutions and
their relationship to the development of society as do educational
leave policies. For the purpose of our discussion it is important
to enumerate the main points of this common background.

Essential in the analysis leading to the postulate of recurrent
education is the observation that it is impossible to prepare an individual for a working life of forty or more years during ten years of
his youth, a few years of adolescence, and the first years of adult
life. Advocates of recurrent education generally relate this observation to the requirements of the modern labor market, the developments of technology, and a notion of the obsolescence of knowledge;
but such subsidiary rationalizations are at least subject to some
doubt, and it is therefore probably preferable to state the case for
recurrent education in its most general terms. The idea that those
who have received education should, and need to, continue to learn
after leaving school or university is part and parcel of the idea of
education itself. What is new in the idea of recurrent education is
the notion that this process of continuing education requires purposive, institutional intervention in later life. Arguments referring
to the labor market, social conditions, and the development of
knowledge serve to justify not the necessity for continued learning
throughout life but purposive intervention at this time (Schwartz,
1974, pp. 11–28; OECD, 1974b; Council of Europe, 1970, p. 9;
UNESCO, 1972). They are essentially four in number and are
discussed below.

Progress of Knowledge and Changes in Technology
Although this is probably the most frequently cited of all reasons
for permanent education, it is also the one with the most limited

application: only those who have received fairly extensive initial training are likely to be affected by the development of new knowledge and new technology in such a way as to require fundamental updating of their education during working life.

Discussion of acceleration in the production of knowledge has been very extensive, even to the point of calculating "depreciation rates" of 5 percent annually (von Wiezsäcker, 1968). This argument, however, applies only to those who are affected by changes in knowledge in its broader applications. The general condition of workers is that changes in knowledge are applied to the work they do in so fragmented and conditional a form that all they can do is adjust to the demands of the labor market for certain skills that can be associated with applying new techniques to the typically fragmented, confined area in which they are active. It can be said that those most affected by new developments in their broad implications are relatively privileged and already have access to a wide variety of formal and informal educative experiences in adult life. A further limiting factor in basing the demand for permanent education on the calculation of rates of depreciation of knowledge lies in the assumption that *formal* educative experiences are required to counterbalance the loss of applicability. A significant proportion of new knowledge can be acquired in adult life through *informal* means, although it is obviously impossible to quantify this process as neatly as one can the depreciation rate.

Changes in Working Life

For the vast majority of the working population, the effects of new knowledge are felt most directly as they impinge upon their place of work. Two arguments are generally advanced in this context. First, the labor market is not static; entire professions disappear and the character of many occupations is transformed several times over during a single working life. Provision must therefore be made to allow people to adjust to these changes. Second, with advances in knowledge and technology, the labor market requires larger and larger numbers of increasingly highly trained people. During the last few years, however, a number of studies have been exploring the developing structure of the labor market and labor qualifications in Europe, and in Germany and Italy researchers have come to the unexpected conclusion that future demand will be greatest for unqualified labor. In other words, a relatively small and decreasing percentage of the working population will require higher levels of qualification, and the greatest demand will be for the minimally qualified (von Blumenthal, 1973, pp. 25–50; Baethge and others, 1973; Kern and Schumann, 1970). This conclusion—known as the "polarization theory"—has led to a vigorous debate still in progress. At issue are the size and character of the growing service sector of the economy and the question of whether the relevant studies are not biased toward the production sector, which is decreasing in size. While discussion of these questions continues, it is necessary to keep in mind that the optimistic projections of rising qualifications may suffer the same fate as the growth projections of higher education have suffered in recent years. It remains palpably true that general levels of qualification have risen over the last few years and are still rising; but the causes of this may lie outside the labor market in political, social, and general economic developments.

In the context of labor market policy there remains the important area of retraining. It is a basic (and relatively new) fact that occupations are changing rapidly, requiring most people to undergo some form of retraining at least once. This can take place at or near their place of work if employment continues; if not, there must be provision for easy return to education and subsequent reentry into the labor force.

Changes in Community Life

Community life has been subject to major changes during the sixty years since World War I. Communities have grown vastly in size; politics and economics are global; and the steering mechanisms of society have become infinitely more complex—from social security legislation to the media. The average citizen must master an increasing number of skills if he is to remain minimally effective in such a society, and particularly in a democratic one. Certainly, literacy alone (the ability to read and write) is not enough; numeracy, articulateness, and some basic analytic skills have become part of the minimal educational requirements of all citizens, regardless of the demands of the labor market. There exists a powerful argument that those citizens who have not had the opportunity to acquire such skills in their initial phase of education should be given the opportunity to acquire them and that those who have received more extensive education should be able to maintain what they have learned in an active and contemporary form. Certainly, this constitutes one of the major arguments in favor of continuing education in a democratic society.

Equality of Opportunity

In the late sixties, the relationship between education and equality of opportunity was a major topic of discussion in all developed countries. This discussion has recently been muted as doubts have arisen as to the effectiveness of education alone as an instrument for the redistribution of social and economic opportunity. Nevertheless, the argument continues to be advanced that recurrent education can provide greater equality of educational opportunity. This line of reasoning has two major threads. The first is that a system of recurrent education will allow those who failed to profit from their initial encounter with education to recover lost ground in later life. The second is that voluntary adult education and retraining is at present utilized by a privileged group; a system of recurrent education will permit other groups in society easy access to these social benefits (Charnley, 1975, p. 17).

The problem is that if adult education is already available to the educationally privileged, providing it for the less privileged will only remove a further relative disadvantage; it will not be a source of relative advancement. The existence of both versions of this argument indicates the difficulty of ascertaining the relevance of recurrent education to equality of educational opportunity. As a working hypothesis, we may assume that educational leave policies can have positive impact in terms of equality of educational opportunity only if they are selectively designed to benefit educationally disadvantaged groups and if opportunities for adult education do not already exist; otherwise their effect will be to extend an existing opportunity to a larger section of the population— certainly an important objective, but one with all the problems which attended the extension of initial schooling to a growing proportion of the population (OECD, 1974a, b).

In the arguments advanced for recurrent education, there

is the underlying hope that it will contribute to the reform of existing institutions. This is no longer considered a primary aim, but it is clearly recognized that any policy of recurrent education requires a root-and-branch reform of the educational system, from preschool to advanced university training. Consequently, any step in the direction of recurrent education policies—as educational leave policies are often considered to be—should reflect an impact of preexisting institutions.

While most of these arguments have been developed in relation to theories of permanent or recurrent education, they apply equally to educational leave. They have always figured directly or indirectly in debates on the implementation of educational leave, and any study of educational leave policies in Europe must consider carefully whether there is evidence to support the contention that such policies are a step in the direction of solving the issues these various arguments raise.

Permanent and recurrent education are generally viewed as ends in themselves; educational leave policies are, however, instrumental—as all implemented policies ultimately must be. This begs the question of what ends an educational leave policy is specifically designed to achieve. While the four major goals listed above certainly provide a broad frame of reference for educational leave policy, they are generally reduced to more immediate concerns. Among these, the most important are the political impulse and the concern for mobility.

Under existing conditions in the countries concerned, increasing social and occupational mobility and the possibility of creating a more highly differentiated system for the certification of rising qualifications are major preoccupations. The strong orientation toward vocational concerns must thus be seen against the background of general social policy. Some advocates of educational leave, however—educationalists and trade unionists for the most part—emphasize political objectives to be achieved through educational leave. This they consider its basic purpose. In its most sophisticated form, this political conception of educational leave aims at a personal emancipation and political enlightenment of the participants that would enable them to participate in political life in such a way as to change the very conditions that produced the narrow perspectives they formerly had—at work as well as in society at large. Educational leave is thus viewed as a key to a democratic society, a society defined by the active participation of all its members in the processes of decision making. Elements of this conception of educational leave are to be found in all justifications that stress equality of opportunity as a principal objective or refer to changes to be brought about in community and working life. In this way, general arguments for social reform tend to be transformed into specific ends of educational leave policy.

4

France

The Events of May 1968

In May 1968, French students erected barricades in Paris in a protest against the government and its social policies. Workers at the Renault automobile works outside Paris showed sympathy through a solidarity strike that led to a general strike. The much-feared coalition between workers and students was short-lived. Nevertheless, it caused an upheaval in French politics and society that continues to be felt nine years later; with the passage of time, the events of May 1968 appear more rather than less important as a turning point.

In the years following World War II, France was engaged in two debilitating colonial wars—first in Indochina and immediately afterwards in Algeria. The end of the Fourth Republic and the accession of Charles de Gaulle in 1958 were connected with the Algerian war and changes in the political structure rather than with social reform. By 1968, however, the country's educational system and its social policies were urgently in need of reform.

After the events of May 1968, two major reform initiatives were taken: university reform was moved forward, and the development of a system of further vocational education for adults was accelerated. These reforms must, however, be seen in the context of the system of primary, secondary, and vocational education, which has changed much more slowly (see Figure 1).

In July 1975, the report of the Commission on the Future of Training (*Commission sur l'avenir de la formation*) recorded that 25 percent of all men drafted into the army had completed upper secondary school with the *baccalauréat,* and then went on to state: "but these figures should not allow us to forget that 75 percent of all young people [have] experienced scholastic failure [*un échec scolaire*] at very different levels of schooling" (Commission sur l'avenir de la formation, 1975, p. 12). This official statement expresses with disarming clarity that the French educational system remains strictly oriented toward the culturally freighted *baccalauréat* leading to university study and that any other form of leaving school is considered a kind of failure. Failure is a basic ingredient of the French educational system—the report quoted above calls it "the ransom for a system based on exams and competitions": 16 percent of any particular age group still do not complete primary education (44 percent in 1958), and more than half the first-time students in higher education—an exam-hardened group—drop out within the first year. In its extremely high level of dropouts at all levels of the educational system, France is comparable to Italy (see Chapter 7) and to Germany (see Chapter 5).

By long-standing tradition, the French educational system has been state run and centralized to a degree unknown elsewhere in Europe. Apart from the fact that this corresponded admirably to the overall administrative structure of the country, a centralized system was also the most adequate form of institutionalizing the strongly hierarchical image of education, with its focus on the university and on a classical and literary conception of culture. In spite of efforts to develop points of exit after lower secondary education, initial vocational education remains the stepchild of the educational system.

As a consequence of this traditional system of education, by the end of the sixties the French labor force was underqualified in terms of international economic competition. Moreover, adult education remained largely undeveloped except for the in-service training activities of private companies, which necessarily had to be relatively substantial. A number of voluntary associations were devoted to making culture available to those members of the adult population who had not completed upper secondary education, but these were not particularly significant in comparison with the voluntary adult education institutions in the Scandinavian countries, Germany, and the United Kingdom. There is a curious divi-

Figure 1. Structure of the educational system of France

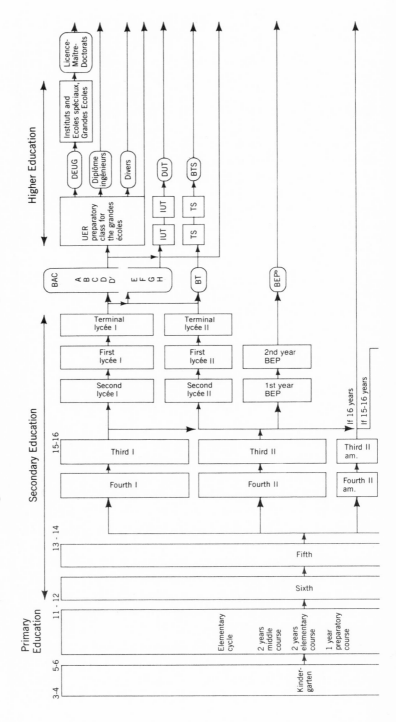

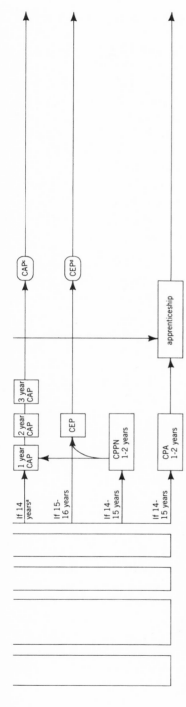

Bac: Baccalauréat (School leaving certificate qualifying for university admission)
BEP: Brevet d'études professionnelles (License of vocational training)
BT: Brevet de technicien (License of technician)
BTS: Brevet de technicien supérieur (License of superior technician)
CAP: Certificat d'aptitude professionnelle (Certificate of vocational aptitude)
CEP: Certificat d'éducation professionnelle (Certificate of vocational education)
CPA: Classe préparatoire à l'apprentissage (Preparatory class for apprenticeship)
CPPN: Classe pré-professionnelle de niveau (Advanced preprofessional class)
DEUG: Diplôme d'études universitaires générales (Diploma of general university studies)
DUT: Diplôme universitaire de technologie (Diploma of Technical College)
IUT: Institut universitaire de technologie (University Institute of Technology)
TS: Classe de techniciens supérieurs (Class of superior technicians)
UER: Unité d'études et de recherche (Units of instruction and research—former universities)

[a] Students must have attained 14 years of age before December 31 of the year of admission to the first class of the technical college leading to the CAP.
[b] The best students holding a BEP may have access to a class of first adaptation to a technical lycée.
[c] The best students holding a CAP may have access to a special class of the second cycle.
[d] The best students holding a CEP may be admitted to prepare for a CAP at a technical college.

Source: Ministère de l'Education, *Le mouvement éducatif en France 1973–1975.* Paris: Institut International de recherche et de documentation pédagogiques, Mémoires et Documents scolaires, 1975.

sion between the countries of Europe as regards the development
of adult education: the predominantly Protestant countries of
northern Europe developed it well in advance of the predominantly
Catholic countries—France, Italy, and Spain.

In France, a further factor contributing to the lack of adult
education activities was the lack of organizations, political and social, to carry them out. Relatively few focal points of decision making
in a large and populous country meant that access to these activities
was generally difficult and that the number of organizations articulating the many different interests in society remained limited.

After 1968, a number of steps were taken to create a system
of further vocational training for adults (*formation professionnelle
continue,* or FPC), culminating in the complex of laws of July 16,
1971, the most important of which was law 71-575 for the organization of FPC in the context of permanent education. This was the
major item of social legislation in the years following 1968 and, in
a certain sense, the first major social-reform legislation in France
after World War II. Inevitably, the policy became a focus for discussion and had to be designed to serve several purposes simultaneously; in particular, the thinness of the infrastructure outside
private companies meant that the new system of FPC had to create
one itself. Since this policy also represents the first educational
leave policy that claims to be comprehensive in any country, it has
received a great deal of attention as such, both nationally and internationally. But an analysis of the French situation reveals particularly vividly how identical terms differently applied in different
countries can lead to misconceptions concerning their real significance. Demonstration of these divergences is one of the virtues
of international comparison.

To understand how the legislation works, it is necessary to
describe its antecedents, both before and after the crisis of 1968,
in some detail. This we will do in terms of institutions and the main
stated objectives of pertinent laws prior to the law of 1971. As a
second step, we will evaluate the main terms and ideas of the legislation as applied within the French frame of reference so as to allow
an analysis of the laws and conventions currently in force. To avoid
any definitional debate that might interfere with a material understanding of the French situation, we will also give French terms

with translation. For the term *formation professionnelle continue* ("further vocational training") we will use the abbreviation FPC: it may help to prevent unwarranted inferences and should become fully intelligible as we proceed. Our third and largest step will consist of an investigation of the present system as it appears in the major source of published information, Document Annexe, 1974, an appendix to the French budget proposition for 1975.

Evolution of the System of Further Training, 1959–1970

Practically all the elements of the law of 1971 were developed in a fragmentary manner, or in nucleus only, before that date. In concentrating on such conspicuous legislation, one often forgets previous experiences that helped to bring it about (Vaudiaux, 1974, p. 13). The historical development is also important in explaining the confusing and complex administrative structures that the law of 1971 required (see Figure 2). The most important of these—the Interministerial Committee, with its General Secretariat under the authority of the prime minister, and the Standing Body of Senior Civil Servants and the bipartite and regional organizations—were created well before 1971, as was the practice of contracting (through *conventions*) between supply and demand of FPC.

Leaving aside the efforts connected with reconstruction directly after the war, as well as the rather unsystematic further vocational training organized during the fifties, the first legal attack on unemployment was the law (no. 159-960) of July 31, 1959, on *promotion sociale* (social advancement), providing for training to facilitate access to a higher position or to new employment (article 1). Coordination committees to study pertinent programs and methods and to circulate information on social advancement policies were instituted at the national level (under the chairmanship of the prime minister), as well as at regional and departmental levels. They were composed of representatives of the interested (twelve!) ministries, professional organizations, and experts. This structure is replicated in the present system. From 1961, a *Délégation générale* worked as a coordinating service and as a permanent secretariat.

The creation of a *Fonds national de l'emploi* ("National Employment Fund") in December 1963 (by law 63-1240) promoted short-term interventions for retraining to prevent unemployment, often

Figure 2. Schematic representation of national policy bodies of FPC in France

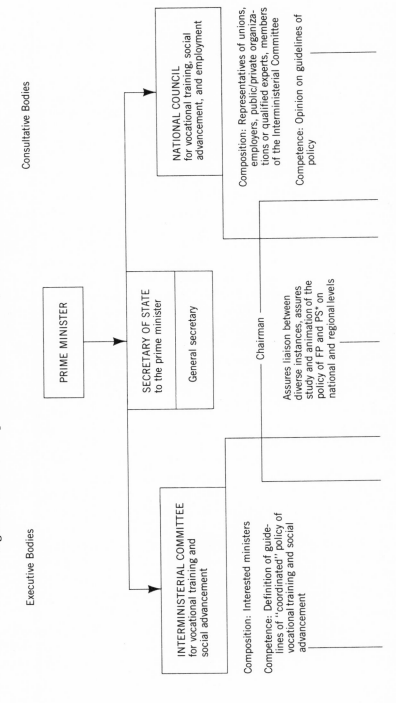

Executive Bodies

Consultative Bodies

PRIME MINISTER

INTERMINISTERIAL COMMITTEE for vocational training and social advancement

Composition: Interested ministers

Competence: Definition of "guidelines" of "coordinated" policy of vocational training and social advancement

SECRETARY OF STATE to the prime minister

General secretary

Chairman

Assures liaison between diverse instances, assures study and animation of the policy of FP and PS* on national and regional levels

NATIONAL COUNCIL for vocational training, social advancement, and employment

Composition: Representatives of unions, employers, public/private organizations or qualified experts, members of the Interministerial Committee

Competence: Opinion on guidelines of policy

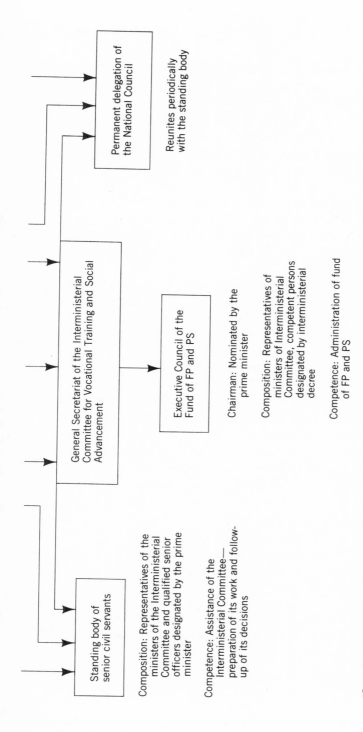

Permanent delegation of the National Council

Reunites periodically with the standing body

General Secretariat of the Interministerial Committee for Vocational Training and Social Advancement

Executive Council of the Fund of FP and PS

Chairman: Nominated by the prime minister

Composition: Representatives of ministers of Interministerial Committee, competent persons designated by interministerial decree

Competence: Administration of fund of FP and PS

Standing body of senior civil servants

Composition: Representatives of the ministers of the Interministerial Committee and qualified senior officers designated by the prime minister

Competence: Assistance of the Interministerial Committee— preparation of its work and follow-up of its decisions

*Formation professionnelle and promotion sociale.
Source: Luttringer, 1974, Cheramy, 1975, p. 90.

by means of contracts (*conventions*) with professional or union organizations or directly with firms. Thus, vocational training was presented as an "integral part of an active employment policy" (Hordern, 1973, p. 63) or as an instrument of "crisis management" by the state (Hein, 1973, p. 6).

The order of magnitude of these actions in favor of social advancement increased continuously during the six years the law was in force (1960 to 1966): from about 180,000 to 440,000 trainees, with budget expenditures rising from 150 million to 360 million francs (Renaix, 1967, pp. 19 and 61). The sharpest increase, between 1963 and 1966, was in agriculture: about 100,000 farmers left this sector each year to look for new employment elsewhere (Renaix, 1967, p. 34).

By 1966, the national education system catered to 260,000 of these 440,000 trainees (Hordern, 1973, p. 64) mainly in evening courses. For the first time, the system was opened to adults, particularly for the training of semiskilled labor (*ouvriers spécialisés*) in centers of adult vocational training (*formation professionnelle des adultes,* or FPA) under the Ministry of Labor; this kind of training activity was formerly the exclusive domain of employers.[1]

Lack of administrative coordination, insufficient financing, and inadequate access, as well as the heavy burden still placed on the individual worker in terms of (spare) time, money, family life, and insecurity, led to the elaboration in 1966 of another law aimed at curing these deficiencies. Certain characteristics that had by then gained prominence were subsequently strengthened: the attention and priority accorded young people and the prevalence of employment and labor market considerations, particularly the promotion of middle-level technicians and executives needed most urgently for industrial development policies. The early law on further vocational training already showed a strong tendency to express fairly limited economic goals in grand but rather vague terms; while the intention of the law was social improvement (*promotion sociale*), implementation was restricted to the narrow labor market concerns—only one element of any policy of social improvement (Renaix, 1967, p. 11).

[1]Hordern, 1973, p. 61, in 1966: 37.000 (p. 64); see also Renaix, 1967, p. 14 and passim; his figure for 1966 AFPA trainees is 47,200; cf. p. 39.

The accent on vocational training was further strengthened by the Orientation and Programatic Law on Vocational Training (*Loi d'orientation et de programme sur la formation professionnelle*), no. 66-892 of December 3, 1966. While the dispositions of 1959 sought social equality through social advancement, the dominant consideration and justification for the 1966 law was economic. In view of the competitive pressures of the Common Market, the policy of industrial expansion and modernization required an elaborate system of vocational training with a strong priority on technical qualifications (Renaix, 1968, pp. 6 ff.) The inclusion of youth in the program can be regarded as an official recognition of the inadequacy of compulsory education and its maladjustment to the needs of the labor market, notwithstanding the school reforms fully implemented by 1967 (Belorgey, Boubli, and Pochard, 1974, p. 2). Presumably in reaction to the unsatisfactory experience with administrative discretion in matters of *promotion sociale* an extensive system of cooperative institutions was created, most of which were later taken over by the regulations of 1971.

An interministerial committee (*Comité interministériel*) presided over by the prime minister (the minister of education served as vice-president) was to define the guidelines of vocational training and social advancement policies, especially in terms of capital expenditures and distribution of the resources of the newly created Fund for Vocational Training and Social Advancement (*Fonds de la formation professionnelle et de la promotion sociale*). The committee was comprised of the ministers of the civil service, economy and finance, agriculture, industry, and social affairs and could be enlarged for specific undertakings. To ensure the permanence and authority of the committee's decisions, a standing body of senior civil servants (*groupe permanent des hauts fonctionnaires*) was to help in preparing and executing them. According to article 3 of the law, it would be presided over by the general secretary of the Ministry of Education: in 1969 this post was abolished in the course of a reorganization of the ministry, and the prime minister was able to assume the presidency (Belorgey, 1972a, p. 10).

The composition of the standing body was identical to the superior committee in terms of ministries represented, which also made up half the membership of the executive council of the Vocational Training and Social Advancement Fund (*Conseil de gestion du Fonds de la formation professionnelle et de la promotion sociale*). The other members were nominated for their personal competence, but also with reference to their membership in, and representation of, the major societal organizations. The fund was fed indirectly by the apprenticeship tax (*Taxe d'apprentissage*), which was raised in 1966 from 0.4 percent to 0.6 percent of the payroll. The council was to redistribute the financial resources under its control to the relevant ministries, who would pass them on to public or private training centers by way of contracts (*conventions*). In the late sixties, however, the fund comprised only 10 percent of all public expenditures on vocational education, a total for this sector of more than 2 billion francs directly attributed in diverse ministry budgets (Renaix, 1968, pp. 15/6).

Resembling the former coordination committee(s) of the law of 1959 in its composition, the National Council of Vocational Training, Social Advancement, and Employment (*Conseil national de la formation professionnelle, de la promotion sociale et de l'emploi*) gave advice on the orientations decreed by the Interministerial Committee on matters of vocational training and social advancement from the viewpoint of the economy and the unions. As a further coordinating link, the standing body, the executive council of the fund, and the national council established a common secretariat, the functions of which were subsequently transferred to the General Secretariat of the Interministerial Committee (*Secrétariat général du comité interministeriel*).

These structures were partly repeated on the regional level. Under the direction of the prefects, a standing body of civil servants in relevant fields and a regional council (*Conseil régional de la formation professionnelle et de l'emploi*) were the counterparts of the national bodies. Since the regional councils representing the administration, employers, and unions for consultative functions were rather large bodies, they also formed a permanent delegation. The Ministry of Education likewise established regional subsidiaries for vocational training. With this organizational structure, almost the entire institutional setting for the 1971 regulations had already been created.

An additional important element was the device of contracts

(*conventions*), which came into general use as the "major means of a policy of orientation, cooperation, and coordination" (Renaix 1968, p. 22). State intervention could be administered more flexibly for the various kinds of training according to priorities set and assigned to public as well as to private institutions. The contracting approach allows devolution in decision making and participation on the part of a multitude of groups to a degree quite unknown under the French administrative system. Within guidelines set by the (admittedly cumbersome) committee structure, those utilizing training (firms, trade unions, and other associations but *not* indivuals) could contract with the purveyors, private or public, thus creating a market for further vocational training.

This impressive apparatus for policy formulation and coordination notwithstanding, coordination does not seem to have been achieved (Hordern, 1973, pp. 68, 70). Civil servants predominated in the tripartite organisms; vocational orientation and information was lacking—notably for adults—as was any consideration of problems connected with pedagogy for adults. Nonvocational education was not covered.

In spite of these difficulties—which, in view of the state of both vocational and adult training before 1966, are hardly surprising—the Vocational Training Law of 1966 represented an important first step toward molding vocational training, initial and continuing, into overall social and economic planning (Hein, 1973, p. 9); it tried to cope with insufficient primary schooling and the problems of maladjusted manual labor in relation to the needs of economic policy in a comprehensive and more or less coordinated manner.

The Vocational Training Law even established "the principle of an employee's *right* to educational leave"; the actual implementation was, however, entirely a matter for employers and trade unions. (Charnley, 1975, p. 125; see also Belorgey, 1972a, p. 10; Renaix, 1968, pp. 25 f.) At any rate, article 11 of the law established for the first time a legal right to claim educational leave for training or promotion programs controlled by the state; leave could be for a maximum of one year, but without remuneration. Article 11 of the law of 1966 was, however, never implemented. In France, laws are only declarations of principle; to take effect, they must subsequently be given administrative detail through executive orders—but this never happened with article 11.

This was the state of affairs in May 1968. One can liken it to patches in a quilt that establish the pattern but do not yet constitute a cover. Without these patches of legislation it would have been impossible to take rapid action in matters of vocational training; the resultant system, however, was largely determined by what had previously been created. The first step after May 1968 was to close the gap in the provision of support for trainees, first through hurried authorization of additional expenditures covered by the law of 1966 (Hordern, 1973, pp. 17 f.) and thereafter through the passage of law 68-1249 of December 31, 1968, on the remuneration of vocational trainees. Five categories of training are specified for which different remuneration rates that vary with the age, the professional status, and the last income of the trainees are applicable (Belorgey, 1972a; Hein, 1973, p. 8; Hordern, 1973, p. 73; Vaudiaux, 1974, pp. 16 f.):

1. Measures enabling youths under eighteen to complement their often insufficient basic education by vocational training to prepare for an occupation.

2. Measures of reconversion in connection with economic adaptation to technological change; these measures are initiated after termination of the working contract. Relatively favorable conditions are designed to provide the acquisition of new qualifications that are in demand; remuneration rates are fixed in close relation to previous earnings.

3. Prevention programs destined to prevent imminent layoffs, and thus unemployment.

4. Measures to maintain or update qualifications (*entretien et actualisation des connaissances*) in order to keep pace with technical progress. The measures involve courses to which the state will give financial assistance on condition that employers and unions conclude agreements over financial and organizational aspects.

5. Promotion programs designed to reestablish a certain equality of opportunity for those who have been unable to pursue their training. The state would guarantee moderate remunerations, mainly for medium levels of qualification (Belorgey, Boubli, and Pochard, 1974, p. 11).

The first three categories of training program carrying the possibility of state aid can be identified as elements of an active manpower-management policy, with a preponderance of employment considerations; this is also the case, though to a lesser degree, for the fourth type of program (refresher training). Only the fifth appears to retain a component reminiscent of the social advancement intentions of the 1959 law; the fact, however, that the promotion is mainly directed toward the recruitment of lower and middle executives needed for purposes of industrial modernization reveals the labor market motivations behind the social objectives. Virtually the same catalog of training schemes was subsequently incorporated in article 10 of the FPC law of July 16, 1971.

The law of 1968 also created the concept of training insurance funds (*Fonds d'assurance formation,* or FAF)—analogous to social security funds—to be established on the basis of *conventions* between employers and employees—to secure the financing of vocational training. The FAF concept extended the contracting approach to areas previously reserved for legislation, thereby marking a further step in the effort by the state to involve the labor market partners more actively in the resolution of the problems revealed by the crisis of May 1968. The FAF concept subsequently became part of the law of 1971 (article 32).

The passage of the "remuneration law" (December 1968) in combination with the Vocational Training Law of December 1966 to which it relates meant the legal acknowledgment, in principle, of the right to *paid* leave for purposes of further vocational training and retraining. Cultural as well as social objectives are espoused by the law. One might infer that a full-fledged legal right to paid educational leave was introduced before the law of 1971, even though—after massive political publicity—the 1971 law was credited in the public mind with its institution. But legal texts often speak a language different from the facts, and we have to bear certain points in mind. First, as we have seen, the modalities of applying article 11 of the Vocational Training Law of December 1966 for educational leave of absence were not promulgated. Second, the types of training announced in the remuneration law of December 1968 are predominantly employment oriented, which implies social motivations only as far as they are justified by priorities of economic policy or to counterbalance negative side effects of economically determined developments. No space is left for civics or culture as ends in themselves or as individual needs.

Since the bias toward economic or labor market concerns is constitutive of French policies in matters of adult education, the provisions of the law of December 1968, marking out the main field of state intervention, contribute an important element, if not a cornerstone, to the edifice of FPC as finalized in the 1971 regulations. For the first time a coherent system of training and remuneration had been designed. It is as yet a design only, for it is important to note that the necessary statutes for the remuneration law were not decreed before June 14, 1969, and then only to provide a 50 percent increase of financial resources (from 250 million to 380 million francs), available under previous regulations; the statutes thereby rearranged the miscellaneous schemes of the past into a more systematic and manageable structure (Belorgey, 1972a, p. 11). In effect, this meant emphasizing the areas listed in the law of 1968. Beyond this administrative clearance (though it was overdue) many of the measures foreseen in the laws of 1966 and 1968 were not promulgated, since the government preferred to await the outcome of negotiations between employers and unions in that domain (Belorgey, Boubli, and Pochard, 1974, p. 2; Vaudiaux, 1974, p. 17).

This attitude, or even strategy, of reserve favored by the state created what is now called a policy of *concertation*. The intention behind this strategy was to foster more active and responsible involvement of the labor market partners in this policy area as a means of encouraging greater cooperation between the labor market partners in general and to help in creating a network of collective bargaining procedures in the area of social policy. It constitutes another pillar of the system of FPC as sanctioned in 1971. It was motivated in the motion for the law of 1971 by the prime minister (Chaban-Delmas) and the minister of labor, employment, and population (Fontanet): "Such a policy [of vocational training] could be a complete success only if its objectives found the support of the heads of enterprises and of the workers. That is why, rather than specifying by statutory texts already existing in 1969 all the modalities of application of the laws of 1966 and 1968, it seemed more consistent with the social philosophy of the government to leave to the social partners the translation of their needs and the realistic means of fulfilling them into a bipartite agreement" (Vaudiaux, 1974, p. 17). This justification post facto sheds light not only on the situation after the events of May 1968 but also on the further evolution of the present system.

The French employers' association (CNPF) and the French trade unions had met in May and June of 1968 to reach a settlement of the crisis. In the ensuing *protocole de Grenelle* (named after the rue de Grenelle in Paris) they "agreed to study the means of ensuring, with the help of the state, vocational training and further training (*la formation et le perfectionnement professionnels*)," while for executive training a special agreement was to be examined by both sides (Hordern, 1973, p. 71).

As an immediate result of the new power relationship, agreements on all levels (for individual enterprises, for sectors of industry, or nationwide for certain groups of employees) were signed; these created commissions to deliberate and decide on professional training courses of all kinds, mostly effectuated on company time, and to provide for better employment and promotion opportunities (Hordern, 1973, pp. 71 f.).

The National Interoccupational Agreement on the Security of Employment (*Accord national interprofessionnel sur la sécurité de l'emploi*) of February 10, 1969, is the first realization on a broad scale of the declarations of intent proclaimed in the *protocole de Grenelle*. The agreement contains regulations to improve the standing of workers in cases of collective notice motivated economically or due to reorganization or merger, approves the creation of bipartite employment commissions (*commissions paritaires de*

l'emploi, or CPE) on branch level, and stipulates obligatory consultation of the works councils on employment questions—all elements
of the later system of 1971. The first section of the preamble con-
firms the determination of both sides to take up the examination
of training possibilities in the second trimester of 1969 (CGT, 1972,
pp. 28 ff.). Negotiations began in May 1969, and it was fourteen
months before an agreement was signed on July 9, 1970 (Belorgey,
1972a, p. 12).

With the National Interoccupational Agreement of July 9,
1970, on Vocational Training and Further Training (*Accord national
interprofessionnel du 9 juillet 1970 sur la formation, et le perfectionnement
professionnels*) (CFDT Formation, 1972, no. 5, pp. 4 ff.; Belorgey,
1972a, pp. 12 f.; Hordern, 1973, pp. 76 ff.) we come to the present
system of FPC in France, of which it is part and parcel; this might
account for the fact that many discussions of the French experience
commence with this agreement. It is, however, difficult to understand the exceedingly complex structure of the present system
without knowing how it developed in its principal outlines between
1959 and 1970.

The agreement of July 1970 covers primary training (*première
formation*), complementary training (*formation complémentaire*) with
the provisions for "educational leave," and the role of bipartite
organizations (*organisations paritaires*). In other words—and this
extraordinary phenomenon deserves particular emphasis—the
labor market partners convene, in the wake of a severe upheaval
of the sociopolitical system, to revise the entire educational structure of the country, a domain traditionally (and legally) falling
under state responsibility. They arrive at suggestions for solutions
to be implemented on the basis of a mutual agreement and for
which they seek the support of the state. The state subsequently
sanctioned most of their solutions through a series of corresponding laws and statutory texts.

To increase the coherence of, and continuity between, primary and complementary training, the preamble of the agreement
suggests a renovation of primary education, the introduction of
technological education at the lower secondary level, and the institution of a preprofessional year for those with deficient basic

schooling. These propositions were to find official acknowledgment in two of the laws of July 16, 1971.[2]

Within the field of their own responsibility, the signatories agreed to settle the financial, pedagogical, and contractual conditions for apprentices and young workers. The special conditions for apprenticeship and for particular professional diplomas providing for adaptation courses and on-the-job training on company time need not concern us in detail, but they bear witness to the comprehensiveness of the agreement. It should be added that the third of the four laws of July 16, 1971 (no. 71-576, *relative à l'apprentissage*) and the four ordinances of April 12, 1972, take up and enlarge on the framework of apprenticeship laid down in the interoccupational agreement.

The dispositions concerning "complementary training" (title II) are most interesting in that they contain the origin and the core of the present regulations for educational leave, although they never use this term; *autorisation d'absence* ("authorization for [leave of] absence") is the wording used for such training opportunities. The agreement distinguishes two major cases: workers affected by a collective notice (as defined by the Agreement on the Security of Employment of February 10, 1969) and workers actively employed.

Workers given collective notice can ask for leave of absence for training of their choice as soon as they are informed of the coming dismissal. They are paid their full salary by the employer for the period of notice. Courses exceeding the period of notice are possible for a total duration of one year, since the UNEDIC (*Union nationale pour l'emploi dans l'industrie et le commerce*, "National Union for Employment in Industry and Commerce") pays the entire salary for the remainder of the period of training.

Every actively employed worker can demand leave of absence for full-time training of one year at most (exceptions being pos-

---

[2]Law 71-577 *d'orientation sur l'enseignement technologique* ("on orientation about technological instruction") and law 71-578 *sur la participation des employeurs au financement des premières formations technologiques et professionnelles* ("on the participation of employers in the financing of primary technological and professional training") and pertinent decrees.

sible by special agreement) or for 1200 hours of part-time or discontinuous training. To qualify, a worker must have not less than five years until retirement, must have at least two years of seniority within the firm (not applicable to workers reemployed after previous collective layoff with no subsequent training), may not have obtained a university diploma within the previous five years or a professional diploma within the previous three years, and may not have benefited from training leave within a period of at least one year (up to twelve years), the necessary minimal delay being a function of the length of the previous training period.

The percentage of workers simultaneously absent for training is fixed at maximally 2 percent of all workers of a productive unit. Workers sent for training at the sole initiative of the employer count as half, so that the maximum of absentees can rise to 4 percent. Priority is given (1) to those whose request had previously been postponed to assure proper functioning of the enterprise and (2) to those with the highest seniority within the firm. The maximum period of postponement of a request for reasons of production may not exceed one year; requests for training leaves of six months or more have to be submitted at least sixty days in advance, indicating precisely the date of commencement, the designation and the length of the training, and the name of the responsible agency. The deadline is thirty days in advance for training shorter than six months or for part-time training. The employer has to reply to the request within ten days. The employer assumes the full training cost as well as the full salary *if* the employee was sent to training "organized at the initiative of the enterprise" (article 34). The case is much more complicated for training requested solely on the initiative of the employee.

In its third chapter, the agreement imposes the function of consultation, implementation, and control or arbitration on the Bipartite Employment Commissions (*Commissions paritaires de l'emploi,* or CPE) created by the Interoccupational Agreement on the Security of Employment of February 10, 1969. Their most important tasks are (1) to draw up lists of training courses "considered to represent a recognized interest for the profession," according to criteria of content and pedagogy to be defined by the commissions themselves, and (2) to determine the categories of workers for which these courses were destined (article 33). If the training course requested by the employee on his own initiative corresponds to his category and is on the list of the competent CPE, then the enterprise will supplement payments he receives under existing legislative or contractual dispositions to ensure his income during the first four weeks of full-time training. It is also up to the CPE to fix the conditions for training leaves, paid in part or in total, for periods longer than these first four weeks, or 160 hours of part-time training (article 35). Should a worker ask for training other than that mentioned in articles 34 and 35, his authorized absence is not remunerated, and the costs of the training are not borne by the enterprise (article 36).

The foregoing provisions, as well as those concerning the remuneration of collectively dismissed workers, all assume that possible assistance from the state under the laws of December 3, 1966, and December 31, 1968, is taken into account. These conditions apply to roughly 10 million workers employed by enterprises represented by the CNPF and the CGPME (Confederation of Small and Medium-sized Enterprises). Only a few groups of enterprises employing about 600,000 workers did not participate in the agreement (Belorgey, 1972a, p. 12). A special agreement for executives was concluded in April 1971.

The Supplementary Agreement of April 30, 1971, to the National Interoccupational Agreement of July 9, 1970, regarding Complementary Dispositions Concerning Executives (*Avenant du 30 avril 1971 à l'accord national interprofessionnel du 9 juillet relatif aux dispositions complémentaires concernant les cadres*) is justified by the signatories in terms of the particular nature of the work of executives and their specific responsibilities and functions. These, according to the preamble of the 1971 Supplement, are considered so essential to technological and technical progress and to the efficiency of enterprises as to warrant the special treatment of this group. To this end, the regulations of the interoccupational agreement of July 9, 1970, are modified as follows: further training (or education) may comprise the acquisition, maintenance, updating, and deepening of basic qualifications as well as the enlargement of general training (article 2). This particular emphasis leads one to infer that corresponding options are not available for "ordinary" workers[3] with the consent of the trade unions. The same observation holds for the extension to executives of the agreement's favorable paid training-leave provisions for workers given collective notice; executives who are given individual notice for reasons of merger or intracompany reorganization are also entitled to these provisions. Similarly, the proportion of executives simultaneously absent for training purposes is raised to 3 percent (instead of 2 percent) for the enterprise (and not for a production unit). This rate is also doubled for executives sent for training at the decision of their employers. One should note that according to the supplementary agreement, "cadres" include engineers and senior officers as defined by collective agreement, as well as foremen and technicians included in special lists established by bipartite agreement between the trades.

The supplementary agreement further provides for leaves of absence without pay of less than one year's duration for executives who intend to teach part-time or full-time; leaves of more than one year and less than five years for full-time teaching give rise to a priority claim to reemployment (or contractual indemnification); the teaching leaves are subject to seniority conditions (two to five years) and periods of delay between two terms; they are also included in the 3 percent rate of absence.

The Law of 1971

To attempt to understand the law of 1971 is like undertaking an archaeological expedition under a national monument. Unquestionably, political considerations have led to an overemphasis on the law of 1971 as a radically new initiative providing comprehensive rights to educational leave as part of a reform of the entire system of vocational education. As the major social reform of the late sixties and early seventies, the law of 1971 had to serve many, sometimes contradictory, purposes. This ambiguity of purpose is already reflected in the law's overgrown title: Law 71-575 of July 16, 1971, for the Organization of Further Vocational Training (*formation professionnelle continue*) in the Framework of Permanent

---

[3]Belorgey, 1972a, p. 13: "One hesitates to consider that this means, *a contrario*, that the same possibility is refused to other employees." Belorgey, Boubli, and Pochard, 1974: "It does not seem that one may infer, *a contrario*, that these courses are closed to other workers but that they are particularly necessary for executives."

Education. The reference to permanent education in the title—which recurs only once in the introductory article to the text—is intended to legitimize the law as an act of educational reform. But closer examination reveals that this edifice has been erected on the precise foundations created by developments between 1958 and 1970; the law of 1971 basically generalized and reinforced the provisions of the agreement of July 1970 (Belorgey, Boubli, and Pochard, 1974, p. 3). "The question was not so much to try a new experience as to generalize previous experiences" (Vaudiaux, 1974, p. 27). Together with the law on FPC, the French parliament enacted laws to reform the organization of apprenticeship (law 71-576), to put technological instruction on an equal footing with general education (law 71-577), and to regulate the participation of employers in the financing of primary technological and professional training (law 71-578)—all passed on the same day.

Some general observations can be made concerning the relationship of previous arrangements, mainly of the agreement of 1970, to this new law on FPC within the framework of permanent education (Belorgey, 1972a, p. 13; Belorgey, Boubli, and Pochard, 1974, p. 154; Vaudiaux, 1974, pp. 17–22). The law generalizes the right of *all* workers to FPC at state-approved training courses; this right was formerly limited to workers covered by the agreement. The passage of the law must be seen in connection with the perspective of the sixth plan for 1971 to 1975, which sees economic expansion through industrialization as a means of social progress. Vocational training, primary as well as continuing, is considered an essential means to this end (Intergroupe Formation, 1971; Vaudiaux, 1974, pp. 37 ff.) if the labor force is to be adapted to the needs of the economy. For this purpose, the sixth plan foresaw a doubling of postschool training activities until 1976, which made continuing training one of the key factors in industrial modernization (Charnley, 1975, p. 121; Vaudiaux, 1974, pp. 17 f., 34 ff.). "The laws of July 16, 1971, intend to realize this aim in giving the country a complete and renewed potential in matters of training [*formation*]. They intend to favor economic expansion while assuring full employment. The rapid industrialization in fact demands a qualified labor force. Continuing training (*formation continue*) therefore becomes the only guarantee for employment and the best means for the workers to achieve promotion" (Belorgey, Boubli, and Pochard, 1974, p. 7). This passage expresses the tenor of all the legal and contractual initiatives since 1959.

The reference to permanent education in the title of the law and the sleight of hand by which this is equated with measures for further vocational training as distinct from all other aspects of the educational system have given rise to many misunderstandings concerning its true purpose. It represents the codification of an elaborate program of labor market interventions essentially comparable to those existing in Germany and Sweden and "elaborated in two movements: a phase of experimentation from 1959 to 1968, and a phase of codification in 1970 to 1971. The publicity given to the last stage and the mobilization provoked by the coming into force of the law of July 16, 1971, may lead to neglecting the previous initiatives and the very object of this text, which was to complete and codify existing measures" (Vaudiaux, 1974, p. 13).

The substantive provisions of the law are essentially those of the agreements of 1970 and 1971, with some modifications. Ordinary employees now have a claim to unpaid leave as instructors that is equivalent to that accorded cadres under the agreements. The clause excluding employees with less than five years to retirement was eliminated. The employer's obligation to pay for the first 160 hours of leave to attend courses listed by the relevant CPE was not taken over by the law and thus remains restricted to employees covered by the agreements. Consequently, the law creates no legal unconditional claim to paid educational leave at the initiative of the individual. Article 7.7 stipulates that workers benefiting from the right to leave at their own initiative may be remunerated by their employers under contractual dispositions—such as the agreements. The state may remunerate them or participate in their remuneration.

The law speaks of *congé formation* ("training leave"), a much broader term than the *autorisation d'absence* ("authorized absence") of the agreements. Theoretically, only the employee could initiate educational leave requests; the activities of the employer are considered apart from these initiatives. Simultaneously, however, the agreements are used as points of reference and are in fact raised to the status of executive orders. This contradiction meant that in practice the *congé formation* envisaged by the law has not gone beyond the *authorisation d'absence* of the agreements, while giving rise to many misconceptions about the law's effect (Luttringer, 1975).

The major innovations of the law lie in its financial provisions. It created two financing mechanisms: a minimum financial obligation for employers and a system of state subsidies. This had the effect of extending the financial obligations incurred by the signatories of the agreements to all employers with ten or more employees.

The legal financial obligation for employers with at least ten employees was 0.8 percent of the payroll to be spent for FPC purposes. It was to be raised to 2 percent in 1976. In fact, it was 0.8 percent for 1972 and 1973 and 1 percent for 1974 and 1975. Taking into account that in 1969, enterprises with fifty or more employees, representing about two thirds of the total payroll of industry, spent 1.11 percent for *formation* ("training") expenses of all kinds (Belorgey, 1972b, pp. 6ff.), the rate of 1.3 percent of the payroll for the new system (the initial rate in 1972 of 0.8 percent plus 0.5 percent of the apprenticeship tax) cannot be regarded as an extraordinary increase over three years.

In other words, even financially the new system does not represent a major departure. Employers can spend these resources, on the condition of prior *délibération* with the works councils (in firms with at least fifty employees), in any of the following ways or a combination thereof:

1. For training to the benefit of their personnel, either within the firm or by way of contracting public or private purveyors of training on the free market of vocational training
2. By payments to a training insurance fund (FAF)
3. By transmitting up to 10 percent of their obligation to agreed institutions satisfying a national or regional interest in the field of vocational training (research, orientation, training of trainers, and so forth)
4. By depositing the difference between their financial obligation and the factual training expenses with the Treasury

Expenses exceeding the obligation can be carried forward over the following three years. Training expenses under the law include the salaries and social charges of trainees, teachers, and admin-

istrative personnel; outlays for equipment and material, if not used
for general production purposes within three years after acquisition; and expenses for the training of tutors and amortization of
teaching premises.

To be legally accredited, training courses must be approved
by an ordinance of the prime minister, on the advice of the standing body of senior civil servants (article 7.8). Since the burgeoning
market for vocational training would have overwhelmed the competent authorities with approval procedures, an ordinance of January 11, 1972, determined in a generic fashion types of courses
which were automatically approved:

> Courses organized by public institutions of instruction
>
> Courses of the Association for the Vocational Training of
> Adults (AFPA) and other collective training centers under
> the tutelage of the Ministry of Labor, Employment, and
> Population
>
> Courses covered by a *convention* providing state aid or other
> state-subsidized courses
>
> Courses organized by chambers of commerce, industry, trades
> and agriculture
>
> Courses approved by the state with reference to (state) re-
> muneration of trainees

The ordinance further stipulated which other courses may also
be approved:

> Courses entered on (special) lists established by the labor mar-
> ket partners
>
> Courses not covered by any of the foregoing categories nor
> profiting from any state aid that have the characteristic of
> a course of prevention, adaptation, professional advancement
> or refresher courses, as in article 10 of the law

This liberal regulation would make it difficult for any course *not*
to be approved; hence the approval procedure does not constitute
a barrier to the fulfillment of the vocational training obligation
stipulated by the system of 1971.

Matters become much more complicated when state aid is at stake. Under the law, an approval mechanism for state subsidies was established that paralleled the approval procedure for courses that can be credited against the obligations of employers; in this instance, however, decisions have not been delegated, and the state continues to exercise detailed control. The financial contribution of the state may include "functioning costs" and equipment outlays, on the basis of *conventions* (according to article 4). Furthermore, the state participates in the remuneration of trainees, for which the most complex regulations are laid down in title VI of the law and further detailed in various decrees and circulars (Belorgey, Boubli, and Pochard, 1974, part 3, Chap. 3).

In principle, state aid for the remuneration of trainees is limited to the five categories of training listed in article 10 of the law (see above discussion on the evolution of the system of further training). Conditions for this aid and the subsidies as such vary with the training category and with the status of the trainee. The courses have to satisfy minimal length requirements, again differentiated by kind of training. The relevant courses must either have been covered by a special *convention* foreseeing the remuneration of trainees (which is the case mainly in the context of the National Employment Fund) or they must have received specific state approval concerning the remuneration of trainees—it is accorded by the prime minister on the recommendation of the standing body.

Law of 1971: Analysis of Experience

The application, and thus the outcome, of the complex set of legal and contractual dispositions which constitute the French system of *formation professionnelle continue* (FPC) is characterized by a "burden sharing" between the state and employers. Guidelines for the division of responsibilities were established by the prime minister in January 1973 and revised in February 1975 (see Table 2).

The differences between the two sets of guidelines are subtle but very significant. In the 1975 version the problem of unemployment clearly predominates; the elimination of specific reference to youth in connection with programs to assist entry into working life is intended not only to favor women but also to provide further help to the long-term unemployed. The fact that the problems of

Table 2. Distribution of Responsibility for FPC Between the State and Employers in France, January 1973 and February 1975

	January 1973	February 1975
Responsibilities of the state	Intervention to facilitate the entrance of youth into professional life	Intervention to facilitate solutions to employment problems
	Conversion programs designed to give new qualifications and employment to unemployed workers	Intervention assisting entrance into professional life
	Vocational upgrading programs (*promotion professionnelle*) to allow an increasing number of employees to rise in the professional hierarchy and assume functions for which a serious shortage of qualified personnel exists	Vocational upgrading programs allowing selected employees to rise in the professional hierarchy
Responsibilities of enterprises and professional groups	Adaptation and refresher training to maintain the capabilities of employed workers	Adaptation training to new jobs or new technologies
	Internal advancement as already practiced by a good number of enterprises	Internal advancement

Sources: Data for 1973 from Document Annexe, 1974; data for 1975 from a memorandum of Feb. 20, 1975, from the secretary general for vocational training in the prime minister's office.

employment now receive first consideration is a further indication of a shift in priorities toward the labor market and away from education. The changes in the list of activities that are the responsibility of enterprises are linked to the reformulation of the state's role in vocational upgrading programs: whereas the 1973 list of state responsibilities still called for the upgrading of an "increasing number" of workers, the 1975 list refers only to selected workers and assigns basic responsibility for upgrading to the enterprises. To make this clear, the category of refresher courses is separated from adaptation training with the remark that the state will no longer support such activities through *conventions* with enterprises; that is, it will restrict itself to those programs that it carries out by itself for reasons of priority. The clear shift toward labor market concerns over the first years of the program tends to reinforce the orientation of the antecedent programs toward vocational training. This priority is also clearly borne out by the statistical evidence.

The principal source of statistical information on the FPC system in France is the government's budget proposal, which contains an account of the previous year's activities. All analyses of French experience are derived from this material, since no other information describing the entire system is available. The information in this document is compiled by the agencies which disburse funds and also serves as a basis for justifying budget requests. There is, consequently, no interest in maintaining year-by-year comparability—the contrary may on occasion be the case. Cross-checking further reveals that the published material has been drawn from diverse sources whose information does not necessarily mesh. In consequence of these difficulties, it is possible to draw only general conclusions, the very detailed nature of the available information notwithstanding.

The State Program of FPC

All public aid to FPC is comprehended under the *enveloppe globale de la formation professionnelle* ("comprehensive budget for vocational training"). The larger part of the budget constitutes the Vocational Training and Social Advancement Fund (*Fonds de la formation professionnelle et de la promotion sociale*), a pooling of pertinent items attached to the budget of the prime minister and mainly serving to

cover contracts (*conventions*). An estimated 666,000 trainees benefited from this aid during 1974 (Document Annexe, 1974, p. 12;
see also Cheramy, 1976, p. 51). The remainder (often also referred
to as the *enveloppe*) is directly subject to the budgets of the interested
ministries and encompasses the Association for the Training of
Adults (AFPA—Ministry of Labor), serving an estimated 85,000
trainees in 1974; the National Employment Fund (no corporate
body, but a pooling of budgetary items under the supervision of
the Ministry of Labor), serving an estimated 28,000; the National
Center for Tele-instruction (CNTE—Ministry of Education), serving 111,000; and the National Center of Arts and Crafts (CNAM—
Ministry of Education), serving 30,000; as well as several institutions
serving as means of orientation, information, research, and documentation that do not, however, engage in teaching (Belorgey,
Boubli, and Pochard, 1974; Luttringer, 1974, pp. 96f). The *enveloppe globale* is intended to provide for the better coordination of
FPC measures undertaken by the state at all levels. The often-cited
global figures on the development of state subsidies to trainees in
all programs subsumed under FPC are particularly interesting:
in 1969, the number of state-subsidized trainees was 566,000; in
1970, 702,000; in 1971, 790,000; in 1972, 956,000; in 1973, 954,000;
and in 1974, an estimated 920,000 (Document Annexe, 1974, p. 9).

While the increase from 1969 to 1974 is impressive—63.7
percent—the figures reveal that much the greater part of the
increase occurred before the law of 1971 came into effect, immediately after the events of May 1968. In the year 1972–73, participation had reached approximately 4.6 percent of the work force.
Between 1972 and 1974 the increasingly restrictive interpretation
of the state's mandate had even led to a decrease of 3.8 percent.
Thus the figures confirm the increasing reliance of the public authorities on the system of *concertation* through *conventions* for all
activities not related to structural labor market concerns.

The employment preoccupation of state aid to FPC is also
reflected in Table 3. The total number of trainees relating directly
to employment was 443,000 in 1973 (46 percent); this number is
up from 28 percent in 1969 and is projected at more than 48 percent for 1974. Refresher courses must also be considered as essentially employment oriented, which raises the employment-related
element of state-aided FPC to three quarters in 1973. Apart from

"subsidized social advancement" courses for 100,000 persons, mainly taking place during spare time, and apart from courses of tele-instruction, practically all FPC activities receiving any kind of state aid are employment related.

As to the introduction of youths into professional life, it should be noted that besides the 83,000 mentioned under the pertinent heading (50,000 of whom were trained within the armed forces during national service), most participants of FPC at large are young: 57 percent (more than 530,000 trainees) are no older than twenty-five years, 30 percent (or about 280,000) of all trainees are sixteen to twenty years old, raising questions as to where the dividing line between initial and further vocational training is located.

To further complicate matters, 220,000 of 954,000 trainees who have followed courses subsidized by public funds in 1973 were also supported by their employer (Document Annexe, p. 9, n. 1 and p. 28, n. 1; Cheramy, 1976, pp. 16, 49). There is no specification of how this burden sharing was effected that would have demonstrated the interplay or *concertation* of public and private endeavors in practical solutions.

Among the contractual measures of vocational training, face-to-face instruction which in 1974 enrolled an estimated 490,000 trainees of the 666,000 supported by the Vocational Training and Social Advancement Fund, represents the very essence of the system of FPC as sanctioned in 1971. It is above all in this largest item of the accounting that we have to search for educational leave effects. The five main components of this predominant element of the FPC provisions, asterisked in Table 3, correspond exactly to the five categories of training listed in article 10 of the law of 1971. Taken together, these five components experienced a considerable upswing in the first year of the implementation of the new provisions, namely by 145,000 trainees (or 42.5 percent), to drop to a more modest 38,000 additional trainees (7.8 percent) in 1973 and revert to the level of 1972 in the estimate for 1974 (− 6.7 percent). The step-up in the first year (1972) was largely due to the increase of "maintenance and improvement of capabilities" training by more than 100,000 trainees, which accounted for more than half of all trainees; this share was slightly reduced in the following years in accordance with the priority guidelines which ascribed prime

Table 3. Trainees in FPC Courses in France Subsidized by Public Aid, 1971–1974

	1971	1972	1973	1974 (Estimated)
Pretraining of youth				
*Contractual actions of *preformation*	21,000	25,000	24,000	24,000
AFPA (*preformation*)	6,000	6,000	6,000	6,000
Actions for youth conscripted to national service	54,000	55,000	50,000	50,000
Actions for youth in overseas provinces	2,000	3,000	3,000	3,000
Total	83,000	89,000	83,000	83,000
Conversion, prevention and adaptation				
*Contractual actions of conversion and prevention	38,000	44,000	45,000	45,000
AFPA (conversion)	54,000	70,000	77,000	79,000
*Contractual actions of adaptation	52,000	69,000	68,000	66,000
National Employment Fund (FNE)	24,000	28,000	23,000	28,000
Total	168,000	211,000	213,000	218,000
Advancement of qualified labor				
*Contractual actions of advancement	61,000	76,000	118,000	115,000
CNAM	22,000	29,000	29,000	30,000
Total	83,000	105,000	147,000	145,000

Total of training related to employment	334,000	405,000	443,000	446,000
*Contractual actions of maintenance and improvement of capabilities	170,000	273,000	270,000	240,000
Subsidized social advancement	160,000	140,000	100,000	90,000
Tele-instruction (CNTE and *conventions*)	126,000	138,000	141,000	144,000
Sum total	790,000	956,000	954,000	920,000

*Major components of the PFC system discussed in text.

Source: Document Annexe, 1974, p. 10.

responsibility for this training category to employers. "Conversion" and "prevention" enrollments remained virtually unchanged, in spite of the high priority attached to them. Only "advancement" or professional promotion enrollments rose by more than 50 percent (76,000 to 115,000) from 1972 to 1974, raising their relative share from less than one sixth to almost a quarter of all enrollments.

How many of these can be regarded as educational leave? This question cannot be answered in general terms, since public aid supporting the various training categories encompasses running costs and capital outlays incurred by employers as well as remuneration aids, mostly in the form of reimbursement to enterprises for trainees' maintained salaries. For a tentative answer the different training schemes must be investigated in some detail.

"Preformation" (Pretraining)

Courses of *preformation,* of preparation for working life, or of specialization are open to young unemployed people aged sixteen to eighteen who are without working or apprenticeship contracts and who have no claim to unemployment pay. They normally run for four months. In 1974, the monthly subsidy was 320 francs for participants in preparatory courses and 360 francs for "formation leading to an employment demanding a qualification" (Document Annexe, 1974, p. 25). In the first semester of 1974 approximately 4.5 percent of all remunerations to trainees were spent on these courses (Document Annexe, 1974, p. 25). Here, again, the employment-policy element prevails in an effort to correct the combined deficiencies of basic "general" education and of initial vocational training.

It is interesting to note that one finds a full spectrum of youth programs that aim at improving the situation of young professional beginners or of those who would like to begin their working life but cannot. All these youth programs are distributed under a diversity of headings so that no clear-cut overall picture emerges. The existence per year of 250,000 to 400,000 youths who leave school with no vocational qualification and/or no employment opportunities (according to various unions) gives an indication of the underlying problems and tensions of the educational and economic sectors. These problems are veiled to some extent by this redistribution to different types of (adult) vocational training, although in essence they reflect unsolved questions of primary vocational education.

"Conversion" and "Prevention" Programs

Both schemes are intended for employees aged at least eighteen who are either threatened by a layoff (prevention programs), already out of work (conversion programs), or under notice. They also cover young people in search of an occupation within one year after completion of their military service or their basic education, mothers with at least three children or single mothers who want to reenter the labor market, and other nonsalaried workers (especially from the agricultural sector) looking for different vocational opportunities. Remuneration is pegged to the legally fixed minimum wage.

Conditions of compensation are most favorable for victims of a collective or "economically motivated" layoff and for individually discharged cadres, who receive 100 to 110 percent of their full prior income or at least 120 percent of the legally fixed minimum wage. All other groups receive between 80 and 90 percent of their former salary or 100 to 120 percent of the minimum wage.

The minimum duration for conversion or prevention programs is 120 hours, with at least 30 hours per week for full-time training or 8 hours per week for part-time training; for the farming sector, the minimum duration is 520 hours.

"Adaptation" (Job Induction)

These courses have "as their object to facilitate access to a first employment for workers with an employment contract and receiving pay from an enterprise, especially for young people with a professional diploma" (article 10, no. 2 of the law of 1971). This is essentially part of initial training of newly employed or transferred personnel. Again, a significant but unspecified portion of this program must in reality be considered an extension of initial training for youth.

Advancement

Courses with the objective of socioprofessional advancement are open to salaried employees with or without working contracts, as well as to nonsalaried workers who desire "an elevated qualification" (article 10, no. 3 of the law). Priority is given to employees aged twenty-one or over with at least three years professional experience. Indemnities are paid by lump-sum rates related to the level of qualification attained after finishing the training.

The training is long-term and rather flexible as to the time it takes. Some courses are also held in the evenings. There is a well-established apparatus for *promotion sociale* ("social advancement"), which is, however, undergoing major changes as a consequence of the provisions of the law of 1971. Traditional activities of social advancement supported by the *Fonds de la formation professionnelle* but effectuated directly and without *conventions* by the national education system, mostly taking place during spare time and for persons with low levels of qualification, declined from 160,000 in 1971 to 100,000 in 1973. In contrast, the *conventions* for professional promotion almost doubled from 61,000 to 118,000, but were expected to decrease slightly again from 1974 (115,000). In this field, educational leave effects can be verified in the case of daytime training, and this implies recognizable advantages for the trainees in the vocational sector. But it is not clear how far employment policy considerations play the predominant part.

Maintenance and Improvement of Capabilities

These courses (*d'entretien ou de perfectionnement des connaissances*), which are open to all salaried (or nonsalaried) workers without any age restrictions, are designed to maintain or perfect their qualification or their *culture* (article 10 of the law of 1971). They constitute, quantitatively, the major part and the largest single item of all figures on further training. This category of training, in contrast to all others hitherto mentioned, offers some kind of a choice to the prospective trainee; only in this case is he assumed to be in secure employment; the other program categories were addressed primarily to the not yet employed, to unemployed, or the soon to be unemployed. Here, for the first and last time in the material portion of the law of 1971, the word *culture* and its use as an alternative course content are mentioned.

It is in this context only that the formal requirements for eligibility for a *congé formation* ("training leave" really apply: two years of seniority within the firm, three years at least since the acquisition of a professional diploma, and the formula of minimal delay between two training sessions. It is in this context that conflict might arise between trainees sent by the employer and those asking for leave of absence for some kind of education on their own initiative. And it is for this particular category that the first 160 hours of educational leave have to be paid by the employer, even if the training might *not* be in the immediate interest of the enterprise. But the training envisaged has to be entered on a list established by the *Commission paritaire de l'emploi,* so that even here, the employment preoccupation of the provisions comes in again, and there seems to be little room left for nonvocational endeavors. Notably, state subsidies for the maintenance of trainees' salaries are lowest in this bracket: a maximum of 25 percent (as opposed to 50 percent for *adaptation* and up to 70 percent for *conversion/prévention*) of the remuneration to trainees *can* be reimbursed by the state, but often there is little or nothing left for this category because of the priorities given to the other programs.

In other words, the majority of remunerations for maintenance and perfection courses have to be paid by the employer, and he who pays the piper calls the tune. It is one of the complaints of the unions that these programs are used for retraining courses on the job, retraining that was necessary in any case as part of ordinary modernization and investment procedures.

If one seeks an answer to the problem of paid educational leave being provided for by public aid, matters become still more intricate. As can be seen from Table 3, the National Employment Fund (FNE) covered only 23,000 trainees in 1973. But according to other data, it supported 137,500 in that year (Document Annexe, 1974, p. 25). Furthermore, it is not clear how the figures of the various training categories relate to one another.[4] As a conse-

---

[4]For example, if in 1973 the FNE paid 71,000 trainees in conversion programs, how does this number relate to the 77,000 conversion trainees of the AFPA and to the 45,000 conversion/prevention trainees covered by *conventions* under the *Fonds de formation professionnelle et de la promotion sociale,* which is separate from both the AFPA and the FNE (see Document Annexe, 1974, pp. 12–13) but with which FNE might conclude *conventions* as well. We cannot conclude from the available data the extent to which these figures overlap or exclude one another.

quence, one cannot clearly identify the extent to which public aid provides for paid educational leave, despite the fact that ample statistical material is offered. With the available information only one conclusion seems justified: if more than 90 percent of the 150,000 trainees benefiting in 1973 from public aid to their remuneration were supported by the National Employment Fund, the main aim of which is to intervene in the most pressing and temporary cases of industrial change in favor of the workers affected,[5] practically all paid educational leave financed by the state represents adaptation to critical conditions of the labor market.

Furthermore, the statistical information is presented in such a way that it is impossible to tell whether or not any of the regroupings constitute educational leave in the sense of the definition adopted, the more so since the running costs and capital outlays are not given for any *comparable* time periods, reference groups, or fields of application, nor are the 220,000 trainees receiving aid from public funds and enterprises simultaneously disaggregated as to kinds of training attended or income maintained. In the figures on running costs and capital outlays even apprenticeship contributions are included.

Finally, then, one does not know whether one is dealing with vocational training in general or FPC. One cannot tell whether these activities can at least be considered as educational leave, let alone pin-point educational leave effects. Under these conditions it would be misleading to render the figures showing the levels, durations, contracting parties, and types of training covered by *conventions* in terms of possible educational leave effects. Trainees benefiting from state aid to the appropriate training center reveal nothing of the possible educational leave character of the training program. In short, existing statistics have frequently been used as a basis for discussion of educational leave in France, but they do not allow any qualified conclusions about it.

Employers' Educational Leave Activities

The data base is less ambiguous for FPC financed by enterprises. These data are computed on the basis of the declarations of enter-

[5]See the description of the objectives of the FNE by Belorgey, Boubli, and Pochard, 1974, pp. 274 ff. (esp. p. 276) and Luttringer, 1974, pp. 107 f.

prises with ten or more employees to the state authorities about the use they have made of their financial obligation for FPC. According to article 15 of the law, enterprises with at least fifty employees have to produce additional evidence that the works council has "deliberated" on matters of FPC concerning the enterprise before these matters are decided by the employers (for firms with three hundred or more employees, a special committee for vocational training substitutes for the works council). Only two full years of application, 1972 and 1973, have been recorded and compiled statistically.[6]

In 1973, roughly 130,000 enterprises were subject to the financial obligation to spend 0.8 percent of their payroll for FPC. They represented about 10 million employees (50 percent of the labor force) and a total payroll of 234 billion. The number of firms that submitted their declaration in due course was 111,000 in 1972 (Cheramy, 1975, p. 16) and 114,000 in 1973 (Document Annexe, 1974, p. 29). In 1972, 2,820 billion francs were spent on training; and in 1973, 3,390 billion. This amounted to 1.35 percent of the total payroll in 1972 and 1.45 percent in 1973, as opposed to the legal obligation of 0.8 percent. This provided almost 77.6 million hours of training for 1,040,000 trainees in 1972 and 96 million hours of training for 1,388,000 trainees in 1973.[7]

1973 enrollments were 1,545,200, indicating that a considerable portion of trainees attended more than one course, which is possible only on the employer's initiative. Altogether, 93 percent of all training hours were organized at the initiative of the employers (Cheramy, 1976, p. 111), while 96 percent gave rise to maintained salaries irrespective of possible indemnifications through

[6]See Document Annexe, 1974, pp. 28 ff. and Cheramy, 1976, pp. 16 ff. Some of the figures differ from each other within the original source. In case of doubt, tables were preferred to figures given in the commenting text and were checked as far as possible by recomputation from the component data. This explains some of the divergencies of our figures as compared to the Document Annexe; this is particularly true for percentage or average figures.

[7]Of these 1973 trainees, 220,000 also benefited from public aid evaluated at about 150 million francs; both figures have to be subtracted at least in part from the relevant data on the performance by enterprises for 1973; see Document Annexe, 1974, p. 28, fn. 1.

public funds, the share of which cannot be assessed. By inference, this would mean that only 3 percent of the training hours financed by enterprises were used at the initiative of the employees, equivalent to 40,000 to 50,000 persons.

On the average, each trainee took part in 69 hours of training, while the average course length of training financed by enterprise was 62 hours, due to multiple enrollments. The average training period for training subsidized by public aid, however, was almost 190 hours, or about 180 million hours of training for 954,000 trainees of all kinds (Cheramy, 1976, p. 49); the large difference in number of hours is explained by the fact that training financed by enterprises focused on rather short refresher and adaptation courses: 70.5 percent of all enrollments were in refresher courses (*entretien et perfectionnement*), and 17 percent were in adaptation courses (only 11 percent were in professional advancement courses and 1 percent in prevention.) Refresher and adaptation training can with fairness be considered of immediate interest to the enterprise; it is still safe to maintain that they constituted part and parcel of ordinary business functions even before the dispositions of 1970–71 were in force but it is impossible to say to what extent they have been intensified by the new system.

The training effectuated by means of *conventions*, that is, by contracting with training institutions on the open market (comprising private, public, and associated institutions), was 44 percent of all training financed by enterprises in 1973 (nearly 50 percent in 1972). The shift toward internal training agencies probably reflects the time required by firms to adjust to the new legislation by creating their own training departments. These appear to operate much more economically than outside organizations. Of external training, 75 percent (84 percent in 1972) was devoted to refresher training, a catchall category accounting for more than two-thirds of all training activities of industry. A further sixth covers adaptation training to new employment within the same firm (effectuated more than twice as often within the enterprise than by *convention*). Of the remaining 12 percent, 11 percent is devoted to professional promotion and barely 1 percent to prevention training, a state activity in terms of distribution of responsibility.

There is no indication of expenditure by kind of training; it can be said, though, that in 1973 almost half of all expenditures by enterprises for FPC were for maintained salaries of trainees (45 percent). Nearly 900 million francs (or more than one-fourth of all expenditures) went for training within the enterprises, while a little more than one-fifth of all expenses went directly to the "training market" (730 million francs). The training insurance funds (FAFs) received 4.2 percent of all payments. From the attempts of the budget document to reinterpret this meager contribution, it is apparent that the role of the FAFs remains a sore point. In the proposed text of the law of 1971, the training insurance funds were conceived as the normal vehicle for financing training, allowing wide scope for cooperation between labor market partners. This conception was all but eliminated in the parliamentary process because of the massive intervention of the employers' association. The budget document spuriously argues that the 4.2 percent de facto contribution to the FAFs represents 9 percent of the legal minimum obligation—when in fact it represents 7.8 percent of this notional sum and includes voluntary contributions from 6,500 firms with fewer than ten employees and, consequently, without legal obligation to participate (see Document Annexe, 1974, p. 32). Only a little less than 3 percent was transmitted to nonteaching organizations representing an acknowledged interest in the field of FPC, under the 10 percent rule of article 14.3 of the law of 1971 (see above discussion on the law of 1971).

Impressive though the global figures may be, they do not tell the whole story, since they conceal significant differences in the performance of FPC when broken down by size of enterprise and status and sex of trainees. As can be seen from Table 4, the percentage of trainees to all employed and the rates of FPC expenses in relation to the payroll increase considerably with the size of the

**Table 4. Percentage of Trainees to Employees and
of FPC Expenditures to Payroll, by Size of Enterprise, 1973**

| | Number of Employees | | | | Average |
| | | | | 2,000 or | for all |
	10–19	20–49	50–499	500–1,999	more	enterprises
Trainees/ employees	1.87%	3.70%	10.15%	16.02%	25.37%	14.12%
FPC/payroll	0.49%	0.68%	1.0 %	1.37%	2.39%	1.45%

Source: Adapted from Document Annexe, 1974, pp. 29, 31.

firms. This means, for instance, that an employee of a firm with 2,000 or more employees had thirteen times the chance of taking part in FPC than one employed in a small firm with 10 to 19 employees. The relative share of the payroll devoted to FPC expenditures is nearly five times as high for the large enterprises of 2,000 or more employees compared with small enterprises of 10 to 19 employees. This divergence of the ratios for chances of eligibility (13.6:1) and for expenditures (5:1) between the very large and small firms points to a relatively higher expenditure per trainee in small enterprises; put differently, it means that the training expenses of large firms are employed more efficiently.

This paradoxical relationship between costs and benefits is demonstrated strikingly by the fact that firms with less than 50 employees spent almost twice as much for each of their *trainees* compared with the firms with over 50 employees (4400:2380 francs), and yet the latter devoted nearly three times as many financial resources for FPC per *employee* as did the former (395:140 francs). Thus the greater chance for employees of medium and large enterprises to participate in FPC overcompensates the higher expenses for FPC *trainees* by small firms.

In terms of FPC expenses in relation to the payroll, enterprises with less than 50 employees spent 0.62 percent on the average, compared with 1.64 percent of the payroll of firms with 50 or more employees (in 1972, 0.58:1.55).[8] The latter sector comprises almost 80 percent of all employees. But even within this bracket, differences are substantial. Large firms with 2,000 or more employees devote almost three times as much money to FPC per employee (640 francs) as medium-sized firms with 50 to 499 employees (220 francs). According to Cheramy (1976, p. 23), it was with the largest enterprises, too, that the strongest relative growth, in terms of trainees as well as financial resources spent, could be observed

---

[8]Computed from the table on p. 28 of the Document Annexe, 1974. This table cannot be used for further comparisons since it subdivides firms by numbers of employees differently from the table for 1973, on p. 29 of the same document. Furthermore, the number of trainees by size classes of enterprises is not available for 1972, making comparisons of percentages of employee trainees by year impossible.

between 1972 and 1973. In addition, Cheramy states, "these enterprises, most of the time, did not wait for 1970 and 1971 to take an interest in the training of their workers: the new provisions have not radically changed the previous situation. It must be added that the core of this training, particularly in enterprises of more than 2,000 employees, is furnished within the enterprise, today as well as yesterday" (ibid).

While large enterprises have built up a comparatively costly internal training department, their FPC expenses per employee are a multiple of those incurred by small firms. The efficient operation of these internal training centers brings about, or even calls for, a high turnover of trainees at comparatively low costs per trainee—as compared with small firms that, as a rule, have to "buy" their FPC on the open market, which is more expensive per trainee. This is clearly the case for the small firms in a sample from three regions (*départements*) of France. In the sample, *all* courses of firms with 10 to 19 employees were bought externally, as compared to 83 percent of those with 20 to 49 employees; in firms with over 500 employees, 71 percent of the courses were externally organized (Commission des Finances, 1975, p. 16). For the whole sample, the courses organized internally (25.2 percent) accounted for 76 percent of all trainees.

The figures for FPC also vary significantly among branches of industry. While a detailed analysis is not possible, the dimensions can be indicated by a number of examples: the average rate of expenditures for FPC as a percentage share of the total payroll varies from 0.63 percent for plastics-transformation industries to 4 percent for public utilities (distribution of gas); the rate of trainees to all employees extends from 2.3 percent for lumber industries to 35.9 percent for banks and insurance companies (Cheramy, 1975, pp. 19 f.).

In general, FPC activities vary with the increasing preponderance of large enterprises in a sector of the economy, and with the absolute size of an enterprise as such; for enterprises with less than 50 employees, only a little more than 3 percent of all employees had also been trainees in 1973, whereas almost 17 percent of all employees in firms with 50 or more employees took part in some kind of FPC, as did every fourth employee of the very largest firms with 2,000 or more employees (Document Annexe, 1974, p. 31).

Similar differentiations apply for different categories of trainees. According to the Document Annexe, close to 60 percent of all trainees were unskilled or semiskilled workers or salaried workers (while more than 40 percent were foremen, technicians, engineers, and managers). The absolute numbers of the reference groups are not presented. However, 10 percent of all workers took a course, as against 30 percent of all foremen, technicians, engineers, and managers (Cheramy, 1975, p. 31).

French data traditionally distinguish between four categories in describing occupational structure: (1) laborers, semiskilled and skilled workers; (2) trained workers and employees; (3) technicians and lower level management; and (4) engineers and management. For purposes of comparison of further training these categories are somewhat unfortunate, since data from other countries indicate that the drop-off in participation rates occurs between skilled and semiskilled workers, both of which are included in the French category 1. Even so, certain conclusions can be drawn: a worker in category 1 employed by a small firm with 10 to 19 employees has virtually no chance of taking part in FPC, with the possible exception of adaptation to his place of work. In firms with less than 50 employees, trainees of groups 1 and 2 and those of groups 3 and 4 of the occupational hierarchy are almost equal in participation (51 percent: 49 percent), while for firms with more than 50 employees the national averages hold (59 percent: 41 percent). The above is only another way of stating the insignificance of small enterprises in matters of FPC as a whole: they represent 20 percent of the employees, but only 4.5 percent of the trainees. Returning to the extremes in the professional hierarchy, the differences between small and medium or large enterprises are significant: in small firms, category 1 workers only made up between one-third and one-fourth of the *absolute* number of trainees from category 4. In medium and large firms, these absolute figures are almost equal; but it is only in firms with 500 or more employees that the percentage share of trainees from category 1 to all *employees* of that category surpasses the corresponding relation in category 4, again without reference to the relative portion of the respective groups within the totality, let alone to the quality of the training. In training hours, unskilled workers received relatively more than the other groups (Document Annexe, 1974; Cheramy, 1976, p. 18, table 3).

The greater incidence of training of long duration for workers in category 1 appears to be counterintuitive. It can probably be explained by the inclusion for tax purposes of a significant portion of initial training of skilled workers in these figures. In evaluating the information given, one must not forget that it is supplied by firms that are under a legal obligation to prove certain minimum expenditures in a very imprecisely defined field of endeavor; thus the temptation to include as much of all training activities as possible must be very great.

As to the distribution of trainees by sex, only aggregate figures are available (for 1973 only): 78 percent of all trainees were men, 22 percent women. Stated otherwise, 16 percent of all male employees took part in some kind of FPC, but only 10 percent of all female employees were trainees of FPC (Cheramy, 1976, p. 18; Document Annexe, 1974, p. 31). The share of women is highest in group 1, with nearly a third; it is still high (28 percent) in group 2, but drops to 13 percent in group 3 and to 9 percent in group 4.

The Law of 1971 and the Civil Service[9]

According to article 41 of the law of 1971, the state is to create a policy of vocational training for its employees, taking into account the special character of the public service. Only in June 1973 were measures ordinanced creating a training service for civil servants, and in March 1975 the appropriate measures in favor of public employees without civil service status were adopted. These decrees created the control organs within the various public services. They have not yet affected the training procedures or the number of participants. As in industry, the ultimate decision on attendance rests with the civil servant's superiors. Available figures do not allow a clear distinction between initial and further training; they do show clearly that the higher ranking civil servants benefit disproportionally from training that has been undertaken

[9]This section is based on Cheramy, 1976, pp. 59–64.

thus far. Basically, further education in the civil service has thus far remained unaffected by the law of 1971, and it is probably by now less readily available than in industry, except for highest ranking civil servants.

Further Training for Teachers

Teachers form a special group within the civil services. Thus, while they fall under the general guidelines established in 1973 for extending the law of 1971 to the civil service, special regulations are to be expected for them. Thus far, only elementary school teachers and instructors in technical schools have recognized rights of further education. By ministerial order of June 20, 1972, every civil service teacher in the elementary schools has the right to the equivalent of one academic year of full-time training leave during working life. This right cannot be exercised during the first year or the last five years of service. In other words, the time available can be distributed flexibly over a period of approximately thirty years. This is financially equivalent to 1.7 weeks per year. During the first six years of the program, preference was to be given to teachers under fifty years of age; courses of three months full-time or six weeks full-time equivalent spread over the entire school year were provided in 1972–73.

A first report on the results of these efforts (Regione Lombardia, 1973a, pp. 118–122) indicates that problems have been encountered because of differences in motivation of the participants, depending on whether or not they identify with reform of the educational system; wide differences of experience as well as the lack of basic pedagogic training in the initial phase of teacher training have also created difficulties. Obviously, the introduction of so extensive a right to educational leave for elementary school teachers was seen as an instrument to achieve greater acceptance of intended reforms.

Similarly, teachers in technical institutes (secondary vocational schools) were given educational leave rights as a means of achieving an ulterior purpose. In 1972–73 the 32,000 teachers in this sector went on strike to force an upgrading of their professional status. This was ultimately accorded with the condition that all of the teachers involved undertake a four-month course of full-time supplementary training beginning in late 1974. As presently framed, this leave must be seen as a single grant rather than as a policy such as the one enunciated for elementary school teachers.

The Infrastructure of FPC in France

The law of 1971 provided for the creation, both by the state and by the private sector, of an infrastructure of research, documentation, and information on the FPC system. A large number of public, private and joint organizations now are engaged in providing support services of all kinds (Luttringer, 1974). Universities received annual grants from the state to finance the coordination and implementation of FPC activities.

The majority of organizations that have carried out the tasks of information, documentation, and research were created in the late 1960s and have received additional support through the codification of 1971. The major exception is the agency of the national education authorities, the Association for the Development of Permanent Education (ADEP), which was founded only in 1973 to complete the advisory and coordinate structure that had been developing steadily within the educational system. This delay of approximately five years in the educational sector can be viewed as symptomatic of the fact that the major elements of the French FPC policy evolved outside the educational system.

The system of information and documentation that has developed represents an external infrastructure. Most of the institutions involved do not engage in teaching trainees (although they often train instructors), nor are they directly linked to enterprises. The principal means of information dissemination appear to be the public media and the large-scale distribution of information materials. The effect has been to create a widespread awareness of the existence of FPC and of the general rights of employees (see Table 5), but the decision-making process concerning the exercise of these rights and the accounting for the use of the available resources remain—in accordance with the law—separate from the information and documentation system.

The extremely small number of people exercising their individual right to educational leave is witness to the fact that there also exists an internal infrastructure within the enterprise that differs

Table 5. Information and Attitudes Concerning FPC of Employees in France—Selected Items from a Public Opinion Survey, January 1974

Question: Do you know that the July 16, 1971, law allows all employees to attend educational/training courses?

	Total	Executives	Middle Management	Staff	Manual Workers
Yes	76[a]	96	87	76	67
No	23	4	13	24	32
No answer	1	—	—	—	1

Question: How have you been informed about recurrent education/training?

		Total
Through the mass media		63
Press	24	
Television	22	
Radio	17	
At work		54
By education/training officers	31	
By colleagues	14	
By union representatives	9	
Through a public office		12
No answer		21[b]

Question: Would you be personally interested in attending an educational/training course?

	Total	Executives	Middle Management	Staff	Manual Workers
Very much	31	46	42	33	20
Fairly	24	24	30	26	22
	(55)	(70)	(72)	(59)	(42)
A little	8	5	4	6	12
No interest	34	18	22	33	44
	(42)	(23)	(26)	(39)	(56)
No answer	3	7	2	2	2

Question: What do you expect from an educational/training course?

	Total	Executives	Middle Management	Staff	Manual Workers
To acquire new quali- fications in view of internal promotion	34	31	34	44	30
Refresh your technical skill to ensure the security of your job	28	23	35	21	30
Personal development	19	27	24	16	15
To acquire new quali- fications in order to change your occupation	11	16	5	13	13
No answer	8	3	2	6	12

Question: If an educational/training course was offered to you, what would be the biggest obstacle to accepting it?

	Total	Executives	Middle Management	Staff	Manual Workers
Disruption of family life	44	38	47	49	42
Possible cut in salary during leave	23	27	20	22	25
Going back to school	12	7	6	11	16
Staying away from the firm	8	11	14	8	4
No answer	13	17	13	10	13

[a]All figures shown in these tables refer to percentages.
[b]The total exceeds 100 percent due to multiple answers.

Source: Charnley, 1975, pp. 75 ff., rendering of some of the main findings from a survey based on a representative sample of the French adult population, conducted by the French Institute of Public Opinion (IFOP) in December 1973 and January 1974.

from one firm to another. Where the firm maintains its own training department, it will have an institutional interest in recruiting trainees. Where external agencies are used, the personnel departments or the operating divisions will play a major role in large enterprises (depending on their organizational structure); in small firms training decisions still appear to be very much a matter of management discretion. In the few instances where a local trade union organization or a works council chooses to play an aggressive role in relation to FPC, it too can have an impact, although its legal position is not particularly strong; the most notorious case in this respect is the Lip watch factory, which was occupied and taken over by workers in 1973 (see Vinzier, 1974).

In general, trade unions have not played a very active role in further training, in spite of the fact that through the *protocole de Grenelle* and through the agreements of 1970 they participated in a crucial way in its creation immediately after 1968. The trade unions do not view FPC as an end in itself but as part of their total political strategy. Thus their attitudes are generally determined by whether or not they are willing to cooperate with employers and public authorities in reform projects. It must be said, however, that the system of FPC sanctioned by the law of 1971 strongly favors not only employment concerns but employers' interests more generally.

The relatively generous funding for the external infrastructure and the availability of state aid for equipment have meant that France has developed much the most comprehensive system of support for instructors in further vocational training, including the training of instructors themselves. As a matter of fact, this area of activity has proved to be one of the most important fields of activity for the older voluntary adult education associations within the overall field of FPC.

Educational Leave Outside of the Law of 1971

The law of 1971 has proved such a dominant factor in the development of educational leave in France that other educational leave effects have sometimes been neglected. The law of 1971, however, explicitly confirmed a number of long-standing laws in favor of trade union training and the training of youths. The fact that trade union training existed and continues to exist irrespective of the law of 1971 is probably a contributing factor to the trade unions' attitude toward the law. Their institutional stake in the law of 1971 is relatively low.

The law of July 23,1957, on worker education (*accordant aux travailleurs des congés non rémunérés en vue de favoriser l'éducation ouvrière*) provides a right to twelve days of unpaid leave for any worker interested in worker education or trade union training. The number of beneficiaries ranges from one to eighteen for production units up to a thousand workers, with two additional beneficiaries for every additional five hundred workers. No other conditions of eligibility apply, and the employer can refuse such leave only if he can convince the Works Council that it would impair production.

This law of 1957 does not provide for remuneration, but under a law of December 28, 1959, the state pays the union subsidies that cover the cost of travel, course expenses, and payment of earnings foregone to approximately 16,500 participants. In addition, works councils and trade unions can, and do, support participants from their regular funds so that at least 35,000 persons have the opportunity to attend such courses. Detailed figures are not, however, available. The basic distrust between some of the trade unions and the government is illustrated by the refusal of one of the unions (the CGT) to accept the government subsidies from 1959 to 1968 (CFDT, 1974).

In addition to the law of 1957, a law passed in 1961 established a parallel right to unpaid leave of absence for persons preparing to assume responsibilities in youth programs. In this instance, a variety of interested organizations assume the costs of salaries foregone.

Reforms of the Law of 1971

In the first few years of experience with the law of 1971, a number of defects have become manifest. The contradiction between the terms *congé formation* ("training leave") and *autorisation d'absence* ("authorized absence") continues as a symbol of the fact that a right to paid educational leave to be exercised by the worker at his discretion for purposes of his choosing was not created, in spite of the fact that this was the intention expressed by the law and still continues to be official policy: in fact, the recent Commission on the Future of Training called for an emphasis on elements of further education that are not directly vocational (Commission sur l'Avenir de la Formation, 1975, p. 21). None of these issues, however, is likely to be the subject of supplementary legislation in the foreseeable future. The first legislative initiative is devoted to eliminating the incongruous possibility for enterprises to credit state support for their internal programs to their financial obligation to provide FPC and is attempting a closer regulation of the institutions engaged in offering FPC courses.

The first four years of the law have seen a rapid and virtually uncontrolled growth of the private-sector training institutions. The proposed revision of the law of 1971 brings all of these institutions under state control by requiring them to register and to submit an annual accounting of their activities; it further establishes an accountability of purveyors to purchasers of training.

The approach to the problems that have developed remains purely administrative. No attempt is made to define the possible content of FPC more closely; nor is there a discussion of the difficulties in establishing a *congé éducation,* that is, of the failure of the law of 1971 to meet its major stated objectives. Consequently, while institutions are likely to come under closer control, there remains no control of the utilization of the law by employers who are basically free to contract with any approved institution.

Conclusions

It would clearly be an exaggeration to view the law of 1971 as a paradigmatic educational leave law. Its purposes were too manifold, and its effects in terms of educational leave have been too limited for that. It is probably accurate to say that its impact in terms of educational leave has been exclusively vocational. The inability to provide nonvocational education during working hours was a problem of adult education before 1968 and between 1968 and 1971. It continues to be virtually impossible to provide it today.

While the law of 1971 brought growth in the area of further vocational education, this growth was not exceptionally large. Its primary effect was to draw medium and small enterprises into responsibility for providing continuing training for their employees and to achieve a slight increase in the training efforts of large enterprises. Nevertheless, the effects of the law have been much wider. It has stimulated public interest in further education, including nonvocational education; and on its fringes it has provided much needed support for adult education outside working hours, particularly in rural areas (where it is, of course, more difficult to distinguish between working and leisure time than it is in factories).

While these developments are statistically insignificant, they may represent a developing trend. There are some signs that employers are also increasingly willing to see at least a portion of the funds for FPC devoted to subjects not strictly vocational, a "culturization" of FPC, as one person put it. In this, French employers would be following tendencies developed in countries that have longer experience in further vocational training. In these countries narrow definitions of what constitutes the legitimate objects of further training are viewed with increasing suspicion as time goes by: training in the social sciences, in leadership techniques, and in general learning skills is viewed as a necessary supplement to clearly job-oriented programs (Commission sur l'Avenir de la Formation, 1975, p. 21).

The roundabout way in which these effects are achieved probably reflects conscious social policy in an attempt to reduce social conflict and to integrate marginal groups into society. Sociologically speaking, the main aim of the law of 1971 was harmonization. The law used an approach to reform that was novel in the French context: by encouraging, and on occasion forcing, the active and continuing participation of many social groups, it was attempting to stimulate the development of greater institutional pluralism and to devolve responsibility. By creating a field of education outside direct state control, the law of 1971 provided an incentive to institutional reform in existing public institutions, which were put on a roughly equal footing with private profit and nonprofit institutions.

The effects of these initiatives will take many years to become evident. The slowness with which the educational sector articulated its institutional infrastructure is probably an indication of the slowness with which it will tend to adjust to the challenges that the legislation has created. Thus while the law of 1971 has proved to be rather a disappointment from the point of view of educational leave, it remains to be seen whether or not it was the major social reform it was intended to be.

5

Germany

Federalism

The development of the educational system of the Federal Republic of Germany after World War II can only be understood in the light of two countervailing traditions—federalism on the one hand and centralism on the other—and in terms of the fear of centralism in cultural affairs instilled in the founders of the republic by the experience of National Socialism. Federalism in cultural affairs has a long tradition in German history, interrupted only by a period of vigorous centralism from 1918 to 1945. It is rooted in the multiplicity of sovereignties which have existed in Germany for many centuries. Within these sovereignties, however, it was taken as a matter of course that cultural affairs were highly centralized under the control of the state. Thus, while it is true that in educational affairs the eleven constituent provinces (*Länder*) of the Federal Republic are autonomous, it is also true that a variety of centralizing and coordinating bodies have been created over the years to maintain a fair measure of uniformity. In educational matters, Germany has thus succeeded in combining at least some of the disadvantages of federalism with some of the difficulties of centralization.

Three bodies have played an important role in the development of educational policy at a central level in Germany in recent years: the Federal Ministry of Education and Research (*Bundesministerium für Bildung und Wissenschaft*), the Permanent Conference of the Ministers of Culture (*Kultusministerkonferenz*) of the provinces, and the Joint Commission for Educational Planning (*Bund-Länder-Kommission für Bildungsplanung*).

The Permanent Conference of the Ministers of Culture maintains a secretariat that prepares decisions for the regular meeting of the ministers. All major policy decisions relating to education must be approved by this body, which operates by a rule of unanimity. This has made it an extremely unwieldy instrument of policy making in practice and has proved to be a major obstacle to necessary decision making both at the federal and provincial levels.

The Federal Ministry of Education and Research has only been in existence since a constitutional amendment gave the federal government a measure of authority in educational matters. This constitutional amendment was brought about primarily by the inability of state governments to finance education from the funds available to them at the time. The ministry has no operational responsibilities for institutions of education but can support construction programs of the *Länder* and finance certain kinds of research and educational experiments, often through the Joint Commission. The ministry has an important function in legislation of frames of reference for the *Länder* and participates equally in the development of the system of higher education. The federal government is responsible for financial aid to students at all levels. The Joint Commission for Educational Planning, as the name implies, is intended to coordinate activities of the federal and provincial governments through planning. It has played a central role in developing new concepts and proposals in the educational system but has had great difficulty in getting them accepted and implemented, since it has no firm operational relationship either to the provincial governments or the federal authorities. It also lacks a base in the various parliaments concerned with educational decision making.

These public authorities are complemented by advisory bodies, professional associations, and the associations of institutions of education, even if these are in the public sector and, consequently, nominally under the authority of the ministers of culture. The system of education that these institutions created has been subjected to several reforms in recent years, but its basic structure

Figure 3. Structure of the educational system in the Federal Republic of Germany, 1970

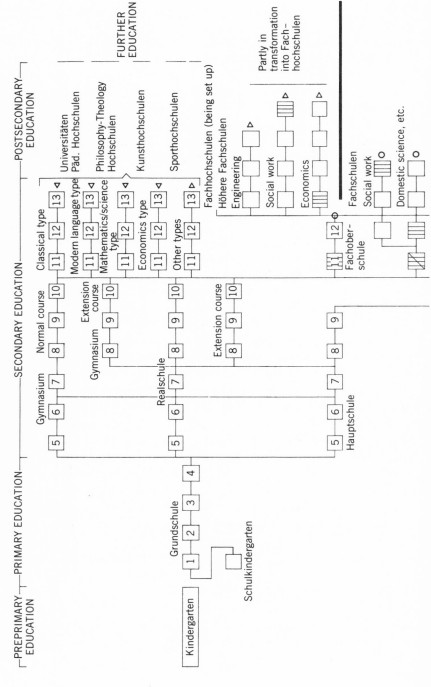

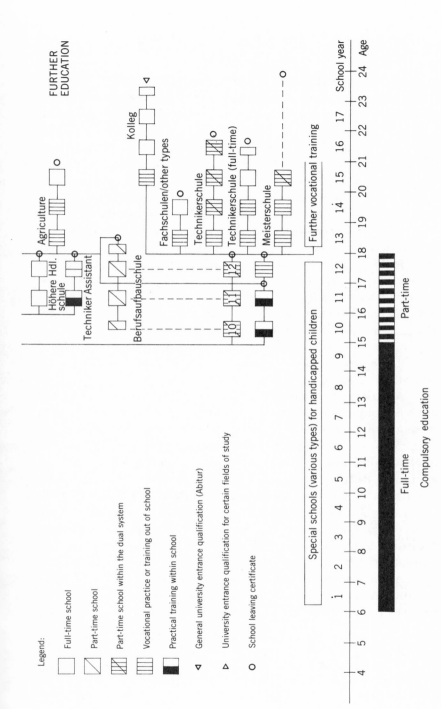

Source: OECD, 1972.

remains unchanged except at the fringes (see Figure 3). It continues to be streamed and highly selective by international standards, with the attendant problems of repeated years of schooling and high dropout rates.[1]

The mosaic of institutions and influence groups has made German educational policy one of the most complex systems of policy making anywhere in Europe, and in the areas of vocational training and adult education it is even more complex. Traditionally, industry, the chambers of commerce (*Handelskammern*), and the craft chambers (*Handelwerkskammern*) have played a central role in vocational training. In terms of the state role, division of responsibility between the state authorities is quite clear, at least in theory; the *Länder* are responsible for all forms of in-school vocational training, and the federal government is responsible for out-of-school training. Since Germany has a dual system of combined apprenticeship and schooling, this theoretically clear distinction is blurred in practice. Germany remains, nevertheless, one of the few European countries whose system of vocational education stands in high regard.

A variety of organizations and institutions contribute to the adult education system. Major portions of the system are organized through folk high schools (*Volkshochschulen*) by the local communities and counties, which do not otherwise play a significant role in educational policy. The church also plays a major role. The organization of the church is also federal: the units of organization are, however, not the provinces of the Federal Republic but traditional church provinces. The trade unions, also important to the adult education structure, are organized regionally and nationally according to major trades and are further organized in a national federation (*Deutscher Gewerkschaftsbund,* or DGB). The employers are represented by a parallel organizational structure. All these institutions have maintained adult education programs at least through the interwar years. Finally, a large number of voluntary

[1]For example, over 10 percent of students in grades 7 to 12 of the *Gymnasium* in Saarland were repeating their grade during the school year 1968–69; and in 1967, only 51 percent of all students in Germany who had been in the seventh grade in 1961 earned the *Abitur* at the end of grade 13 and qualified for university admission (Kornadt, 1974, pp. 18–19).

organizations exist whose sole purpose is the provision of adult education. This diversified, pluralistic structure represents the kind of system which the French policy of *concertation* is trying to create.

In regard to labor market policy, goals and responsibilities are much more clearly defined. The Ministry of Labor is the responsible body, and all legislation must be federal.

All the above institutions participate in some form in programs affecting educational leave in Germany. It is, therefore, not quite accurate to speak of the situation as federalism: the reality of day-to-day administration and policy making is more comparable to a cat's cradle. Nevertheless, the only way to achieve some measure of understanding of the present situation and future responsibilities concerning educational leave in Germany is to consider the question level by level and, if necessary, group by group. No other form of argument would be commensurate with the situation.

Activities at the Federal Level

At the federal level one can distinguish between two quite purposefully unconnected developments in the area of educational leave: the substantial and growing program oriented toward the labor market and the attempts to legislate an educational leave program. In German usage, *Bildungsurlaub* has increasingly come to mean leave for nonvocational education, although the practice in those *Länder* which have introduced legislation for *Bildungsurlaub* is much less clear-cut in this respect than the continuing theoretical debate might lead one to believe (see discussion later in this chapter). At the federal level, this separation continues.

Labor Market Activities

In July 1969, the German *Bundestag* passed the Labor Promotion Act (*Arbeitsförderungsgesetz*), which was designed to develop an instrument to achieve better coordination of vocational education and the labor market. This act systematized and amplified trends that had been present in Germany since the achievement of full employment in the mid-fifties and the attempts to cope with the effects of structural unemployment in the coal-mining regions of the Ruhr. At that time, the need for an active labor market policy designed to avoid major structural unemployment was recognized, and the first large-scale retraining programs were developed in the Ruhr area. Many years of full employment had also meant that large sums of money had accumulated in the unemployment insurance agency.

Since 1927, Germany has provided unemployment insurance through a semipublic independent agency known since 1968 as the *Bundesanstalt für Arbeit,* financed by fluctuating compulsory contributions paid equally by employers and employees (most recently 2 percent of wages). The federal government guarantees the financial position of the employment agency in case payments exceed receipts. After lengthy political argument, the Labor Promotion Act was passed; it authorized the employment agency to engage in programs in support of labor market–oriented education in addition to its traditional services of providing unemployment insurance and job-placement services. The employment agency became responsible for such diverse matters as providing living allowances to apprentices and undertaking rehabilitative education for handicapped workers. Further education was only one segment of these activities. (Deutscher Bundestag, 1973, p. 20). Criteria for intervention were that it should serve an interest transcending the individual enterprise, that it should fulfill an identifiable labor market demand, and that the beneficiary should not have alternative resources.

In essence, this first program was financed by the contributions of employers and employees, and until 1974, when the federal government had to provide financial support to the employment agency for the first time, this remained the case. In 1972 a total of 1.5 billion deutsche marks was spent on further education of individuals. Only in 1975 did the form and volume of labor market training again become a political issue as ways were sought to reduce the deficits of the employment agency.

One of the explicit purposes of the Labor Promotion Act was to increase the mobility of employees. Traditionally, mobility has not been high in German industry, and it was assumed that a more mobile labor force would also of necessity be more adaptable to structural changes in the labor market.

In passing the law, the *Bundestag* (the German parliament)

stated frankly that the demand for such training assistance was unknown. In consequence, no limit was set on the number of participants or on expenditure, but a report was called for after four years to reassess the effectiveness of the measures, and particularly the means of financing them. This report, already published in March 1973 (Deutscher Bundestag, 1973), remains the principal source of information about the volume and scope of activities in labor market training, although recently published figures indicate that with rising unemployment the number of applications for training has also risen steeply. Participants in retraining rose from 23,420 in 1970 to 36,560 in 1974, while the number of participants in all programs under the Labor Promotion Act jumped from 170,166 in 1970 to 288,390 in 1971 and then fluctuated down to 232,597 in 1974 (Deutscher Bundestag, 1973, p. 81; Bundesanstalt für Arbeit, 1975, pp. 130 ff.).

Any person liable to compulsory unemployment insurance contributions is eligible for further vocational education in recognized programs. The grants cover all course-related expenses up to a maximum rate per hour of instruction and provide an allowance for earnings foregone that is modeled on the lines of unemployment payments. Since the agency also provides tuition, the program is an indirect source of support for the institutions providing the education; these are most often private, generally nonprofit, and affiliated to one or the other of the labor market partners.

The parallels between the German Labor Promotion Act of 1969 and the French law of 1971 are striking: the major support categories, the background of the participants, and the division of responsibility between public and private institutions are in practice almost identical, even though the legislative frame of reference is so different. Since the legislative history of the German law is much simpler and its application far more clear and direct, and since the available data are based on a user survey and not on a fiscal document, it is possible to discuss the effects of the German law much more briefly.

The main difference between the French and the German situation is that the German Labor Promotion Act is a supplementary measure that does not affect many coexisting activities in further vocational education, whereas the French legislation seeks to organize the entire field of further education. In Germany the tradition of plurality in adult education is well established, and the state need act only as a balancing factor; in France the state has traditionally been dominant in all educational matters and is seeking to decrease its role.

During the first full year of the Labor Promotion Act in Germany (1970), a total of 170,166 persons were supported in one of the three major areas of activity: upgrading of skills, retraining for new occupations, and the job induction of the newly hired. Of these, 76.1 percent were male. In the following year, 288,390 were supported, of whom 78.3 percent were male; in 1972, 260,285 participated in labor market training courses, with 79.3 percent male enrollment.

A number of clear trends have emerged over the years in the composition of the participants: growth has occurred primarily in the area of upgrading courses, an area most heavily frequented by men and by more highly skilled workers. The total number of retraining and job-induction grants used primarily by workers without any completed training has remained fairly steady. Notably, the 25- to 35-year age group has provided the majority of new male participants so far and nearly a third of the female participants (Deutscher Bundestag, 1973, p. 83):

	Male		Female	
Age Group	*1970*	*1971*	*1970*	*1971*
Under 25	28.8%	25.1%	39.9%	39.5%
25–34	51.2	53.1	29.4	32.6
35–44	15.1	17.3	18.5	18.1
45–54	3.9	3.9	10.4	10.4
55 and over	1.0	0.6	1.8	1.8

In addition to information on the implementation of the Labor Promotion Act, the report of 1973 also contains data on the participation rates of the labor force in any form of further vocational education, based on an analysis of the educational history of a representative sample of employees. This study shows a strong correlation between prior education and further education. Depending on the level attained before leaving school, participation rates in further vocational education range from 9.8 percent for those who have no initial vocational training to 54.4 percent for those who have attended teacher training colleges. This result has since been confirmed by two further independent studies (Deutscher Bundestag, 1973, pp. 29–30).

In spite of fairly extensive advertising efforts, the weaknesses of the Labor Promotion Act in reaching certain groups of workers are almost classic: although this form of vocational education represents a right of the employee enjoyed equally by all, and although support for income foregone is available if the employer is unwilling to provide it, unskilled, semiskilled and agricultural workers, as well as women, remained severely underrepresented relative to the proportion of the labor force they represent (Deutscher Bundestag, 1973, p. 66).

The Study Support Law

In 1971, the federal government undertook a reform of the entire system of financial support for students through the Study Support Law (*Bundesausbildungsförderungsgesetz*). Up to that point, primarily university students had been eligible for federal support (the *Länder* did not provide financial aid), and only if they had above-average ability. Under the new law, every student has a right to financial support, subject to means tests, from completion of compulsory schooling up to the age of thirty-five; support is given beyond the age of thirty-five to complete study begun earlier. Proof of normal progress is required, and support is only given in the form of loans for a second course of studies at a level completed beforehand.

As of August 1974, the amount of support was limited to a maximum of 480 deutsche marks per month, which represents no more than 50 percent of after-tax earnings of the lowest paid workers. While it provides basic support to unmarried students, it can hardly be considered maintenance of salary. On the other hand, it does offer the opportunity for reentry into the educational system up to the age of thirty-five, albeit at considerable financial sacrifice. Since no job security is provided, BAFÖG (as it is widely known in Germany) does not provide educational leave, but it does represent a step in this direction; it eliminates the notion of lock-step education from beginning to end and allows students flexible points of reentry. In recent years, however, the effectiveness of BAFÖG in this respect has been restricted by the introduction of entry limitations in higher education, making effective reentry under BAFÖG possible only at the upper secondary level.

Attempts to Create Federal Legislation for Educational Leave

In the light of the various federal competencies for labor market regulation and initial vocational education, an argument could be made for introducing comprehensive educational leave legislation at the federal level in spite of the constitutional primacy of the *Länder* in cultural matters. This approach would avoid the problem of major differences between the *Länder* and would eliminate the difficult process of negotiating with eleven different parliaments. Because of these advantages, the passage of the Labor Promotion Act, as well as that of two other federal acts pertaining to vocational training in 1969, led to a renewed debate on nonvocational *Bildungsurlaub*.

The basic program of the German trade union federation (*Deutscher Gewerkschaftsbund,* or DGB) called for the provision of educational leave in 1963, and it reiterated this demand after the ILO debates of 1965 in its "action program" (Freyberg and others, 1975, pp. 1 ff.). In these documents, *Bildungsurlaub* is still defined as comprising both vocational and civic education.

The newly installed coalition government under the leadership of the Social Democratic party, with its close ties to the labor movement, declared its intention to legislate an educational leave law as part of the comprehensive program of social and economic reforms announced in 1969. After the passage of the Labor Promotion Act, the term *Bildungsurlaub* increasingly came to be applied to nonvocational education complementing the vocational education provided by labor market legislation.

With departure from the labor market orientation, the educational authorities for the first time also became involved in the debate, which in turn brought the peculiarities of the German federal structure into full play. A large number of studies and position papers were developed by the trade union (Görs, 1974); by the

Deutsche Bildungsrat, an advisory body on educational policy (Deutscher Bildungsrat, 1973); and by the *Bund-Länder-Kommission für Bildungsplanung,* which developed a comprehensive educational plan for the period up to 1978 (*Bund-Länder Kommission für Bildungsplanung, 1973*). The employers played a largely defensive role at this stage. The result of this extensive planning activity, which was supplemented by a number of theoretical publications on *Bildungsurlaub* (Siebert, 1972), was essentially a stalemate, with the paradoxical outcome that discussions of educational leave at a federal level came to a halt almost simultaneously with the adoption of the ILO convention, although the chance of federal legislation appears to have disappeared by the fall of 1971, when the Factory Constitution Law was being prepared.

The initiative for educational leave legislation then passed to the *Länder,* with the federal government financing studies and pilot projects for the time being. After several *Länder* had created educational leave legislation (see discussion later in this chapter), the Joint Commission for Educational Planning was requested by the heads of government of the *Länder* and the federal chancellor (not the ministers of culture) to study the possibilities for uniform legislation on educational leave. After a year of study, the commission developed an Outline for a Sequential Plan for Further Education (*Strukturskizze für einen Stufenplan zur Weiterbildung*) that contained some remarks on educational leave. These remarks tend to confirm, however, the generally held opinion that a federal law on educational leave is not to be expected in the foreseeable future (Deutsche Presse Agentur, 1974), even though the ILO convention is likely to be ratified with existing legislation as justification.

Labor Union Training

In the course of the general debate about *Bildungsurlaub,* provision was made for educational leave for a special group. By means of the Factory Constitution Law of 1972 (*Betriebsverfassungsgesetz*), educational leave was secured for all members of the works councils. In Germany, the works council does not act as a branch of the trade union but plays a role defined solely in terms of the individual factory. While members will generally be members of the trade union, the union must maintain a separate organization at factory level and does not have control over the actions of members of works councils.

Under the 1972 law (Urbach and Winterhager, 1975, pp. 25–26), members of the works councils received the right to attend courses that provided skills necessary to the work of the council without loss of pay. In principle, this right is not subject to a time limit, except that the production requirements of the firm must be taken into account and agreement must be achieved between the council and the employers concerning the timing of courses. In case of conflict, a mediation board arbitrates. The law further stipulates that every member of the works council has the right to three weeks paid leave during his two-year term of office to attend special courses recognized for this purpose by the labor authorities of the *Land,* after consultation with representatives of the unions and the employers. Where a member is elected to the council for the first time, this minimum right is increased to four weeks, unless he was previously a youth representative. The youth representatives have an organization that parallels the works council and represents the particular interests of young employees; youth representatives are treated as members of the works council with regard to educational leave rights.

During the first years of operation not all those with this right to educational leave have been able to exercise it; there has been a lack of suitable courses and facilities. After the necessary expansions, which must be financed by the responsible institutions—primarily trade union institutes but also institutions associated with the employer federations—it can be assumed that this entire group will use the right the law gives them, since candidacy for elective office is probably adequate proof of motivation.

Educational Leave in Labor Contracts

Since it first called for provisions for educational leave in 1963, the labor union movement has made repeated attempts to have educational leave provisions included in the labor contracts they have negotiated. By 1974, 198 branch and factory contracts, covering approximately 2.2 million workers, had been signed (WSI, 1974). In some instances they provide for leave for trade union officials and have therefore been redundant since passage of the Factory Constitution Law in 1972.

Nothing is known about the degree to which these provisions have been utilized in general. Since they are part of the labor contract, utilization depends almost entirely on the trade union. Even where a generalized right to educational leave has been established, workers are unlikely to claim it unless the trade unions actively promote its use. There is certainly no evidence that these sometimes fairly generous provisions have led to the creation of a market for adult education where none existed before. It appears warranted to assume that these contractual provisions have mainly been used to support attendance of courses (including vocational courses) in institutions linked to the trade union movement. This, at least, is the clear inference we draw from the slightly better documented experience of the first year of the public educational leave law in Hamburg (see discussion of activities at the provincial level in this chapter).

An exception to this general rule is the contract that was first negotiated in the corsetry industry in 1964 and has regularly been renewed. Under this complex contract, the employers agreed to the creation of a bipartite industry foundation that was to be fed by payment of a sum equal to 4 percent of the payroll. This foundation in turn paid 25 percent of its income (1 percent of the payroll) to a union foundation whose purpose was to provide education, leisure, and convalescence support to employees in the corsetry industry (Stiftung Miederindustrie, 1974).

This undertaking is unusual in several respects. Dating back more than ten years, it represents one of the earliest attempts to initiate educational leave programs in Germany on a systematic basis; moreover, the employees of the corsetry industry are predominantly unskilled and female and thus represent a group which is habitually underrepresented in further education. The foundation's approach to the peculiar problems of the contract's beneficiaries is interesting: no vocational courses are offered; rather a careful mix of educational and recreational activities is sought, so as to overcome the largely passive attitude of the participants. Time for pure recreation and informal contacts between the participants and the instructors within agreeable surroundings is part of the avowed purpose of the programs offered. Because of the security of the financial position of the foundation and the clearly identified group of beneficiaries, the educational strategy is a fairly long term one: a common introductory course designed to reintroduce participants to the learning processes and to group exploration of political and economic subjects leads to a variety of course sequences on these topics. The entire program covers several years. In comparison with a number of other experiments which have been conducted in Germany with low-status workers (Deutscher Bildungsrat, 1973; Freyberg and others, 1975; Siebert, 1972), the program of the corsetry industry is distinguished by its low-pressure, relatively untheoretical approach, and above all by its ability to undertake programs over longer periods of time with intervals of work.

Educational Leave Rights of Civil Servants

Civil servants are, according to German law, not ordinary employees. Their conditions of employment are regulated by a special law and by a large number of executive orders. Among other restrictions, civil servants are not allowed to undertake additional work in their free time without the approval of their superiors. They cannot receive leave, with or without pay, except in cases regulated by law; this, contrary to the practice in industry, for example, is not a matter left to the discretion of their superiors. As a result, the leave provisions of executive orders concerning the conditions of employment of civil servants are fairly substantial; they are further complicated by the fact that each commune and *Land* has its own provisions within a broad framework set by federal law. Under these circumstances, the relevant provisions must be seen not so much as rights of the civil servants, as guidelines for their superiors (Urbach and Winterhager, 1975, pp. 18–25). The point of comparison for these guidelines should not be the educational leave provisions of the labor contracts but rather the practice of industry in giving leave for in-service training.[2] From this perspective, the provisions are not particularly generous and are heavily weighted in favor of higher civil servants. Apart from provisions

[2]Charnley, 1975, erroneously assumes that these provisions provide some three million civil servants with educational leave rights.

for leave to attend to collective bargaining concerns and to seek elective office, leave can only be granted to attend scientific congresses and to participate in courses offered by the state, and only if these are in the interest of the civil servant's work. In these instances, and for courses of civic education recognized for this purpose, leave of generally three days at a time and not more than six days a year can be granted. For language courses, up to three months can be given. A special provision for leave in cases not explicitly mentioned does allow some flexibility, but it states unequivocally that the criterion for permission is solely its relevance to work.

In 1974, some three thousand courses were approved by the federal authorities, and attendance was rather less than ninety thousand, or less than 7 percent of those eligible. More than 50 percent of these courses were organized by the trade unions or civil service associations, suggesting strongly that they involved activities which are essentially comparable to those provided to members of works councils under the Factory Constitution Law (Stein-Ruegenberg, 1975).

It is difficult to compare these provisions with general practice in industry. They are probably more generous in their effect, even though they do not provide the individual with the right to initiate leave requests against the judgment of his superior. Furthermore, many of the public services—railway, post office, and municipal works—maintain training schools that they use as industry uses its internal training facilities for further vocational education. The legislator obviously does not consider these training activities leave at all, but simply part of the normal work load.

In-Service Training in Industry

The Labor Promotion Act provided support for certain training functions that might otherwise have been undertaken by industry, covering costs for 53.8 percent of all participants in courses attended at the initiative of their employers. All the job-induction courses, as well as an unknown proportion of all other courses under the act, are conducted at the place of work or in the enterprise itself. In-service training is financed directly by industry and through the Labor Promotion Act. It is impossible to determine the relative contributions of both sources of finance; the question of labor market training has not been studied. The 1969 Labor Promotion Act stipulated that courses serving the purposes of a single enterprise or branch of industry could be supported only under exceptional circumstances. This stipulation has caused difficulties in application, and it has meant that persons who were planning to become self-employed or civil servants (who do not contribute unemployment insurance premiums) were excluded from the courses. At the same time, it is likely that the Labor Promotion Act provided a stimulus to further vocational training inside industry, since the existence of an alternative external source of training for workers aspiring to professional advancement required special efforts on the part of industry if they were to be retrained (Sasse, Segenberger, and Weltz, 1974, p. 31).

The training effort financed entirely by industry unquestionably remains a very significant one. A 1971 study showed expenses incurred by industry for further training of 2.1 billion deutsche marks. Since the average cost per participant in industry is much below that in the government program (see discussion above), this would imply industry support of another 600,000 employees, or 2.4 percent of the labor force. Assuming a certain amount of double counting, this would mean that approximately 3.5 percent of the labor force receives some form of further vocational training annually. This estimate of the relative importance of in-service training and external initiatives also corresponds roughly to the data on the educational experiences of persons interviewed in the 1970 "microcensus" (Sasse, Segenberger, and Weltz, 1974, p. 54, n. 43).

During the 1960s, Germany experienced the most acute labor shortage of any major industrial country. Only Sweden, Switzerland, and the Netherlands have had comparable difficulties in meeting their labor needs. Because of the inadequacy of the external labor market as a source of recruitment, firms were increasingly forced to develop internal programs of further education to meet their needs for qualified labor. Germany has therefore had a strong and growing system of further vocational education in industry for the last ten years. It is also one of the best-studied systems of in-service training in Europe, with a large number of studies providing information on many aspects of this system.

A sampling of industries revealed that management and skilled workers are, if anything, more strongly represented in in-service training financed by industry than is any other group, regardless of the form that such training takes. One-third of all firms providing in-service training do so exclusively for management personnel. The present evidence indicates clear-cut priorities. In virtually all branches of industry, in-service training is provided for highly qualified management personnel. Other groups are provided for subsequently and in descending order, depending on prior levels of training, albeit at a lower volume of activity relative to the numbers involved. Only in exceptional cases and insignificant numbers do employees without prior vocational training benefit from these activities.

In the light of the evidence presently available, there can be no doubt that in-service training programs in industry, while very substantial in volume, strongly accentuate differential levels of educational attainment upon entry into the labor force (Sasse, Segenberger, and Weltz, 1974, pp. 60 ff.). One is led to assume that more highly qualified employees will be more aware of the effects of changing social and technological conditions on their positions and will therefore seek to offset these effects actively. From the employers' viewpoint, the more highly qualified employees represent a greater asset in terms of education and experience and are less easily replaced, and this justifies the substantial expenditure on their future training.

The results of these efforts for participants can be much more ambivalent than one would suppose at first glance. The activities of most coordinated industrial programs are aimed at achieving a somewhat paradoxical effect: increasing the qualifications specific to the needs of an enterprise while avoiding an increase in general qualifications great enough to increase the beneficiary's mobility in the external labor market. To the extent that this goal is achieved, one may conclude that "for many, presumably for a majority of employees, the development of in-service further education achieves no, or even negative, change in his position within the overall labor market" (Sasse, Segenberger, and Weltz, 1974, p. 111), thus highlighting the fact that further education does not guarantee benefits to the individual involved.

Educational Leave Effects in the Armed Forces

In nineteenth-century Germany, the army was often referred to as "the nation's school"—a reflection of the militaristic spirit of the age and of the fact that the army, rather than the schools, was considered the principal institution of socialization. The dangers of this tradition were an important element in the discussions on the creation of the West Germany army (*Bundeswehr*) in 1956. Consequently, all educational activities of the *Bundeswehr* were initially viewed with a certain distrust; when two universities of the *Bundeswehr* were founded with the status of "private" universities in 1962, they also encountered strong hostility. Nevertheless, the armed forces have developed a substantial system of education based on the Service Support Law (*Soldatenversorgungsgesetz*) of 1957 and organized in the Vocational Support Service (*Berufsförderungsdienst*) created in 1960. Because of the sometimes controversial nature of these activities in the public mind, the development of education in the *Bundeswehr* has been fairly well documented— better, at any rate, than in any other European country.

The German armed forces are based on conscription. Hence they differ from any other form of employment in that the majority of soldiers view their service as a transitory phase only. Even volunteers with contracts of more than two years expect to enter civilian employment at a later stage. For them, the possibility of obtaining further training at full salary is a major attraction of the armed forces. In this sense they are also a strongly self-selected group, since the opportunities for training rather than a call to national duty form the cornerstone of the recruitment program of the *Bundeswehr*. More than in any other institution, further training is considered an important fringe benefit to obtain "employee" loyalty. In the case of the *Bundeswehr* the increased mobility of beneficiaries is an accepted, and to some extent even a welcomed, side effect.

The educational programs of the *Bundeswehr* cover three elements, depending on length of service: (1) general education and further vocational education during the period of service, (2) support for vocational education after completion of the period of service, and (3) assistance in reentry into civilian employment.

These activities cover elementary through higher education. Examinations providing access to qualified positions are administered by the civilian authorities, except for examinations at the universities of the *Bundeswehr*, which have been authorized to award their own degrees.

It is possible to obtain the *Mittlere Reife*, the tenth-grade certificate, in the *Bundeswehr* during one year of part-time study during service hours, whereas in civilian life the only possibility is a two-year course at evening school. Volunteers with periods of service from five to ten years acquire the right to one to one and a half years of paid training leave at 90 percent of their last salary at the end of their contract, enabling them to finance their training.

No figures are yet available on the universities of the *Bundeswehr*, but the planned capacity of the two institutions is 4,600 students. Attendance at study circles and vocational courses was 92,071 in 1973 and 115,014 in 1974, representing close to 10 percent of organized further vocational activities in Germany (Jäschke, 1975, p. 35).

The greater portion of these armed forces activities represent educational leave effects. The actual extent depends on whether one classifies members of the armed forces as employees—they certainly qualify for educational leave in the formal sense of our definition. A study on the motivation of participants and its effect on the courses would be particularly interesting; participants' motivation for further education is often strong enough to overcome resistances to the dependency that service in the armed forces implies. Clearly, the degree of involvement and the satisfaction of participants in this kind of environment would provide insight into the conditions in less authoritarian situations, with less rigorously screened participants.

Activities at the Provincial (Länder) Level

A good rule of thumb concerning federal distribution of authority in educational matters is "when in doubt, provincial authority." Adult education thus falls under provincial authority wherever it is not covered by explicit federal legislation linked to some ulterior purpose—labor market regulation, industrial democracy, or the military—that clearly falls under federal responsibility.

For many years, the development of adult education in Germany has been largely haphazard and voluntary, with minimal provincial legislation. Only more recently have the provinces begun to intervene and guide this process. In the course of this intervention, information is beginning to be developed in most provinces concerning the scope of present activities (Marten,1974; Meister, 1971; Wema Institut KG, 1974). The Joint Commission for Educational Planning is currently undertaking a survey of all activities of further education in the Federal Republic that is due to be ready by early 1976. The most important element of the adult education system are the *Volkshochschulen* (VHS), locally based institutions offering courses on all subjects (including vocational courses and preparation for school examinations for adults) to voluntary participants. In 1973, a total of 3.2 million course participants were registered in *Volkshochschulen*, and a further 3.8 million attended lectures or other single events. The instructors in this largely uncoordinated system are mostly part-time; the proportion of full-time to part-time nonclerical staff has remained approximately 1:100 over the past four years (Deutscher Volkshochschulverband, 1974).

The courses include a significant number that are clearly vocationally oriented, many of which will be attended on released time as part of the in-service training effort of small and medium-size firms. In 1968, 7.82 percent of the courses in the Bavarian *Volkshochschulen* clearly fell into this category, and a further 13.05 percent were language courses (Meister, 1971, p. 121); both categories have since grown much faster than the very rapid expansion of the VHS themselves. By 1973, languages constituted 26 percent of the VHS courses both in Bavaria and in the Federal Republic as a whole, and administrative and commercial subjects alone accounted for a further 9 percent (Deutscher Volkshochschulverband, 1974, table 5a).

In addition to the *Volkshochschulen,* the Protestant and Catholic churches, the major trade unions, the trade union federation, and a variety of rural organizations offer adult education courses. In 1968, these groupings accounted for 61.27 percent of all courses and 63.37 percent of all enrollments in Bavaria (Meister, 1971, p. 76, table 24), allowing us to assume that by 1973 in the Federal

Republic of Germany as a whole at least 6 million enrollments were registered annually in adult education (representing 9.7 percent of the population). These figures exclude the activities of the chambers of commerce and of the residential *Volkshochschulen,* which would raise the participation rate to approximately 11 percent for 1973. In all of these institutions, at least the vocationally oriented activities are being supported indirectly by released time for attendees, either from industry or—in considerable numbers— from the civil service. Although it is impossible to estimate the numbers involved, they are clearly very substantial, probably several hundred thousand annually, and they would be directly affected by any legislation in favor of educational leave.

The approach of the *Länder* to the problem of adult education and educational leave has been a two-pronged one: the establishment of legal guidelines for adult education and the discussion and in some instances adoption of explicit educational leave laws. All of the *Länder* have by now passed laws on adult education, regulating the conditions under which institutions can receive financial support and setting out basic requirements in terms of organization and legal responsibility (Marten, 1974). In Hessen the relevant law has gone further in prescribing that each of the administrative districts of the *Land* must have at least one public *Volkshochschule.* Thus first steps are being taken to fill gaps in the provision of adult education.

In 1973, the *Volkshochschulen* had a combined budget of 187 million deutsche marks. Of this, 59 percent was received in the form of subsidies. Of the subsidies, 46 percent were supplied by the local authority, 40 percent by the *Land,* and only 2 percent by the federal government. (Deutscher Volkshochschulverband, 1974).

The actions of the various states are contentious issues, as any further regulative measures are likely to be: unlike the "mainstream" educational institutions, adult education is a field in which private institutions predominate. Insofar as the state is active in this field at all, the responsible authority tends to be more local than the *Land,* either the *Kreis* (county) or one of the municipalities. Consequently, state regulation is something entirely new and not always viewed as beneficial, even attached to attractive subventions.

The variety of institutions and sponsors remains one of the characteristics of the field of adult education, and it is unclear what effect state regulation may have.

Five of the *Länder* have passed educational leave laws. But the five *Länder* form two distinct groups: Berlin and Hessen have laws for the further education of young people up to twenty-five (Hessen) or twenty-one (Berlin), while Hamburg, Lower Saxony, and Bremen have educational leave laws covering all workers. The fact that laws with such diverse groups of beneficiaries can still have the same name is one further indication of how diffuse the concept of educational leave (*Bildungsurlaub*) remains (see Table 6).

The Berlin law is the oldest of this set of relatively new laws; passed in 1970, it provides unlimited unpaid leave and up to ten days of paid leave for all workers and trainees up to their twenty-first birthday. The law allows both vocational and civic education, as well as courses leading to a school diploma, provided these are offered by a recognized institution or one that has been given special approval (Urbach and Winterhager, 1975, pp. 42–44). In its initial stages only an estimated 2 percent of the beneficiaries of the Berlin law actually exercised their right. Since the majority of beneficiaries who are not in full-time education are likely to have had negative experiences at school, one must assume that the law was designed to assist in special cases rather than to provide a broad range of opportunities. Young workers willing to take an active part in the work of the trade unions or the political parties, those in youth organizations, or those engaged in part-time study to reenter the educational system are the most likely beneficiaries under these circumstances.

The educational leave law in Hessen came into effect on January 1, 1975. It provides one week of leave for vocational or civic education in approved institutions. Approval is given by the Ministry of Social Affairs rather than by the Education Ministry, indicating that the thrust of the law is social rather than directly educational. The law provides for accumulation of leave rights from one year to the next, and states that educational leave rights existing under labor contracts can be applied only if the contract explicitly says so. The Hessian law extends the definition of workers who are covered to include those working in the household or in similar positions who are not independent.

Table 6. Overview of Laws for Educational Leave of Absence in the Länder

State of the Federal Republic	Principle	Persons entitled to leave	Length of leave
Berlin	Educational Leave Act of July 16, 1970; leave for vocational and political education	All workers and trainees until completion of their 21st birthday	Unlimited unpaid leave; maximum of 10 days paid leave annually
Hamburg	Hamburg's Educational Leave Act of January 21, 1974; leave for political education and advanced vocational training	All workers and trainees with place of principal employment in Hamburg; school and university teachers, social work teachers only during school/university/institution vacation	10 working days every 2 years; if 6-day working week, then a total of 12 days during same period
Bremen	Educational Leave Act of December 18, 1974	All workers and trainees with place of principal employment in Bremen; school and university teachers, social work teachers only during school/university/institution vacation	10 working days every 2 years; if 6-day working week, then a total of 12 days during same period
Lower Saxony	Lower Saxony Act on Educational Leave for Workers of May 10, 1974; right to leave for political, vocational and general education courses	All workers and trainees except for state officials and judges. No. of total educ. vac. days an employer must grant equals total no. of employees as of April 15 of each given year times 1.5	10 working days per annum, 12 per annum for 6-day work week
Hessen	Educational Leave Act of June 19, 1974; leave for vocational and political education	All workers until the age of 25	5 working days per annum

Source: OECD, 1975; Urbach, 1975 (for Bremen).

After it became apparent that no educational leave legislation was to be expected at the federal level, three *Länder* undertook to pass such laws themselves. The provisions in these three *Länder* differ slightly, but in the main they are comparable. Hamburg's law was the first of the three and represents the standard against which the other two laws were developed. To some extent, the differences between Hamburg and the other two *Länder* have been obscured administratively, since the practice has been to recognize courses mutually; that is, any course which is approved under the Hamburg law will also be recognized in the two other *Länder*.

The Hamburg law provides up to five days of educational leave per employee per year for all employees whose principal place of work is Hamburg. Employers are obliged to grant leave simultaneously to up to 2 percent of their work force unless production can be shown to be jeopardized. Only state-approved courses can be attended. Both vocational and general courses can be considered, and courses from the in-service training program of industries are eligible if they do not tend to decrease the participant's mobility; increased mobility is, in fact, one of the expressed goals of the Hamburg law. The three laws make no provision for the payment of course fees, which can be substantial in cases where extensive travel is involved. These must be paid either by the participant or by some interested organization.

The state's function under the law is simply to approve courses. During the first eighteen months, nearly three thousand courses were approved in Hamburg, many of them outside Hamburg (Amt für Berufs-und Weiterbildung, 1975). From the list of approved courses it is quite apparent that most of the principal institutions of adult and further vocational education have submitted all or part of their regular catalogs for approval, which has been fairly generously given. In several instances enterprises with large in-service training establishments have also submitted their catalogs and have received approval for all courses that the authorities felt might have relevance beyond the individual enterprise. The effect of this procedure is to transfer the cost of income maintenance to the employer without changing the preexisting institutional and course structure.

During the first year, 1,630 courses were approved. Of these 849, or 52 percent, were for further vocational education, while

781 were for civic education. In the following four months, a further 988 courses were approved, but of these 75 percent were devoted to vocational education. The strong trend toward vocational education can be explained by considering the institutions offering the courses. During the initial phase, trade unions and voluntary adult education institutions predominated because they had a vital interest in providing course participants with salary maintenance if they were not already receiving it. Industrial training departments had no participants who were not receiving salaries during in-service training. Their interest in applying for approval could only lie in a modest expansion of their enrollments and in a defensive strategy of the enterprises: insofar as they were able to have their internal courses recognized, they could apply workers attending these courses to the 2 percent limit for all educational leave absences, thus reducing the potential additional burden.

Only the number of courses approved is known. These courses are also open to participants not benefiting from educational leave, and thus it is not possible to determine how vigorously the right to educational leave has been exercised. The state authorities are not empowered to require institutions offering courses to provide this information. A recent informal survey of firms in Hamburg showed that utilization of educational leave benefits is extremely limited; between 0.3 percent and 0.4 percent of all eligible employees applied for leave, and they represented only about 5 percent of all employees engaging in some form of further training during working hours. According to this survey, 72 percent of the participants in 1974 were salaried employees. This corresponds fairly accurately with the structure of the course offerings: the vocational courses are oriented toward the salaried employees. Only 21 percent of the courses offered were not in the categories of lower-level management and languages. These 21 percent also comprise courses for engineering and advanced technical skills requiring substantial prior education. There are no courses which would allow reentry into the educational system, and not more than 1 percent of all vocational courses could be taken by workers without prior completed training. There are no courses designed to accommodate foreign unskilled workers.

One must assume that the necessity of paying course costs has proved an important selective device. Only those strongly motivated will be willing to do so from their own resources, and this generally means those with previous education. Otherwise, only members of organizations willing to finance course costs (the trade unions and the political parties; to a far less extent other groupings such as clubs and associations) will be able to participate; but active membership in such organizations is in itself a strongly selective characteristic.

From the available evidence, one must assume that the trade unions have been the primary beneficiaries of the laws: members of works councils are eligible for educational leave in addition to that provided under federal law (The Factory Constitution Law; see above) and the laws create a means of providing training for those who are not yet members of works councils or some other representative body. The trade unions can now conduct the training of their prospective middle-echelon representatives without the need for providing salary maintenance.

The existing institutions of adult and further vocational education without established links with individual firms and special branches of industry are also likely to experience some improvement in their recruitment prospects. Since they do not have access to the place of work, the effect is likely to be much more limited than in the case of the trade unions. While the law does stipulate that firms must formally approve applications for leave until the quota is filled, the actual decision requires action by the worker's immediate superior. Except in the case of very strong-willed people, or where the trade unions are willing to play an active role, this fact alone is bound to have a powerfully inhibiting influence. Employer-employee relationships are determined by a large number of factors, and the mutual attitude toward educational leave is necessarily only a subsidiary factor in this relationship—a fact which is often overlooked in studying educational leave. The laws of Hamburg, Lower Saxony, and Bremen are clearly trade unions laws, in the sense that they will change existing conditions only to the extent that the trade unions are committed to this.

Conclusions

The peculiarities of German federalism often obscure what can be and has been achieved. In the face of multiple competencies and highly fragmented practice, an analysis of so indeterminate a concept as educational leave appears to be impossible. Nevertheless, in tracing the various means by which educational leave effects can be achieved, one is struck by the manifold possibilities that exist. The various components have been patched together over many years without being considered as parts of a single, comprehensive policy, but the result is nevertheless fully adequate provision of further vocational training in all areas, a well-established system of adult education, and an emerging complex of possibilities for non-vocational further training during working hours, beginning with, and heavily dependent on, the trade unions. The debate on *Bildungsurlaub* has been restricted to the nonvocational policies, both because this remains the area of greatest need and because it would tend to complement available programs.

A number of options available in other countries do not, however, exist in Germany. The most important element in the German situation in respect to educational leave is the relative unavailability of the system of initial education. The federal structure, and even more the many unsolved problems of structure and access, have meant that further education has taken place almost exclusively outside the "mainstream" institutions. Even the relatively generous program of support for long-term studies through the Federal Study Assistance Law has failed to create new opportunities for those who have already been employed to reenter the "regular" institutions of education; in many instances, new institutions have had to be created to accommodate these students.

Another striking feature of the German situation is that relative to the substantial amount of educational leave effects that are available, it has not proved possible to extend these effects to workers with the lowest level of prior education, or to workers of foreign nationality—migratory workers in particular. While there are a number of declarations of intent in favor of such an extension, there has been little effort to realize them, and this generalization also applies to the role of trade unions. In general it must be said that because of the piecemeal fashion in which educational leave effects have been created in Germany, they tend to conform fairly closely to the existing distribution of social benefits and do not actively promote greater equality of educational opportunity.

6

Sweden

The Context for an Educational Leave Policy

The official Swedish attitude to education is stated in the 1970 government proposition on adult education, endorsed by parliament: "Education is an important means to change the present society: it is of decisive importance for the social and economic standard of the individual, for his work satisfaction, and for his possibilities to influence his working environment. Education also affects relations between people and contributes to an increasing community of values among men that is a prerequisite for the realization of equality. Education plays a great role in the strengthening of democracy. It can enhance the individual's interest in social issues and enlarge his opportunities for participating in cultural life" (NU 1974:10, p. 107). Convinced of the strategic role of education for a society of self-determined and socially responsible citizens, Sweden has undertaken great efforts to reshape the educational system, root and branch, in order to improve the educational opportunities for everyone. After a period of experimentation, Sweden established the nine-year comprehensive school (*grundskola*) in the early sixties as minimal obligatory schooling for every child; this was succeeded by the institution of the integrated secondary school (*gymnasieskola*) in the late sixties (see Figure 4).

About 85 to 90 percent of all sixteen-year-old graduates from the comprehensive school continue their education, either directly or after a few years, in one of the more than twenty programs of the integrated secondary school, which cover all the fields of the former gymnasium and vocational schools; they are orga-

Figure 4. Structure of the educational system in Sweden

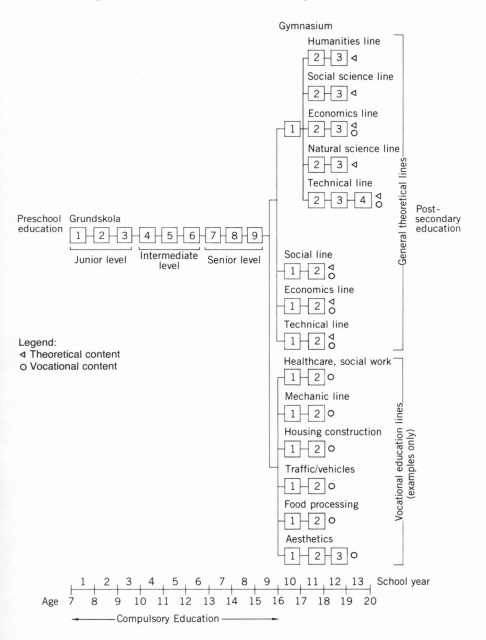

Source: *School Systems. A Guide,* 2nd edition. Strasbourg: Council of Europe, 1970.

nized in two-year courses within the major sectors: "arts and social subjects," "economics and commercial subjects," and "technical and scientific subjects." About 30 percent of the students go on for a third year.

According to a law of 1972, a minimum of two years of secondary education in Swedish and English constitutes the basic qualification for higher education. Special courses in each of the main sectors of the *gymnasieskola* serve as a preparation for studies of specific subjects. In this way the differences between the former gymnasium, now represented mainly by the 3-year program, and the former vocational schools, now incorporated in the two-year lines, are leveled further.

The most recent postsecondary school reforms provide for a structural reorganization of this sector and for the general institution of the "comprehensive university" (*högskola*). These reforms, still in their implementation phase until January 1977, give "widened access" (*vidgat tillträde*) to the former universities for people reentering from working life according to the formula 25:4. Applicants with a minimum age of twenty-five and four years of working experience plus capabilities in Swedish and English corresponding to two years of secondary school (and, if required, in additional specific subjects) may take up studies on the postsecondary level. This capacity may also have been acquired through participation in folk high school courses, municipal adult education, or any other of the many forms of adult education.

This latest step in the staggered fundamental reform of the Swedish educational system over the last twenty-five years highlights a crucial problem that has been engendered in turn by the reforms of the fifties and sixties. The new standards of personal development and education of those who have benefited from the reform at the primary and secondary levels and the increasing share of young postsecondary students (25 to 30 percent of the twenty-year-olds) put the majority of the older members of the Swedish population at a considerable disadvantage in socioeconomic and cultural life, since more than 50 percent of the Swedish work force and 68 percent of the adult population received their basic education prior to the reforms and attended school only for seven years or less. The percentage having earned the second degree of secondary school (*studentexamen*) as of 1970 was as follows (Prop., 1975, pp. 59 f.):

Age Group	Percentage
20–24	23
25–29	11
30–34	4
35–39	3
40–44	3
45–49	3
50–54	3
55–59	2
60–64	2

Nevertheless, the Swedish situation is singular since in system and scope its adult education programs are among the most highly developed in the world. In terms of enrollments, more than one fourth of the entire Swedish population, or more than 40 percent of its active members, participate in some kind of adult education activity every year.

In Sweden, the concept of recurrent education is considered a planning instrument to realize the high aspirations attached to education. Recent initiatives in favor of educational leave are seen as a means to establish a full-fledged system of recurrent education. Since 1970, the conditions of access and public aid to renewed studies were gradually improved in order to recruit an increasing proportion of those most disadvantaged educationally, particularly those whose educational level corresponds to grades 7 to 9 of the new comprehensive school.

The Swedish Adult Education System[1]

Sweden had a tradition in adult education long before the term *vuxenutbildning* received currency in the sixties. The popular movements (*folkrörelse*), mostly founded toward the end of the nineteenth century, were created to improve the social and personal conditions

[1]The description of Swedish adult education is based on SOU 1974:54, pp. 93 ff.; SOU 1974:62, pp. 75 ff.; Prop., 1975, pp. 37 ff.; NU 1974:10, pp. 107 ff.; B. Johansson, 1973.

of their members, and nearly all of the voluntary study associations (*studieförbund*) can be traced back to such political or cultural movements. They are now affiliated with labor market organizations, political parties, and religious and temperance movements. Together with the residential folk high schools (*folkhögskolor*), the first of which were founded in the middle of the nineteenth century to improve educational opportunities, particularly for young farmers, the study associations represent the traditional core of education for adults in Sweden. In addition to their educational function, these popular movements have played a significant role in furthering the coherence of Swedish society. They offered opportunities for social contact and communication and promoted the participation of major parts of the Swedish population in articulating social and political demands; this fact is quite important when considering the geographical character of a sparsely populated country with few urban centers.

The Swedish adult education system of today is the outcome of a considerable upswing and restructuring of this sector in recent years on the basis of characteristics that had developed historically. Because of this strong traditional element, most courses or activities in adult education are still conducted during leisure time; they call for the initiative and commitment of those who are to take part in them. As of 1972–73, these were the major sectors and their enrollments or participants (NU 1974:10, p. 116):

Educational association study circles, enrollments	2,143,482
Folk high schools, participants in subject courses	33,885
Folk high schools, participants in winter courses and subject courses of 30 weeks or longer duration	13,554
Municipal adult education, participants	230,140
Municipal adult education, new entrants for winter term	148,933
State schools for adults, participants in combined courses	2,500

State schools for adults, participants in correspondence courses	2,000
Trade union training, course participants	18,126
Labor market training, enrollments	142,821

With regard to the educational generation gap referred to above, it became increasingly obvious that the majority of the Swedish work force—with only six or seven years of primary schooling—would not be able to close the gap through available programs that left the major burden on the individual. The problem is compounded by the fact that those with the lowest levels of primary education generally reveal the least motivation for, and involvement in, further education.[2] It is to this group, therefore, that recent reforms pay special attention, in particular the experimental schemes designed to actively recruit the most underprivileged into adult education and to involve them in positive educational experiences. If continued, these are supposed to eventually improve the social standing of the participants. This so-called outreach activity (*uppsökande verksamhet*) clearly reflects the conviction of Swedish policy makers that legal or even financial measures are not sufficient, by themselves, to change the prevalent patterns of adult education so as to insure greater equality of opportunities. The first and decisive impediment—lack of motivation—is to be removed for those who might not even realize their deficiency with the aid of study organizers from the same work environment who search for the undermotivated people at work places or at home and help them develop the necessary motivation.

This approach, pragmatic and missionary at the same time, is unique and typical of the Swedish stance in matters of social and educational policy for several reasons. It demonstrates the pivotal significance attributed to education, the combination of theoretical insights and practical measures, and the intimate intermingling of educational with social policy. This instance of the Swedish "reform spirit" is not, however, representative of the introduc-

---

[2]Unfortunately, there is no indication of the distribution of *all* participants in adult education by levels of prior education. The available evidence in SCB Statistical Reports, Nr.U 1974:54, p. 5, fig. 1, suggests that this trend has not changed.

tion of an educational leave policy as such that was, and still is, characterized rather by an additive approach: that is, paid educational leave by installments.

For educational leave Sweden relies on her elaborate adult education system as a basis, supplemented first by legal claims to educational leave—paid for specific groups (immigrants (1973), unions representatives (1974)), and unpaid for all employees (1975)—and then by an improvement of the financial provisions, with special regard to short first-time educational leaves (valid as of 1976). It is now heading for a long-term process of industrial democratization to be triggered off by a law proposed for 1977 on democracy at the work place. As a well-established procedure, all these reform steps and measures were prepared for, or accompanied, by experimental schemes and/or by the creation of particular government task forces commissioned to investigate the relevant substantial or financial aspects of the problem areas.

We will trace this development of Swedish educational leave policies, taking the present supply of adult education as a point of departure, and identify possible present educational leave effects as well as those to be expected from reforms under way; these reforms we must consider also in the light of the ultimate aim assigned to them—to transform the character of Swedish society into a more fully participatory and emancipatory democracy.

Study Circles

The "study circle" or study group (*studiecirkel*) is the most widespread and typical form of adult education in Sweden. In 1973–74, this most important, and most "Swedish," form of adult education attracted over 2.1 million enrollments of considerably more than 1 million participants (SOU 1974:62, p. 76), while the figures expected for 1974–75 point to another increase of more than 10 percent, or about 2.5 million enrollments.

In the main, study circles are organized by the ten state approved educational associations, the largest of which is the Workers' Educational Association (ABF), with strong ties to the ruling social democratic party (SAP), and the Swedish Confederation of Trade Unions (LO). The ABF accounted for nearly 30 percent of all study circle enrollments in 1973–74 and for slightly more of the total meeting hours (Prop., 1975, p. 39):

	Enrollments	Meeting Hours
Workers' Educational Association (ABF)	29.3	30.6
Study Association Adult School (SV)	15.0	17.1
Study Association Fellow Citizen School (MBSK)	11.5	11.9
Salaried Employees' Educational Work (TBV)	10.1	10.3
Sweden's Church Study Association (SKS)	8.5	6.1
Free Church Study Association (FS)	7.7	4.8
Folk University (FU)	7.4	7.3
Temperance Movement Educational Work (NBV)	5.1	5.5
Study Promotion Association (SFR)	4.1	5.1
YWCA/WMCA Study Association (KFUK-M)	1.4	1.1

Since the introduction of state aid to study associations in 1948, the number of study circles increased almost ninefold from about 27,000 to over 230,000 in 1973, roughly doubling every ten years until 1970.

In principle, a study circle is the most unconstrained setting in which adults may further educate themselves: "an informal group that meets for the common pursuit of well-planned studies of a subject or problem area decided on beforehand" (according to the 1970 decree on adult education, NU 1974:10, p. 108). The key to this kind of activity is its voluntary nature regarding choice of subjects, materials, working methods, and so forth. The group leader or "animator" does not work as a teacher, but as convener and coordinator.

Study circles deal with all kinds of subjects, from languages to geography.[3] They can even be concerned with immediate social or political problems; in this way they can be instrumental in policy formation. For example, the Swedish government launched a campaign on the energy problem, providing the basic material to be discussed and decided on in study circles. More than seven thousand study circles with over forty thousand participants were formed to take up these questions, the answers to which served as a basis for the traditional political process.

In spite of the freedom of content and working conditions, study circles are not organized and carried through at will. One reason for this is the state subsidies to the running costs. To be subsidized, study circles must present a sufficiently detailed study plan, a time frame of at least 4 study weeks and 20 meeting hours, with no more than 2 meetings per week and 3 study hours per meeting, for 5 to 20 members including the leader. In 1973–74, almost all study circles recorded have complied with these organizational conditions; 98 percent of all study hours were covered by state subsidies. They are supposed to cover up to 75 percent of the combined costs of leaders' fees (max. 26 kronor per hour) and study materials, with an upper limit, at present, of 32 kronor per study hour for the so-called "general study circles" (*allmäna studiecirklar*). Of the study circles, 34 percent were conducted in high-priority subjects such as Swedish, English, mathematics, and civics on levels corresponding to grades 7 to 9 of the (new) nine-year compulsory comprehensive school (*grundskola*); these "priority circles" (*prioriterade cirklar*) obtain an additional state aid of 15 kronor per study hour. A special subsidy is granted to the study associations for administrative costs and for outreach activities to involve the least educated in adult education (see below). As a general condition for state approval, a study association must have conducted at least 50,000 study circle hours per year during the last three budget years.

[3]As of 1972–73, the study circle subjects ranked in this order: languages, 27.6 percent; literature, art, and theater, 19.4; social science and law, 16.0; music, 14.0; economics, employment, and livelihood, 10.3; religion, philosophy, and psychology, 4.3; science, medicine, and sports, 3.7; technology, industry, and communications, 2.5; and history and geography, 2.2 percent (SOU 1974:62, p. 83).

Guidelines established by the Swedish Municipal Federation (*Kommunförbund*) recommend that municipalities support the study circle activities by providing 25 percent of the running costs and 75 percent of the outlays for premises and administration, but in fact modalities of communal aid vary considerably. The same observation holds for participants' fees; they differ widely according to subject, sponsor, and local conditions. On the average, public aid covers more than half of the costs. As the Committee for Study Aid to Adults (SVUX) notes, the participants' fees, even if moderate, constitute another obstacle to participation in adult education, particularly for those with little or no motivation for studies, that is, often the least educated (SOU 1974:62, pp. 81f.). Priority circles indeed are cheapest because of the additional state subsidies; some study associations even try to offer them free of tuition.

As an illustration, revenues of an average AEF local subdivision in 1972–73 originated as follows: state subsidies, 51 percent; municipal subsidies, 32 percent; participant fees, 13 percent; fees from member organizations, 2 percent; diverse revenues, 2 percent (from SOU 1974:62, p. 82). According to a representative survey from a sample of more than 3,000 study circle participants in 1970 (R. Johansson, 1973), about two-thirds of the participants are women. Their median age is 40 (men: 37). Of the study circle members, 42 percent are 18 to 33 years of age, 31 percent are from 34 to 49 years old, and 7 percent are older than 66 years. Of the women, 49 percent have children at home; of the men, 46 percent. A third of the participants live in towns of less than 40,000 inhabitants (23.1 percent) or in rural areas (10.4 percent).

Data on the educational background of study circle participants in 1970 reveals that 38 percent had *folkskola* ("elementary school") education, while 16 percent had completed upper secondary school; 46 percent were at intermediate levels. For those 18 to 33 years old, 16.2 percent of the women and 13.1 percent of the men had *folkskola* education, while for those between 34 and 49 years of age, 47.8 percent of the women and 46.7 percent of the men had reached this education level; more than half of those 50 to 65 years old had *folkskola* education, as did more than two-thirds of those over 66 years of age. Comparing these figures with the overall distribution of the Swedish population by formal education and age, it becomes evident that the degree of underrepresentation of persons with low levels of education is greatest in the youngest group. In other words, it may prove increasingly difficult to attract persons with low levels of formal education into further education as the general level of schooling of an age group rises. At the same time, those who have benefited from the increase in initial education are participating in further education most actively. According to other surveys, the share of participants with prior education on the *folkskola* level was 55 percent (7 percent *gymnasium* or university graduates) for the Workers' Educational Association during the fall of 1971, while in the priority courses at large it was 60 percent in the fall of 1970 (4 percent gymnasium or university graduates), with 60 to 70 percent of the participants older than 36 years (SOU 1974:62, p. 84).

Three groups of subjects are predominant in the nine subject areas of the general study circles: languages (particularly English), aesthetic subjects (particularly instrumental music and handicrafts), and civics and social sciences. This information at the national level conceals the great differences between the various study associations as to preferred subject areas and preoccupations in relation to their main political or cultural orientation; the general principle, however, holds for all study circle activities that they be geared to the participants' background, interests, and needs, with respect to working and interaction methods, utilization of materials, and educational targets. While very few of these activities constitute educational leave effects at present, the study circles provide the organization and pedagogy on which to base educational leave programs in the future.

University study circles. These circles are open for everybody, regardless of prior level of education. With some 30,000 enrollments projected for 1974–75, they can be regarded as the largest "university of recurrent education" in Sweden at present. Course contents either relate closely to university curricula (in which case optional exams with university credits can be taken) or are carried out independently but on university level. University courses are not restricted to university sites but provide an opportunity for extramural studies. A circle leader must satisfy the formal qualification required for teaching of his subject within regular university faculties.

University study circles must have at least 48 meeting hours and 16 meetings of 5 to 25 participants. State aid covers 75 percent of the circle leader's honorarium (a maximum of 60 kronor per study hour) plus study materials up to a total of 75 kronor per meeting hour; an additional subsidy allows for 75 percent of travel expenses and per diem to the circle leader.

Swedish for immigrants. In response to a rising tide of immigrants, the Swedish authorities provided, in 1964–65, possibilities for immigrants to learn Swedish free of charge in study circles. As is characteristic of Swedish practice, this program was launched as an experiment jointly run by the National School Board (SÖ), the labor market agency (AMS), and the state office for immigrants (SIV) in cooperation with study associations. Although it is still called an experimental activity (*försöksverksamhet*), Swedish for immigrants has by now become a significant component of the study associations' work, in 1973–74 comprising 6 percent of the circles and 5 percent of enrollments. The social concern for the immigrants' situation in a foreign country is predominant; in December 1972, this concern was sanctioned by a legal right to paid educational leave for those taking instruction in Swedish for immigrants (*rätt till ledighet och lön vid deltagande i svenskundervisning för invandrare*—SFS 1972:650), effective January 1, 1973. This was the first full-fledged paid educational leave regulation in Sweden. It entitles immigrants to a maximum of 240 paid working hours of educational leave; if the participants continue working full shift, the employer has to pay course hours as overtime. That the first beneficiaries of an educational leave program were foreigners, representing the weakest group in society, is characteristic, too, of the social dimension of Swedish educational policy.

Since 1971, courses in Swedish for immigrants have been conducted according to one of the following schemes:

1. Light instruction (*glesundervisning*) of at least 20 meeting hours, with 1 to 3 hours per meeting and at most 10 hours per week.

2. Intensive instruction (*intensivundervisning*), with up to 240
    meeting hours per study circle, 4 to 6 hours per meeting,
    and at least 3 meetings or 16 hours per week (in this cate-
    gory courses are typified as A, B, and C, meaning, respec-
    tively, that none, some, or all of the participants obtain a
    study grant—*AMU-bidrag*—from the county labor market
    agency).
3. Courses (since 1973) ensuing from the law on the right to
    paid educational leave to participate in Swedish for immi-
    grants (so-called L-courses), with 1 to 6 study hours per
    meeting and at most 36 meeting hours per week. Partici-
    pants are accepted on the basis of a language test.
4. Special civics courses of 10 meeting hours, often with one
    or two interpreters and experts, to increase understanding
    of the operation of Swedish society (*särskild samhällsunder-
    visning*). Up to one seventh of the general immigrants'
    courses may also be devoted to civics.

L-courses are to be organized to supplement light or intensive instruction; this does not preclude some of the L-courses being per-
formed in the format of the regular instruction. A central register of
immigrants exempted from the law reveals that more than 43,000
immigrant employees were exempted on August 13, 1975 (SÖ,
1975, annex 6), because of previous instruction and/or sufficient
knowledge in Swedish: the qualification indicates that the claim of
immigrants to paid educational leave for learning Swedish is not
unconditional. A memorandum of June 7, 1974, fixed the total
number of meeting hours of Swedish for immigrants, including
orientation to Swedish society, to be subsidized by state aid—that
is, free of charge for the participants—at 550,000 hours, 300,000
of which are to be covered by the law on paid educational leave for
immigrants. An additional 100,000 hours for instruction not covered by the educational leave law was granted through a royal
decree of April 24, 1975.

Compared with more than 713,000 meeting hours and about
142,500 enrollments in all 17,690 immigrant study circles in 1974–
75, the special L-courses, with 322,203 meeting hours and about

51,000 enrollments in 7,438 circles (SÖ, 1975, annex 2), account for far less than half of all immigrant instruction. In view of these findings, the right to *paid* educational leave must be considered as an additional incentive, particularly for new immigrants, who have the greatest need for instruction in Swedish and on Swedish conditions of social life, and for whom it would be most difficult to obtain without maintained income. The majority of older immigrants are still privileged compared to other study circle attendants insofar as they are instructed free of charge. Those citizens of foreign origin who can be considered integrated into the Swedish society are expected to utilize the adult education system under the same conditions as native Swedes.

Even with the quantitative limitations, expenditures for the instruction of immigrants have risen considerably since the institution of the measures, in response to the immigration waves over the years. Though the increase has not been constant, expenses rose from 6.3 million kronor in 1965–66 to a first peak of 49 million kronor in 1970–71, then declined to 34 million kronor in 1972–73; for 1974–75, about 57 million kronor are expected. Expenses per study circle increased from 1506 kronor (140 per enrolled person) in the first year to 3224 kronor (400 per person) in 1974–1975 (SÖ, 1975, p. 5).

Some folk high schools organize residential courses in Swedish and social orientation, particularly in summer courses of up to four weeks duration, in which entire families can take part; in 1974, only 356 adults with 185 children in 14 courses participated in this new approach.

Since information disseminated by the usual channels does not reach immigrants working at home, a particular outreach effort has been undertaken by seven of the study associations. Offering, among others, special short technical courses, such as sewing and cooking, through 47 local offices, these study associations devoted 500,000 kronor to this program in 1974–75. Many older immigrants were to be induced to first-time participation that would possibly motivate them to further studies in language and more general subjects. In 1974–75, these direct-recruitment endeavors engendered more than 27,000 meeting hours distributed among

692 study circles, of which 377 were in Swedish, 34 in courses of special civic instruction, 256 in sewing and like subjects, and 25 in priority circle subjects (SÖ, 1975, p. 6).

Folk High Schools

The folk high school, or people's college (*folkhögskola*), represents another principal element of the traditional Swedish adult education system that is constantly widening and modifying its scope of activities; it now ranges from programs for the handicapped to university level education.

The 108 extant, mostly residential, schools (with seven additional branch campuses) developed pedagogical concepts for adult education very early in their history. Because they provided freedom for the pursuit of personal development, folk high schools have traditionally played a decisive part in the training of political, social, and cultural leadership at all levels of the country: they used to be the only means of further education and career promotion for proven (though poorly educated) leaders from the lower ranks of society, and even today, many leading personalities (including up to a third of the members of various parliaments) are folk high school graduates. Their success is recognized by the Swedish Folk High School Code (SFS 1974:279), which regulates modalities of operation and state support in very unconstraining terms. There is no nationally prescribed curriculum; each folk high school establishes its own program according to its primary social, cultural, or political concerns. The wide variations in characteristics and curricula of individual folk high schools are also determined by regional conditions, affiliation to different popular movements, and diversity in present ownership. Forty-seven of them (plus branch campuses) are affiliated with county councils, 17 with free religious communities, 12 with the Swedish church, 11 with foundations supported by county councils or municipalities, 9 (plus 1 branch campus) with the labor movement, 4 with the temperance movement, and 8 (plus 2 branch campuses) with other organizations.

The most significant activities are the so-called winter courses of 22 to 34 weeks duration and the subject courses (*ämneskurser*) of generally one or two weeks; subject courses may vary, however, from a few days to more than 34 weeks.

Winter courses are conducted at two or three different levels, which can be considered grades if followed in sequence; they often lead to a general competence equivalent to the new nine-year *grundskola* for participants who had seven years of the old *folkskola* as primary education. While music is an obligatory subject for all grades, only the first year's (winter) course must comprise Swedish, literature, history, civics, psychology, and mathematics, with either geography, physics, or biology as elective subjects. Recently, two-year sequences on a level corresponding to the gymnasium have been introduced by various folk high schools. About a quarter of the roughly ten thousand students of winter courses were sent to participate in these folk high school programs through the labor market agencies, with their incomes maintained according to the AMU conditions (see discussion later in this chapter). These students in fact enjoy paid educational leave for one to three years.

While the long courses are expected to decline in the future, shorter specialized subject courses have been increasing steadily— from 6,049 students in 1966–67 to 18,637 by 1970–71 and to 46,165 by 1973–74. Here, variations in subject areas and course arrangements are most marked. Subject courses are likely to comprise a larger part of the folk high school offerings when the new study support law becomes effective in 1976. The main folk high school course type is expected then to be of two to four weeks duration, conducted all through the year. Special courses for municipal youth leaders and leisure time organizers (about five hundred participants per year), study circle leaders, journalists, and social workers are also held as long, vocation-oriented subject courses; some of these prepare students for higher studies at professional schools or universities.

Increasing attention is directed to the handicapped, for whom residential folk high schools can provide a more favorable learning environment than many other forms of education or therapy. Therapy often is the idea, too, behind programs for older people (pensioners) whose educational "treatment" could possibly prevent their hospitalization. To integrate them in prophylactic educational processes is considered a social obligation, particularly by the county councils, who also operate the medical system.

Significant as these endeavors to help the aging may be, they still are marginal in terms of the overall scope of the folk high schools. The folk high school commission, established in December 1972 (*folkhögskoleutredning*) to investigate the future role of folk high schools in cultural and educational life, showed an average age of 21.3 years for participants in 1973–74, with 40 percent of the students under 20 years of age. Of the students in winter or long subject courses, 61 percent are women and 39 percent are men. Forty percent of the students had *folkskola* or *grundskola* as prior education; 22 percent had previously dropped out of school, with 10 percent of the male and 8 percent of female students doing so at secondary levels (Prop., 1975, pp. 42 f.).

The state covers 100 percent of the teachers' and school leaders' salaries and subsidizes administrative and special costs to varying degrees according to special regulations. The owners of the folk high schools provide for the remainder, often aided by the local authorities, the county councils (if not owners themselves), and various sponsors for scholarships. Students not belonging to preferred groups have to pay for room and board plus study materials. They can apply for state aid (grants and loans) under the same conditions as university students; these conditions will be improved by the new study support law (see discussion later in this chapter).

Present educational leave effects in folk high schools mainly must be attributed to labor market training, which utilizes this sector of Swedish adult education as it does other institutions. This example of coöperation as well as the multitude of other activities, many of them closely coordinated with various organizations, prove the capability of folk high schools to provide qualified staff, appealing premises, flexibility, and cooperation that can easily be harnessed to diverse programs of educational leave.

Municipal Adult Schools

Another means of offering a second chance to those with insufficient primary education was provided by the adult education law of 1967. The law, by increasing central state subsidies to municipal adult education (*kommunal vuxenutbildning*), prompted a growth of municipal adult schools; while in 1967, such schools existed in less than 10 percent of all municipalities, they are available, by now, in almost all of them, although with considerable imbalances, locally and regionally, as to quality and extent of supply. Generally speaking, municipal adult schools provide instruction corresponding directly to the curricula of grades 7 through 9 of the new compulsory *grundskola* and to the various lines of the integrated secondary school (*gymnasieskola*) beginning with grade 10; in addition, a spectrum of vocational and technical courses are offered. The adult school utilizes premises, equipment, and usually also teachers of the regular schools for youth, but each has a director for adult studies and, where necessary, a separate administration.

Most students study part time and in the evenings, but the share of full-time students is growing. Studies are organized in concentrated, or "intensive," courses so that only one or very few subjects are studied at a time. In 1973, an estimated 3,000 students finished their studies with a certificate corresponding to the *grundskola* diploma, while nearly 2,000 completed one of the full *gymnasieskola* programs.

Although the overall figures for student enrollments have been on a decrease in the last years, after a peak in the early seventies, those of new entrants have been rising again, particularly because of a growing number of participants who are aged 35 or older. The number of younger new entrants is practically stable, although in the vocational courses the number of new students is still rising for all age groups. Of the more than 33,000 new entrants in the spring of 1974, 90 percent are older than 25 years of age, 35 percent are older than 35 years. About a third of all new entrants attended *folkskola* (a maximum of 8 years) as their prior education, 25 percent attended *grundskola* or the equivalent, while 14 percent took an exam qualifying them for admission to university (*studentexam*).

The average share of women in municipal adult education is 64 percent: 67 in *grundskola* courses, 37 in the two-year lines, 62 in the three- or four-year lines of *gymnasieskola,* and 65 in vocation-oriented courses (SCB, Nr.U 1974:42).

The state subsidies cover 100 percent of the teachers' and directors' salaries. Additional support is given to the handicapped, and 25 percent of the total teaching hours of the compulsory school (*grundskola*) division are devoted to counseling and orientation, including supplementary instruction and the imparting of study techniques to those with the least previous education; another 2 percent of the outlays for salaries are apportioned to outreach and recruitment activities; more favorable conditions apply for adult schools in those parts of the country that have a poor infrastructure. As with other educational schemes, special investigations to improve the pedagogical methods of municipal adult education were initiated by the government. Special two-semester adult teacher training courses have been provided at Stockholm Teachers' College since 1971.

Financial assistance to students is the exception rather than the rule. It is given only to full-time students or those who have to cut down full-time employment to part-time in order to master their heavy course load. Since this assistance is mainly on a loan basis, there are practically no educational leave effects in municipal adult education: this is liable to change to some extent with the new study support provisions (see discussion later in this chapter). Nevertheless, the figures on educational background and age distribution of municipal adult students indicate that this form of adult education in Sweden represents a first step toward recurrent education. Those students who obtain a certificate fully equivalent to graduation from the school system for youth are a small minority of less than 5,000 per year compared to more than 60,000 students (in the spring of 1973) in courses equivalent to secondary school level; most of the latter group study individual subjects, many at upper secondary level, to brush up their knowledge at a later age.

Adults with vocational experience have access to regular daytime *gymnasieskola* for youth, especially where municipal adult education is not developed satisfactorily. In the fall of 1972, 1.7 percent of the then over 235,000 *gymnasieskola* students were older than 35, and 10.5 percent were between 21 and 35 years of age—taken together, nearly 29,000 students. They are found primarily in special courses of less than one year's duration and in the ordinary technical lines of two to four years. On September 14, 1973, 1,800 students of the first group and 2,700 of the second group collected the so-called training grant from the labor market agencies (*utbildningsbidrag*); in other words, they enjoyed long educational leaves. The others, since 1973, have been able to apply for loans (SOU 1974:62, pp. 112–114).

The other elements of the public adult education system in

Sweden, though interesting in themselves because of their variety and often unusual pedagogical approach, need not interest us in detail from an educational leave point of view. The two state adult schools cater to about five thousand students, half of them through correspondence courses only, the other half through correspondence combined with short intensive sessions at the school. Another promising approach is that of TRU, the government task force to investigate and experiment with educational television and radio programs for the benefit, in particular, of those most educationally and socially underprivileged. TRU also works together with other institutions of adult education, and at all levels, from programs for the handicapped to university programs, often by a media mix combining their programs with correspondence instruction and study circles.

In the universities, the proportion of students older than 25 years had reached 38 percent in the fall of 1973 because of reduced new matriculation of younger students. The experiments with "widened access" (*vidgat tillträde*) to universities for older students, according to the formula 25:4 (see the first section of this chapter), are as yet of too little importance quantitatively to account for this high rate of older students, 77 percent of whom did not intend to pass any exams (SOU 1974:62, p. 117). This constellation may be interpreted as another trend pointing to a readiness for recurrent education.

Labor Market Training

The aims of labor market training in Sweden (*arbetsmarknadsutbildning,* or AMU) do not differ very much from those in other countries. In principle, labor market training is supposed to counteract the effects of structural, cyclical, and seasonal changes that occur for various reasons in all modern economies and that leave an increasing number of people at the margin of the labor force, unable to satisfy altered qualification patterns. Until 1957, when Sweden also experienced economic slowdown, mainly handicapped people and refugees were affected by this training. Since then, the charges of labor market training have continuously been extended, quantitatively and qualitatively. Within a labor force of, by now, nearly 4 million, the number of people undertaking training for reasons of labor market adaptation soared more than thirtyfold, from 3,325 in 1958 to over 108,000 in 1973. Course offerings now range from general education on the compulsory school level and orientation courses to over four hundred specialized curricula, about half of which are currently being given. The proportion of women in labor market training increased from about 20 percent to nearly half of all trainees, foreigners account for 10 to 15 percent of trainees, while still almost every third trainee is afflicted by a personal handicap of some kind. Outlays multiplied almost fivefold within less than ten years: from more than 200 million kronor in the fiscal year 1966–67 to over 1 billion kronor in 1974–75 (SOU 1974:79, p. 57). Regular follow-up studies revealed "that of those who have undergone vocational training courses and who are available for the labor market, some 85 percent have obtained work within three months after completing their labor market training. Approximately 85 percent of these people have, in turn, obtained work within the occupational branch for which they have received training" (SOU 1974:79, pp. 58, 93).

Enrollments have increased from about 12,000 in 1959–60 to about 98,000 in 1969–70 and about 143,000 in 1972–73 (SOU 1974:62, p. 105). Participants' figures differ in various sources by 2 to 10 percent because of different time frames (calendar year versus fiscal year) and because there are no uniform terms of instruction in AMU; the intake of labor market trainees occurs successively as need dictates.

To be eligible for labor market training, individuals must be unemployed or in danger of being so, or be experiencing difficulties in placement on the labor market (for example, untrained housewives or the handicapped). They must be registered with the employment agencies as seeking permanent employment. Employed persons are eligible for training in occupations for which there exists particular demand; a maximum of 3,000 persons were eligible for this retraining in 1974–75. The minimum age of twenty years can be waived for single parents, handicapped persons, and refugees. In 1973–74, another exception was introduced on an experimental basis; those eighteen or nineteen years old were eligible if their primary education fell short of the nine years of compulsory schooling or if they had two years of active employment plus subsequent unemployment of six months or more (SOU 1974:79, pp. 71, 181 f.; Prop., 1975, p. 45).

Labor market training enjoys comparatively favorable economic conditions, being the largest single recipient of state aid for education of adults. The government proposition on widened adult education and study support for adults (Prop., 1975) states that this was the only scheme of support adapted to the needs of adults (p. 163). The regulations in force until the end of 1975 provide for a basic allowance, allowances for rent outlays, for per diem, for children, and for special costs incurred. As of 1974, the basic rent and children's allowances combined may reach a maximum of 1,700 kronor per month (taxable since 1974) and are reduced progressively, depending on other income, including the spouse's, to half of the basic allowance and children's allowance (SOU 1974:79, p. 73). The rules for compensation will be changed by the new study support law, effective January 1, 1976 (see discussion later in this chapter).

Labor market training is organized cooperatively by the National Labor Market Board (AMS) and the National Board of Education (SÖ). SÖ contributes administrative, pedagogic, technical, and economic assistance in addition to organizing courses. AMS is responsible for the evaluation of the volume and for the vocational as well as regional distribution of training, the recruitment and subsequent placement of trainees, and the concession of training allowances. A consultative delegation (SAMS) comprises representatives of both AMS and SÖ and partners of the labor market.

Both administrations have regional offices with some cross-relationships, and SÖ conducts some fifty so-called AMU centers with about a hundred local branches, where the training organized by SÖ (57 percent) takes place (SOU 1974:62, p. 108). Of all new entrants in labor market training in 1972–73, 23 percent were instructed in the regular education system, 11 percent by educational organizations, associations, and public authorities, while 9 percent (without the so-called local placement training—*lokaliseringsutbildning*) received training in enterprises (SOU 1974:62, p. 106, table 2.10).

The figures for new entrants have increased annually from 3,325 in 1958 to 108,245 in 1973. Figures for the average number of participants computed in terms of main providers of training indicate that 41 percent of the participants enrolled in SÖ courses, 30 percent in the regular education system, 23 percent in enterprises (including placement training), and 7 percent in other courses. The roughly 19,000 participants in SÖ courses must be viewed against the 25,000 to 30,000 full-time training places available per year in all AMU centers and local branches taken together (SOU 1974:62, p. 108); this comparison reveals a utilization rate of only 65 to 80 percent and points out difficulties in prognostic planning in view of the vagaries of labor market developments.

Pedagogically, SÖ courses are among the most refined in Europe. They are specifically geared to the preconditions of individuals and to the necessities of particular trades. The trade-related courses are worked out in several steps and modified in close cooperation with the labor market partners. In view of the varied prior experience and diverse primary education of the participants, highly individualized instruction methods have been developed and are constantly being improved on. Study material designed for extensive, though teacher-guided, self-instruction is preferred (programed instruction); course schedules for specific curricula can be extended for individual cases. Wherever possible, courses are built in a modular system with different stations, the passage of which can be accommodated to individual needs; the same holds for basic and continuing courses. There are no separate terms, and the intake of trainees is in most cases continuous. Since 1969, general subjects (Swedish, English, mathematics, physics, chemistry, and civics) have been introduced, and since July 1, 1973, these have been an obligatory element, in principle, of all courses longer than eight weeks; the reason for this, among other considerations, is that about three quarters of all AMU participants have only six or seven years of *folkskola* as previous formal education (SOU 1974:62, p. 110), which is another way of stating that those with poorest primary education have the most difficulty in complying with the demands of the labor market. However, the educational element without direct vocational orientation to labor market training by now accounts for about one third of all AMU activities in terms of participants, bearing witness, once again, to the strong social concern in Swedish adult education policies. In its effort to increase equality of opportunities, labor market training in Sweden promotes as one of its outspoken objectives the kind of education that would be considered an abuse of comparable schemes in other countries.

The nonvocational education within labor market training mainly consists of preparatory courses for different target groups and purposes, ranging from Swedish for immigrants to driver training, the largest being a course called Working Life and Training (*Arbetsliv och utbildning*—ALU). In about four weeks it gives general information and orientation on labor market and social conditions and counseling as to the individual's aptitude for training and/or work and combines this with diverse practical working experiences of about two weeks' duration. Since its introduction in 1969, ALU has grown at a fast pace and is attended to a considerable degree by women previously working at home.

A similar course (*anpassningskurs*), generally of forty-two weeks, is especially designed and administered to the handicapped to adjust them to working life and the conduct of every day life and includes training in the application of technical appliances; an additional four-weeks course is provided for people with defective sight. Theoretical preparatory courses (*preparandkurser*) of two to twenty (normally sixteen) weeks on *grundskola* level are offered to those with insufficient knowledge of general subjects to lay a foundation for further vocational training. A more extended version (*kompletteringskurser*) of three or four terms is conducted within municipal adult education.

These introductory courses should not be confused with the eight weeks of instruction in general subjects that, since July 1973, precedes the special vocational training of all AMU trainees with only six or seven years of *folkskola* as primary education and gives them an improved basis for their vocational training as well as for their labor market competitiveness.

More conventional vocational labor market courses account for the other two thirds of labor market training. The bulk of these are retraining courses (*omskolningskurser*). Continuation courses lasting from a few days to about three months constitute a minor element in labor market training, as do so-called beginners courses for youths of fifteen to twenty-one years. The latter courses taking place either in municipalities or in five of the six national vocational schools, represent genuine basic vocational education for unemployed youths who would not or could not find a vocational education through the ordinary channels.

The main part of retraining (about one third of all AMU) takes place in manufacturing of all kinds. Like the nonvocational training, it has almost doubled since 1969, and in terms of new entrants the volume of both activities was almost balanced in 1973 (SOU 1974:79, p. 77, table 1.2; SOU 1974:62, p. 104, table 2.8); about 15 percent of all new entrants are trained for technical, scientific, social, or artistic occupations; more than half of them (or about 8 percent of the total) are trained in health care. About as many are trained in accounting and clerical work and in domestic work (all data are for 1973).

Almost two thirds of AMU carried out in enterprise concerns so-called localization training (*lokaliseringsutbildning*), a measure of regional policies, which normally consists of a standard payment from the state to enterprises of 5 kronor per work hour for newly employed persons during six months in particular regional development areas. Similar devices apply to on-the-job training of youths and women, in the latter case to alter established role patterns in certain trades, as well as to older and handicapped persons. The median age of AMU participants is 30 years. The age distribution of new entrants into labor market training in 1972–73 was: 36 percent under 25 years of age and 23 percent older than 35 (15 percent over 45 and 3 percent over 55—SOU 1974:62, p. 106). Though older people are underrepresented as compared with the age distribution of the unemployed, AMU participation of this group tends to rise; for youth under 25 years of age this relationship is balanced.

The picture of labor market training would not be complete without mentioning at least a few details from the dropout investigation done in the fall of 1972 in four counties with reference to AMU courses organized by the National Board of Education (SÖ). In 1972, only about 70 percent of participants in retraining courses finished their training; 15 percent dropped out without stating any reason, 4 percent left because of illness, and another 5 percent left for new employment or other training (SOU 1974:79, p. 90). Although there were many imperfections in the dropout records, certain reasons for leaving training emerge as significant. The most common reason for dropping out was economic (15 percent): of the economic dropouts 37 percent found economic conditions harder than expected, 57 percent found their expectations fulfilled, while 6 percent even experienced less economic hardship than expected. As to possible continuation of vocational training, 12 percent would settle for less than half of their previous income compensated for, 11 percent would settle for three quarters of their income, and 45 percent would continue training only if their full previous income was maintained; 19 percent could not make up their minds, and 12 percent would not train themselves further, irrespective of the remuneration. The other reasons for dropping out were change of training program (11 percent), discontent with the course and kind of training (11 percent felt uneasy with the course they were in, 8 percent thought they were in the wrong course, 6 percent could not keep pace with the schedule, 5 percent found training too difficult), nervous difficulties (10 percent), too much travel (6 percent), and family reasons (5 percent). In addition, about two thirds of the AMU participants had families to provide for.

Rates of failure were highest among young male or immigrant trainees and among the handicapped; as to subject areas, dropout rates were higher in manufacturing or in such theoretically oriented courses as the preparatory course "working life and training" or in Swedish for immigrants (SOU 1974:79, pp. 90 ff.). Yet for those who finished vocational training and were available for the labor market, nearly 85 percent found an occupation within three months, even in the difficult years of 1971 and 1972 (SOU 1974:79, p. 93), although conditions varied considerably in different branches.

The success as well as the shortcomings of the then prevailing labor market training, the need for expansion combined with high flexibility of the future AMU system, and the paramount significance of labor market training both for the individual and for the economic and social order in a time of rapid and unforeseeable change have led the Royal Committee to Review Labor Market Training (*Kommittén för översyn av arbetsmarknadsutbildningen,* or KAMU) to stress the predominant role of labor market training in future adult education, also in view of recurrent education. The more generous economic conditions for labor market training therefore ought to be preserved and even strengthened.

To underline the priority attached to labor market training, new conditions obtain from January 1, 1976. These new dispositions are, in the main, based on the proposals put forward by KAMU in its final report (SOU 1974:79). The role and objectives of labor market training are considered in terms of economic and labor market, redistributional, and educational aspects; in their socio-economic significance, they are considered from the viewpoint of the individual, as well. Possible conflicts between these concerns are evaluated under both short-term and long-term perspectives, to the effect that individual aspirations and long-term goals of a more general scope should be strengthened provided that the immediate social and economic needs not be neglected. But, in principle, both objectives are deemed reconcilable: a broader and more general instruction would enhance the individual's chances for a second employment with meaningful work and would impart to the trainee a heightened flexibility for further adaptation to changing employment conditions.

The primary importance attributed to labor market training is reflected, in particular, by even more advantageous financial conditions for this kind of adult education:

> The training allowance (*utbildningsbidrag*) shall be granted in accordance with the principle of income maintenance; it will be bound, in future, to the unemployment insurance. Under the new scheme insured trainees will receive, depending on their last income, 80 to 120 kronor per day (maximum 2,860 kronor per month); uninsured trainees are paid the minimum daily allowance: 80 kronor per day (maximum about 1,980 kronor per month); youths under 20 years of age are paid 35 kronor per day; if they have children to care for or are entitled to unemployment pay the same conditions as for adults obtain. All trainees receive an additional 10 kronor as training stimulus (*stimulansbidrag*). There is *no* reduction, henceforth, for other income (trainee or spouse's). The allow-

ances are accorded for five days a week, are taxable, and are included in the computation of pension rights.

The concept of risk of unemployment shall be widened for carefully assessed individual cases to allow for AMU training and recompensation before actual unemployment occurs. Likewise, the annual quota of training allowances in "shortage occupations" (*bristyrkesutbildning*) will be raised from 3,000 to 10,000.

Training shall be directed to particular occupations rather than to comprehensive occupational fields. Instruction in general subjects must be concentrated on the specific competence required and should be shorter than in other education.

Provisions for flexible course offerings adapted to adults' needs without rigid terms shall be improved; possibilities to "buy" courses from the regular education system or from enterprises shall be given; the introduction of recurrent education shall be furthered, as well as the equalization between men and women and between low income groups and those with more extended previous education.

All trainees with a previous schooling below the nine-year comprehensive school shall be given instruction in general subjects for eight weeks; where vocational training objectives require, preparatory courses (of regularly sixteen weeks) in general subjects shall be offered. Handicapped people shall be integrated as far as possible into the ordinary labor market training, notwithstanding required deployment of specific pedagogical or social resources on their behalf.

Swedish for immigrants as a part of labor market training shall, as a rule, be limited to two months as has been the case before. Where individual conditions so require, an additional two months term shall be granted. Vocational instruction for immigrants shall also be effectuated in their mother tongue, together with instruction in Swedish.

Training of detained persons shall come under the tutelage of the National Boards of Labor and Education on decision by parliament in 1976.

Training in enterprises shall be conducted under employment terms, except for the practical part of Working Life and Training (ALU) courses. Public support for training in enterprises is paid to employers: allowances for job induction (introductory allowance: 5 kronor per hour, or more for training according to established curricula) shall be paid for six months as before (for shorter or longer periods in the latter case). For older and handicapped on-the-job trainees the allowance shall be 8 kronor per hour; the same applies for training as an alternative to dismissal. The introductory training support for the handicapped in protected workshops remains unchanged at 10 kronor per hour. For occupations dominated by either sex, training experiments conducted in enterprises to change this pattern are supported with 6 kronor per hour. Experts are called upon to develop and evaluate training in enterprises.

Along with minor reforms in organizational responsibilities, better codetermination by representation of participants' delegates are provided for, together with improved information procedures, particularly with the help of union study organizers.

The cost increase for these measures is estimated at 690 million kronor per year; 160 million thereof are covered by increased income taxes on raised training allowances. The remainder shall be balanced by an employers' levy of a suggested 0.4 percent of the payroll, effective from 1976, to be put into a new labor market training fund (*Nytt om högskolan*, 1975, pp. 124 ff.).

Labor market training in Sweden seems to fairly well satisfy the definition of educational leave adopted for this study. The self-evident and primary concern for problems of reemployment notwithstanding, AMU produces considerable educational leave effects. This observation holds for the present system and conditions of labor market training and seems even more justified for the future regulations just presented.

If one weakens the requirement that security of employment be maintained in all educational leave policies, Swedish labor market training could almost be considered a comprehensive educational leave policy, particularly as more than 70 percent of the AMU participants who completed their training obtained employment in corresponding occupations within three months.

Certainly, the elements of Swedish labor market training that purposefully stress social and educational objectives along with employment policies go beyond the limits of traditional labor market policy. The consideration of long-term perspectives of the individual in the labor market and, thereby, in society that accounts for the unusually high proportion of general education within labor market training is an instance of this; the prospect of AMU as a nucleus for recurrent education is another.

As a conclusion, labor market training in Sweden, by its intentions as by its effects, blends into educational leave—sometimes of rather wide scope and duration—without any clear lines of demarcation. Even if it is not identified as such, labor market training occasionally satisfies the purposes and goals assigned to educational leave more comprehensively than many outspoken educational leave programs.

In-Service Training in Industry

Although in-service training in industry represents a major field of training with educational leave effects, the government has paid little attention to it thus far, nor have independent research institutions. In 1975, the Swedish government established an additional commission to study in-service training in industry. In view of the Swedish style of educational research, closely linked to policy development but with relatively little independent research, this is an infallible sign that very little is presently known about this activity.

Clearly, firms are engaged in in-service training programs; in all likelihood, the extensive system of adult education means that not as much education needs to be provided through the firms as is needed in most other countries. In several instances, large firms provide organizational support and the use of their facilities to voluntary adult education activities. The last studies on in-service training were undertaken in the late sixties and no longer provide an accurate picture, particularly since they are weighted in favor of large enterprises, which tend to undertake more such activities. The studies reported by Eliasson and Höglund (1971, pp. 2.1–2.33) tend to concentrate on an analysis of in-service training in selected enterprises rather than attempting an overall evaluation of the phenomenon. Thus no satisfactory assessment can be made until the new commission presents its findings.

In view of the highly developed and well-documented system of education and adult education, it is surprising that the Swedish government has also taken a long time to turn systematically to the educational needs of its own employees. From the sparse available information, it appears that the state acts much as most private employers in the area of further training: while it is, in principle, available, it does not represent a major priority.

Outreach Activities

The Committee on Methods Testing in Adult Education (*Kommittén för försöksverksamhet med vuxenutbildning,* or FÖVUX) has, since 1970, conducted an experimental program for adult education, involving direct recruitment of participants by personal contact. Concluded in 1974, these activities are not conspicuous for the number of participants (about 4,500 in five years) nor are educational leave effects always present, but the approach and the basic ideas behind outreach activities (*uppsökande verksamhet*) should be considered in the context of educational leave.

In Sweden, as in other countries, there is a marked tendency for adult education to be utilized mainly by younger and better educated people. This has led the Swedish Confederation of Trade Unions (LO) and the Workers' Educational Association (ABF) to suggest, in 1969, an experimental scheme especially designed to reach out to people with inadequate primary education, or with psychological, economic, and social impediments, to convince them in personal contacts with "study organizers" that participation in educational activities would be reasonable and helpful for them. Recruitment took place at places of work and, starting with the second year, also at homes of prospective participants. The outreach by personal contacts was done by study organizers from two unions (LO and TCO—Tjanslemanners Central Organization) who had been specifically trained in short courses for this activity and were to be familiar with the working and living reality of their contacts. Since one of the objectives of the experiments was to identify those most favorable conditions of enrollment that would remove obstacles to the participation of diverse groups of potential attendants, the test plans and results have become rather complex and detailed, with no overall summary tabulation possible. Different years have been reported separately in all details—geographic, demographic, and so forth.

In the third and fourth trial years, for example (SOU 1974:54), employees with regular working hours, industrial and mining shift workers, health care personnel working under duty rosters, women working at home, physically handicapped persons, and people in sparsely populated areas were contacted for study circle participation under varying enrollment conditions. Some circles were to be conducted during spare time, some during paid working hours, some half and half; some people were offered additional incentive allowances if they attended. Since the reference groups were of very diverse sizes, the percentages for persons willing to participate on first contact are not fully comparable; their relative magnitudes, however, permit some inferences on the possibilities and limitations of efforts to actively recruit disadvantaged persons for adult education. For example, in the third trial year 81 percent of the health care personnel under duty rosters applied to attend, but only 40 percent, on the average, of those with regular working hours applied, and only 37 percent of housewives (SOU 1974:54, p. 40). In general, spare time studies were considerably less attractive than studies conducted half during paid working hours and half during spare time. Interest in participation also decreased with rising age and shorter prior education, and interest was particularly low in sparsely populated areas—during the fourth trial year, between 33 and 37 percent (SOU 1974:54, p. 49). Incentive allowances did not play an important role for those with normal working hours: at the end of the year, only 13 percent adduced them as a prime motivation for participation, while for 79 percent the possibility of studying during paid working hours had been of great importance. Seventy-six percent of the shift workers and even 90 percent of the nursing personnel considered the enrollment conditions (paid working hours) very significant. Besides the interest in a particular subject, for many people the personal contact with the study organizer constituted the real reason for participation (SOU 1974:54, p. 44). About two thirds of the attendees completed their studies; but, for various reasons, between 7 and 24 percent of those enrolled never appeared, and between 3 and 30 percent of the various groups dropped out before the end.

Between 61 and 74 percent, however, intended to continue their studies after the first experience. About two thirds of those who completed their studies found their expectations fulfilled or even surpassed (SOU 1974:54, p. 47). In all, during the third trial year 1,045 individuals out of more than 4,500 contacted took part in 110 study circles of, on the average, 46 study hours (SOU 1974:54, pp. 40 and 44). Participation in all cases was free of charge. The study circle activities (some in combination with short folk high school courses during the fourth and fifth year) were carried out by two educational associations (ABF and TBV—Salaried Employees' Educational Work) in cooperation with the unions, employers, and organizations of the handicapped.

The FÖVUX committee concluded that by properly conducted outreach activities "a very large proportion of those with brief schooling can be recruited to studies" (SOU 1974:54, p. 50). Among those contacted at home about a third were recruited, and at places of work, about half of those personally contacted participated. For certain people in the target population, such as shift workers or nursing personnel under duty rosters, the need for further study was great, but motivation had been suppressed because of unfavorable working conditions. When the major obstacle was removed by providing for study during paid working hours, more than two thirds of this group were recruited.

The importance of well-prepared study organizers with backgrounds similar to the target group is stressed; they should preferably be recruited from the popular movements, the study and political associations, and the unions. Their training and activities (also to be carried out during paid working hours) have been sanctioned through the union representative law, effective July 1, 1974. The proposed study allowances (an hourly assistance of 10 to 35 study hours per half year and a daily assistance of 2 to 5 days per half year) are incorporated in the new study support law, effective from 1976. They are mainly designed as a supplement to outreach activities for those groups in which a suppressed need for studies can be ascertained, and allows them to participate in first-time experiences of adult education without loss of income: a "Head Start program" for underprivileged adults.

Detailed organizational, pedagogic, and financial measures to improve the opportunities of these people to participate in adult education over the next five years have been worked out as additional proposals. The major portion of the increase is to go to the ordinary study circle activities and to increase in the hourly study grants. Significant sums in absolute terms are to be devoted to work with the handicapped and with those in sparsely populated areas.

The results of the experiments with outreach activities clearly demonstrate that passing an educational leave law is a far from sufficient means of giving those who most need to further educate themselves the opportunity to do so. At the same time, the pragmatic approach tried in Sweden to remove the obstacles for those who are unable to do so by themselves is an invaluable aid to a realistic assessment of both the potential and limitations of any comprehensive educational leave policy.

The Development of Educational Leave Legislation

The Swedish system of adult education, highly developed and able to cater to diverse needs, is changing further in order to fully reflect the demographic composition of the population. This change is not to be achieved by educational policies alone; they constitute but one strategic element of structural social reforms. To this end, Sweden has chosen to institute educational leave by installments through a series of laws.

A law adopted in December 1972 on a right to paid educational leave for participants of instruction in Swedish for immigrants (*rätt till Ledighet och Lön vid deltagande i svensk undervisning för invandrare*) entitling immigrants to support while learning Swedish (see discussion above).

A law effective as of July 1974 on the position of the trade union representative at the place of work (*lagen om facklig förtroendemans ställning på arbetsplatsen*–SFS 1974:358) providing trade union representatives with substantial educational leave rights to fulfill their functions; it also covers employed study organizers.

A law on the employees' right to unpaid educational leave (*lag om arbetstagares rätt till ledighet för utbildning*—SFS 1974:981) of December 23, 1974, effective as of January 1, 1975, with practically no limitations as to the kind or length of the training or education; the law sets a frame to be substantiated by collective bargaining.

A law concerning the amendment of the study support law (*lag om ändring i studiestödslagen*—SFS 1975:359) was passed in the spring of 1975 to be effective fully on January 1, 1976.

All these laws are accompanied by a number of government-initiated task force investigations (*utredningar*) in the relevant fields, often combined with experimental schemes of a pragmatic character: FÖVUX (outreach activities), SVUX (reform of the study grant system), KAMU (review of labor market training), TRU (television and radio instruction for adults). Again, these building blocks have to be seen in a perspective which is guided by reformist political convictions; they all serve the general goal of approaching more justice in terms of opportunity and social benefits, for which a proposed law on democracy at the work place (*förslag till lag om demokrati på arbetsplatsen*), most likely to be effective January 1, 1977, seems to constitute a preliminary culmination.

Trade Union Representatives. The law on the position of the trade union representative at the work place must be seen in connection with the introduction, in 1970, of a new kind of state aid to the educational activities of the professional organizations. The trade union spokesmen are considered an important factor of the socio-economic balance and development of Swedish society, but often their basic education is insufficient. Therefore it seemed logical financially to support the efforts of professional organizations in

providing shop stewards and union spokesmen with the basic qualifications required (Prop., 1975, p. 163). The union representative
law can be regarded as the legal corollary to this strengthening of
the trade union position, and as such, it aims at rather far-reaching
reforms of working life.

The law provides a wide framework of rather indistinct general rights that can be further specified by collective agreements between the competent trade unions and the employers according to
the special conditions of a branch or an enterprise. The law covers
all forms of trade union activities that are important for the conditions at the work place and that are to be undertaken in appropriate measure during paid working hours. These include, among
others, education and instruction enabling the spokesman to better
perform his job. According to the law, the union spokesman may
not be impeded in the exercise of his functions, nor suffer disadvantages from them; he enjoys special employment protection, even
in cases of economic slump. He has free access to the place of work
but must not hinder the proper operation of the plant. All these
privileges only apply to elected union representatives (and/or employed study organizers) of unions competent to contract for the
kind of work or workers for which the spokesman is responsible.
The position of the trade union is invigorated by its having been
granted primacy of interpretation (*tolkningsföreträde*) in disputed
matters—until such time as these conflicts are tried at the labor
court.

There are no figures on company time spent for educational
concerns and/or other union matters by union representatives.
Only from firms covered by the commercial clerks' union within
LO are some figures known, and these cannot be properly assessed
because of lack of comparison. In firms with 25 to 50 employees,
50 minutes per employee were spent during half a year by the
union representative in pursuing union tasks, while in firms with
451 to 750 employees the time input averaged at 10 minutes per
employee during half a year. Due to economic limitations the maximum number of hours spent seems to be 20 to 30 per half-year,
the educational leave share of which cannot be measured at all
(communication by Mauritz Sköld, LO, June 1975). While big
companies pay for these activities in terms of paid company time,

the smaller ones only lose productive hours, because the wage payment is taken over by the state. It seems safe to say that the union representatives take time out as they need it and negotiate later with the employer.

Unpaid Educational Leave. The law on the employees' right to educational leave is the next link in the evolutionary chain of measures to change the conditions of working life. It gives each employee a virtually unconditional right to absent himself from work in order to participate in any kind of education of his choice—vocational, trade union, or general—if it shows some regularity; in other words, only individual private studies are excluded. The law applies equally to the public and the private sector, even to substitute and part-time workers. It does not hold for the self-employed. The only stipulation is that a beneficiary must have been employed for at least the last six months or twelve months during the last two years; this restriction does not hold for trade union training, though this law, like the union representative law, constitutes a frame of reference that may be substantiated by collective agreement. Such agreement, however, may only modify technicalities; none of the essentials, such as the right to educational leave and the right to sue for it and for the related employment protection, may be changed.

In principle, the right to educational leave is unlimited; according to the educational purpose, it can range from a few hours to several years. There also is no required intermittence between two educational leaves. But as the French experience of a right—in principle—to individual educational leave without guarantee of continued income payments demonstrates, such general principles in most cases do not effect much change. As long as the economic problem of maintained income is not solved, they remain paper rights. This issue was left to be regulated by a subsequent law with the expectation that it would partially answer the demand for maintained income by providing for paid leave for short periods of study—the kind that are considered socially most desirable.

The employer can postpone demands of educational leave if the proper operation of the plant would seriously be impaired or in order to reorganize the plant. The law establishes no percentage limit to determine the maximum number of simultaneous absentees for educational leave purposes. It is up to the employer to decide initially on this matter. Applications for educational leave of one week or the equivalent or for trade union training may be postponed by two weeks; those for longer studies can be delayed for six months. In any case, the applicant as well as the competent trade union have to be informed about the reasons for postponement. For any longer postponements the employer has to obtain the consent of the union. The union again has primacy of interpretation until a labor court decides otherwise. If workers (particularly those not represented by a union) are unable to begin their leave within two years of application (one year for leaves of less than one week), they can seek recourse in court. These conditions are designed to incite joint advance planning of study leave measures by the social partners.

The law suggests an order of priority among applicants for educational leave, preferring trade union training and short courses to the education of those with less than the equivalent of nine years of previous education. Among these, preference should be given to those with the most arduous shift-working arrangements.

A person on educational leave may interrupt his education at his own discretion or upon advice without losing the right to return to work immediately if the leave was intended for one week only; he has to observe a period of notice of two weeks in case the leave has been shorter and of one month if the leave has been equal to or longer than a year. The beneficiary of an educational leave is guaranteed job security and can ask for damages and reemployment if he is given notice with reference to his demand for educational leave. He has claim to the same or an equivalent occupation on return from the educational leave.

This educational leave law also gives the primacy of interpretation to the local branch of the labor unions or, in more general cases, to the national organization. It is up to the employer to go to court. Trade unions normally represent the applicant in lawsuits. Employers can also be sentenced to pay damages to the trade unions, including damages for insult. Inversely, the union can be made liable for damages caused by abuse of their primary-interpretation rights, as can the individual employee for fraudulent applications.

Study Support. The provisions of the newly adopted law on socio-economic support for adult studies will constitute the following scheme of public assistance, to take effect on January 1, 1976 (*Nytt om högskolan,* 1975):

1. Shift and hard workers will get 18 kronor per hour of study circle attendance of 10 up to 35 hours per half-year for compensation of loss of income. These study-hour grants (*timstudiestöd*) are taxable. This new form of support for brief adult education is applicable to studies in priority study circles, and in special cases also to studies in municipal adult education. This support is restricted to the actively employed. For the first half year of 1976, about 10,000 individuals can be granted a study-hour grant (the FÖVUX committee had proposed 29,000 35-hour allowances).

2. There will be a daily taxable income grant of 90 kronor as well as 70 kronor per day, tax free, for accommodation and travel for short courses of between two and five days per half year. The per diem study allowance (*dagstudiestöd*) is intended to compensate for the income foregone for students who participate in short subject courses at folk high schools. It is destined for employed persons, but can also be granted to homeworkers, the handicapped, and people living in sparsely populated areas: 3,750 income and accommodation allowances are available for the first half-year of 1976 (FÖVUX suggested 6,500 combined allowances, 3,000 income allowances for external studies, and 3,000 accommodation allowances for people without employment).

Because of their brief duration, these two new types of study assistance are not designed to achieve any formal qualifications. They are regarded as a possibility to give the most underprivileged a chance to experience an educative process again in order to motivate them to take part in more extended programs. Both short term study allowances are the financial counterpart to the (unpaid) educational leave law, and thus will constitute two new schemes of paid educational leave in Sweden from 1976 on. In accordance with the FÖVUX suggestions, they are particularly designed for those with the most adverse working conditions and brief prior education. Application will mainly be collective through the intermediary of the unions; but individuals may also apply, and they may complain at the central level against decisions taken at the county level by newly created adult education boards (*vuxenutbildningsnämnd*).

3. Within the labor market training (AMU) scheme, participants (those unemployed or threatened with unemployment) will be subsidized by 90 to 130 kronor per day, which is subject to taxation; this is 10 kronor above the ordinary unemployment pay.

4. Longer adult education efforts are supported by the same amounts as in the AMU case, but only 65 percent of the special adult education allowance (*särskild vuxenstudiestöd*) consists of direct grants; the remaining 35 percent constitutes a loan repayable after employment begins again. Preconditions for this kind of support are four years of vocational experience, with a certain minimal income qualifying for old-age pension computation. Child care for children under ten years of age is also counted as equivalent to vocational experience. Priority is given to those with short basic education who are attending courses at upper compulsory or secondary school levels or in a continued vocational education program at a technical college (*yrkeshögskola*) with limited admissions. The aid also applies to half-time students and part-time workers. Eligibility is conditioned on the actual economic need, with special regard to persons with dependents. Preference will be given to people with brief prior education for studies at the compulsory school level. The precise distribution of some 7,000 study allowances for the first half-year of 1976 is to be decided by government; studies on postsecondary level shall at first be restricted to new experimental vocational colleges (*yrkeshögskola*) to allow all new entrants in the fall of 1975 to benefit from the scheme.

The law also revised the system of regular loans and grants in secondary and higher education.

These schemes will require a new system of administration with stronger union influence and a political decision procedure within the regional adult education boards.

Schemes 1, 2, and 4 will be financed through a new employers' contribution (*arbetsgivaravgift*) of 0.15 percent of the annual payroll, introduced by a specific law (on a contribution for adult education—*lag om vuxenutbildningsavgift*—SFS 1975:358 of May 29, 1975).

Trade Union Education. In the next few years, the responsibilities of Swedish unions are going to increase significantly. In addition to representing workers in contract negotiations and local management-worker relationships, the unions will play an increasing role in adult education as they develop their outreach activities through study organizers.

The training of the study organizers is initiated on the local level in different ways that the various unions themselves will decide on. The common denominator is a similarity of background and experience between the outreach worker and the target group(s) together with his ability to link individual conditions with the social framework in which they occur. This analytical ability and the capacity to create a consciousness for the necessity of further education are the main objectives of the outreach training.

In the Swedish Confederation of Trade Unions (LO), the training on union structures and objectives takes place in the evenings in study circles of twenty to thirty hours; sometimes the Workers' Educational Association (ABF) holds study circles of up to 60 hours. This training accounts for roughly one third of all union study circle activities, other subjects being working environment, industrial or enterprise democracy, and the like. The circles include an estimated 100,000 participants per year.

Educational leave effects are realized in residential courses ranging from one week to three months. When union functionaries with legally prescribed responsibilities (such as security commissioners at the working place or labor representative board members) are trained, their continued incomes are paid by the firms or from working environment funds established by the employers; other union members receive payments from the union. About 20,000 participants annually attend the longer union programs of paid educational leave. These are not clearly defined in content and may have many different names, although the general outlook and qualification they convey is similar.

Since these courses reached less than the number of elected union representatives in the firms newly elected each year, LO started an ambitious empirical research project to investigate in detail the specific activities and functions their representatives have to perform in the workshops, trying to clarify how representatives could better be prepared by union training.

In the future, study circles will be the most widely used form (80 to 90 percent) of disseminating methodological knowledge and experience, while residential courses are intended to decrease drastically in importance.

Participatory Democracy. The most far-reaching reform of industrial organization and social life is intended by a proposal for a law on the right to collective bargaining (*lag om förhandlingsrätt och kollektivavtal*) developed by the Committee on Labor Law (*Arbetsrättskommittén*) with representatives from the political parties, the unions, and the employers. It is to be deliberated in parliament in the spring of 1976 after having been submitted to the societal organizations for comment and revision, and will be effective as of January 1, 1977. The salient points of this gradual revolution of working life are (1) that all questions concerning the relationship between employers and employees shall be subject to negotiation between the former and the employees' representatives (unions)— which means the elimination of any inherent rights of the employers—and (2) that the scope and procedures of these bargaining rights shall, in turn, be determined through collective agreements; in other words, the negotiating skill and strength of the employees and their unions will determine their influence within broad guidelines set by the law. This conception of a democracy at the place of work from bottom to top leaves the decisive rights with the local workshops. The central organizations are called in only in cases of conflict or principle. State arbitration is previewed also. Within the first ten days of a conflict, the employer's interpretation prevails (*tolkningsföreträde*). Unless legal proceedings are instituted within this time, this right is ceded to the unions. The employers also must, under threat of paying damages, contact union representatives to inform them about all important questions, imminent measures of importance, prospects of the enterprise and the economy. They have to grant leave for bargaining: two employees must be given paid bargaining leave for negotiations with their own employer. This is particularly important for representatives of minority groups that cannot contract collective agreements of their own. In principle, the bargaining rights also apply to the public service.

The proposed law further strengthens the positions of the unions, whose influence on the bill is not to be denied. In preparing for the new law, the unions are planning to utilize the educational leave provisions that have recently become available. A major project is being developed to eventually reach all members. LO intends to implement study circles of ten meetings each, beginning at the workshop level, in an effort to apply a new problem-solving strategy to practical problems. This participatory education will be undertaken in close cooperation between functionaries and members. The primary target group of 100,000 regional union club members will, together with 500,000 cooperative union members, try to recruit 300,000 additional nonclub members to form working groups at the factory level as study circles. The first three meetings will be devoted to the perspectives of the reforms and pertinent LO plans and policies; the fourth would then deal with personnel guidance and rationalization; the fifth would try to find solutions—and so on to the tenth meeting, which would undertake the formulation of an action program. Since the study circles would concentrate on different sectors, such as working environment, supervision of work, and rationalization, they will result in an array of action plans in the respective fields. These plans would be coordinated by special action plan committees, on the common basis of LO ideology and would have immediate feedback with the study circles.

Serving both to further internal union democratization and to inhibit structural rigidity, these study circles would also help remodel industrial relations completely by stimulating individuals and groups to reflect on their situation, to make use of union resources, to express themselves, and to take part, by teamwork, in social decision making. As a next step, each LO member is to be involved in one week of further education. This action program will also have a considerable political impact for the simple reason that 80 to 90 percent of the some 1.8 million LO members are also active members in the Social Democratic Party (SAP). The full program would cost 200 million kronor per year, equal to 0.3 percent of the total wage bill, while LO now spends 50 to 100 million kronor on education.

The unions gathered in LO seem prepared to use the possibilities of educational leave and adult education as far as possible to restructure society and the economy, in particular, by instituting new forms of mass participation, that aims at a full democratization of industry on the basis of their ideology. In this way they are also trying to precondition the expected law on the right to collective bargaining.

Conclusions

Since most of the Swedish reform measures directed toward educational leave have only had a short period of application or are still in their preparatory stages, it is too early to draw any inferences about their eventual results. The Swedish initiatives closely or remotely linked with educational leave all have a strong programmatic tinge pointing to a "new society." The distribution of legislative power is such that few obstacles are to be expected from that quarter. Major portions of the new social order are appearing in outline, but most of the new order is still only at the blueprint stage; Sweden is neither an isolated adult educational province nor a monolithic progressist country (although conditions for a balanced change apparently are among the most favorable of all countries considered). In any case, the new approaches will have to go through the test of social, political, and economic strife and of practical application on a large scale before one can ascertain whether they can carry their share of the new society. While many of the social and educational programs of the sixties have had an important impact, the Swedes would be the first to admit that they have not fully eliminated the problems they were designed to solve. In a sense, Sweden's educational leave policies are "futuristic" as compared to the other three countries, notwithstanding the fact that the country already has one of the most highly evolved adult educational systems to date.

7

Italy

The Italian Educational System

Throughout most of Western Europe, the major historical periods in the twentieth century are roughly comparable: the most significant events are World War I and World War II, and the interwar years are divided into the periods before and after the international economic crisis of 1929 to 1933. For Italy, however, this is not the case. The advent of fascism in 1922 meant that there was no period of democratic rule before the economic crisis, and the interwar years are years not of civilian but of paramilitary rule. This historical fact is reflected, understandably, in the educational system, both in the institutions of initial schooling and in the adult education sector.

Whereas in most European countries there was a period of democratic, even progressive, reform and experimentation in education immediately following World War I, the reforms undertaken in Italy between 1923 and 1929 (known as *la riforma Gentile,* after the responsible minister of culture) tended to reaffirm social and professional divisions rather than to mitigate them. This put Italy at a disadvantage in attempting to create an educational system corresponding to the needs of a pluralistic democracy after World War II. Whereas the typical educational reforms for greater equality of opportunity—comprehensive institutions for compulsory education, liberalization of access to advanced education, reform of vocational education, delay of selection decisions and increased possibilities for reentry into the educational system, liberalization of curricula, and increased participation of parents and students in decision making—have all been legislated or are in the process of being implemented, their effect has been much more limited than in other countries.[1] This has left Italy with some far-reaching contradictions between stated policy and the present condition of the educational system. Since recent initiatives of an educational leave character are aimed at eliminating these very contradictions, they must be described in some detail.

There is virtually no analphabetism among young people who are not mentally unable to acquire the necessary skills. Historically, however, analphabetism was a problem, and it continues to be an area of special activity in adult education. In 1973, 1.4 percent of the active labor force and 5.1 percent of the population were still listed as analphabets (Censis, 1974, table 5, p. 961, and table 4, p. 951).

At the present time, the Italian system of education provides for eight years of comprehensive, compulsory education, divided between five years of elementary and three years of middle (*scuola media*) schools (see Figure 5). The middle schools lead to a certificate (*licenza media*) which is universally considered the minimum level of attainment required of all citizens. In fact, both historically and at the present time, a significant number of students do not reach this basic level of attainment—49 percent of them in 1959–60, 26 percent in 1966–67, and 13 percent in 1973–74 (ISTAT, 1968; Censis, 1974, p. 946). The primary reasons for this are the practice of streaming in the *scuola media* and the large number of students who are forced to repeat one or more classes in the elementary or middle schools, mostly for academic reasons, but occasionally still for lack of teachers and facilities. This phenomenon of "delay" relative to the theoretical course of studies is one of the basic characteristics of the Italian educational system, causing major discrepancies between average actual time spent in school when compared with the time required in theory. In 1967–68, for example, 30.5 percent of the eighth-grade students had repeated at least one year of school, and 12.0 percent had repeated two or more years (CNEL, 1968, vol. 1, table II.3). The average

[1] Fadiga Zanatta, 1972; the basic thrust of Italian educational policy is presented on p. 13, whereas the following chapters give details on the difficulties of implementation.

Figure 5. Structure of the educational system in Italy

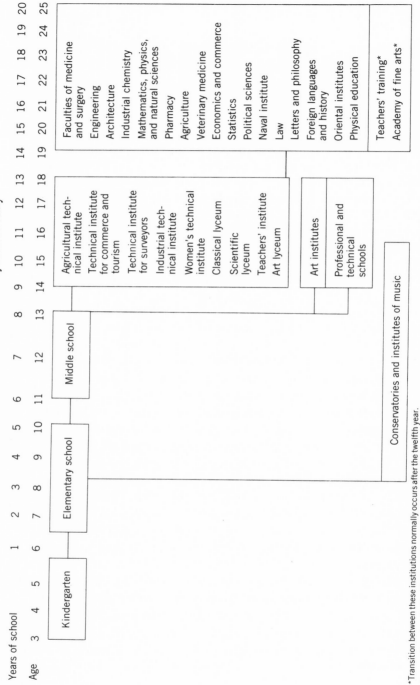

*Transition between these institutions normally occurs after the twelfth year.

Source: Based on Fadiga Zanatta, 1972, p. 22, modified to take into account later changes.

time required to complete the eighth grade is more than 8.5 years; and upper secondary school, which ends with grade 13, actually represents closer to 14 years of schooling on the average. Moreover, 52.0 percent of all students leaving the educational system after the 1972–73 academic year did so without having completed the course of studies they were enrolled in (Censis, 1974).

The school curriculum also poses a number of serious problems. Until 1969, mastery of Latin and classical Italian were the main criteria for selection into the universities. The specialized nature of the skills required is illustrated by the fact that, in spite of the highly selective course of studies, Italian students in an international study of student achievement showed the lowest relative increase in all subjects considered (Trivellato and Bernardi, 1974, p. xiv, n. 5; Scuola di Barbiana, p. 130).

Some liberalization of the curriculum has occurred in the early seventies, but the curriculum continues to pose serious problems for those whose background does not correspond to the basic pattern of the majority culture reflected in the schools.

Vocational Education

We do not really know what happens to students who drop out of the scholastic system of education. A significant number go directly into the labor force as unskilled and semiskilled workers, often only sporadically employed. Although a wide variety of courses are offered, ranging from apprenticeship without schooling to purely institutional vocational education, no reliable statistics on the number of students involved are available. A recent study showed variations of up to 140 percent between sets of statistics (Trivellato and Bernardi, 1974, p. 25). One reason for this large variation may be that formally all young people between fifteen and eighteen were hired as apprentices, even though they did not participate in a training program.

The situation is made even more complex by the changes that have recently taken place in administrative responsibility for vocational training. After years of hesitation, basic responsibility for vocational education was transferred to the regions in 1972. In many areas this has clarified the situation, but the transferral was not complete; whereas all courses that used to be the responsibility of the Ministry of Labor have been transferred, the Ministry of Education continues to play a major role in adult education (Trivellato and Bernardi, 1974, p. 20). It retains responsibility for the *Istituti Professionali*, the upper secondary vocational schools; the Ministry of Defense retains authority for vocational training in the army, and the Ministry of Justice retains a role in courses conducted in correctional institutions.

Whereas the effect of the transfer has indeed been to allow closer supervision and to ease identification of the locus of decision making, it has also made generalization concerning vocational education even more difficult. The response of the regions has varied; the reporting on developments has varied even more; and available reports cover, at best, only the first year of regional responsibility. There are, however, signs that in some regions there has been a fairly vigorous development of the vocational education sector; this in turn means that what research there was on conditions as they previously existed may rapidly become outdated (Fondazione Giovanni Agnelli, 1972; Trivellato and Bernardi, 1974).

Taking into account these difficulties, some broad generalizations are still possible. The report on the first year of experience in the Lombardy region—probably the region with the best provisions for vocational education—describes the system taken over from the Ministry of Labor as follows: "In sum the efforts were disaggregated and poor in technical and financial means, a system of planning and execution that was counterproductive relative to its expressed goals, the guidelines were irrational and, most serious of all, it constituted a system removed from public control." (Regione Lombardia, 1974, p. 7). A comparison of information on the years 1961 to 1973 for various regions of Italy reveals that although the growth in this sector has been substantial since 1971–72, by 1973–74 in Lombardy no more than 20 percent of the youth between fifteen and nineteen years of age who were not in the secondary schools were in some form of vocational training.[2] By all accounts

[2]Trivellato and Bernardi (1974, table 114, p. 49) state that in 1971, 6.1 percent of the resident population in Italy aged 15 to 19 were attending *"corsi normali."* In Lombardy, the total number of students in vocational education courses under the auspices of the Ministry of Labor, excluding agricultural students, was 20,858. The

even those presently enrolled are being ill served by their experience. The system has many diverse elements that are categorized
differently in different reports, making comparisons all but impossible. No one approach has been given general priority. A dual
system of apprenticeship and supporting instruction exists for
many professions; purely institutional vocational education is offered in many areas, often including those where apprenticeships
are available; and for some trades—especially building trades—
instruction takes place entirely at the work place. Each of these
approaches (which include all basic models of vocational education
being discussed in other countries) has been trenchantly criticized
as practiced in Italy. Apprenticeship, it is thought, serves as a source
of cheap labor and provides poor training, with only a small percentage of apprentices participating in the supporting institutional
instruction (Trivellato and Bernardi, 1974, p. 33). Institutional
vocational education is highly fragmented, not oriented toward the
labor market, and too specialized; this is especially true of the agricultural sector, in which more than 90 percent of the students ultimately seek employment outside the area they were trained for
(Fondazione Giovanni Agnelli, 1972, p. 15; Trivellato and Bernardi,
1974, pp. 33–35).

When one combines the experience of students in vocational
education with what happened to them in schools, the dominant
factor is the experience of failure. Only a small proportion of the
youths who are not in school are in the vocational education system, and their prior educational profile is not encouraging: 35.4
percent of all those who attended vocational education in the Veneto
region in 1970–71 had not completed the *terza media* (eighth grade,
or third grade in secondary school) and a further 29.7 percent had

growth for the total group not broken down by category was 44.43 percent (Regione
Lombardia, 1973, p. 80). Between 1972 and 1974 the growth rate was in excess of 100
percent in all categories; for unexplained reasons, however, the figures are not
comparable. The education authorities themselves point out that 65 percent of all
courses are devoted to retraining or upgrading, which may not include the basic age
group. Courses devoted only to initial training accommodate roughly 9 percent of the
15- to 19-year-olds not in secondary schools, 4.5 percent of the age group (Regione
Lombardia, 1974a). We have assumed at least another 10 percent of the 15- to 19-
year-olds not in secondary school are attending the retraining and upgrading
courses.

repeated at least one class (Trivellato and Bernardi 1974, p. 177).

Even on the assumption that the transfer of responsibility for vocational education to the regions will have the intended effect of inducing sustained growth and effective reform, and that the reform of the *scuola media* will take hold as intended, the Italian population will have to be considered, on the average, inadequately educated and trained for years to come, as the following summary indicates (Censis, 1974, p. 1059):

> *Population.* According to the latest census (1971), 76.6 percent of the Italian population sixteen years or older did not have the *licenza media* (in 1961, 84.8 percent); 32.8 percent did not have the *licenza elementare* (successful completion of five years of elementary school). Differences according to region, sex, and age revealed particular disadvantages for the South, for women, and for the older population.
>
> *Labor force.* In 1973, 65.8 percent of the labor force did not have the *licenza media* (81.8 percent of all industrial workers).
>
> *Employed.* In 1973, 66.7 percent of all persons employed had not completed the *licenza media* (in 1972, 68.5 percent).
>
> *First-time employment.* Of those seeking first-time employment in 1973, 24.1 percent were without *licenza media,* 35.8 percent had the *licenza media* only, 33.3 percent had an upper secondary certificate, and 7.4 percent, a university degree.

Adult Education

Improvement in the educational system for the young and the ensuing rise in educational qualification of those entering the work force initially exacerbates differences between young graduates and the working population and creates substantial demand for adult education. For years to come, the major concern of adult education—and hence also of most educational leave programs—will have to be remedial (Trivellato, 1975). The budget for adult education represented 0.53 percent of all expenditures of the Ministry of Education in 1974 (Censis, 1974, p. 1068), but, unfortunately, the statistics on adult vocational education are most misleading. The "normal courses" for unemployed youths and workers in employment are generally divided into four categories: (1) basic training for those without a vocational degree, (2) courses to requalify or improve the qualifications of employed workers, (3) courses of specialization, and (4) agricultural courses. While there are wide variations between the regions, it is generally true that a significant portion of the total training effort is devoted to the second category of courses. This might lead to the conclusion that there exists a field of adult vocational training comparable in size to that for first qualification.[3] A more careful study of who is actually attending courses for requalification and specialization shows that the percentage of employed or formerly employed actually attending courses is insignificant and that their average age is only two years higher than the average of those who have not yet been in employment (Trivellato and Bernardi, 1974, p. 194, table II.25).

The only source of national statistics on general adult education is the Ministry of Education. Since the ministry mainly provides subventions to other organizations that conduct the courses, the ministry statistics do not necessarily reflect the entire effort of these organizations. At the same time, to consult decentralized statistics becomes futile, since they often include a significant but not clearly identified portion of activities supported by ministry subventions. The problematic nature of any analysis is reflected in the fact that the education ministry's Directory of Adult Education Institutions lists 1,134 addresses (Ministero Della Pubblica Istruzione, 1975), while the statistics for 1972–73 list only a total of 8,625 courses, showing either extreme fragmentation or—more probably—incomplete information (Trivellato, 1975, p. 41, table 16).

Adult education is subdivided into two sectors: popular education (*educazione popolare*) and adult education (*educazione degli*

---

[3]Available figures on first qualification are highly contradictory. Fondazione Giovanni Agnelli (1972, p. 51) states that, in 1968–69, 89.2 percent of all *courses* in Italy in the industrial sector were devoted to basic qualification; Trivellato and Bernardi (1974, p. 41, table 19) in the same year state that 69.9 percent of students in Veneto were in courses for basic qualification; Assessorato regionale all'Istruzione (Regione Lombardia, 1974a, p. 79) states that in 1972–73 and 1973–74 only about 25 percent of all courses and students were concerned with initial training.

adulti). The former includes basically remedial courses at elementary school level, whereas the latter covers all forms of activities specific to adult audiences. Both sectors have shown a clear decline according to the ministry's statistics—for instance, from 7,920 courses of popular education and 7,358 courses of adult education in 1971–1972 down to 4,280 and 4,694 courses respectively in 1973–1974 (Censis, 1974, p. 1068).

The entire field of adult education has not yet received concerted attention. In 1967, the first major effort was undertaken to create a serviceable network of institutions of adult education. The state authority for development of Southern Italy (*Cassa del Mezzogiorno*) created eighty-four centers of cultural services and began to support them with significant funding. By the mid-seventies, however, this effort was largely dissipated; the centers never having been fully staffed, the funds being steadily withdrawn.

In terms of popular education, the Ministry of Education, in addition to the alphabetization program, has maintained a series of courses for the completion of compulsory schooling (CRACIS). These courses normally require three years, with eighteen hours of instruction a week for seven months a year, or a total of more than 1,500 hours of instruction, during the participants' free time. Since 1969, special arrangements have been made for members of the armed forces, involving 23 percent of the participants. Between 1964 and 1973, a total of 167,000 course enrollments had been registered. The year-on-year rate of failure was 22 percent on the average, so that not more than 75,000 completed the entire course of study by 1974 (Trivellato, 1975, p. 11).

In an attempt to provide greater focus to the adult education effort, the Ministry of Education began to create Centers for Permanent Education—by 1975 a total of 1,201—which received an increasing proportion of the diminishing funds. This initiative is now also considered to be floundering (Bechelloni, 1973, p. 75; Castello, 1970). The main reason is probably that the resources, both financial and personal, that have been brought to bear on the problems of adult education at large have not been adequate to the huge tasks. The constant redefinition of programs and priorities (with the signal exception of the continuing effort against analphabetism) is rather a symptom than a cause of the difficulties. In the face of failure to achieve an impact with the meager resources, there is a constant temptation to reallocate them and to create new programs to meet the many and pressing needs that remain unattended to.

The one area in which there exists a continuous and to some extent successful tradition of adult education in Italy is in the fight against analphabetism (Censis, 1974). Over the last ten years, this program has gone through a steady evolution: initially aimed primarily at the eradication of the "symptoms" of analphabetism, by the late sixties it was already espousing a much broader view of the problem, as expressed in the notion of "integral alphabetization," which tried to provide the student with basic social and political skills beyond those of simply being able to read and to write (Avveduto, 1973, p. 64). Certainly, the steady fall in the number of analphabets in the Italian population is attributable not only to the increased level of educational attainment among young people but also to the effort at remediation through programs for adults.

In spite of this, Italy cannot be said to have an adult education sector of any consequence by international standards, even by the relatively more modest ones of France before 1971. Moreover, virtually none of these activities have had educational leave effects, since employers have not felt constrained to grant special privileges, such as paid absence from work, to those who participate. The only exception is that employers have been contractually obliged to give five days' paid leave to any employee preparing for an exam leading to a recognized degree. Until 1974, most such exams were being taken for an upper secondary school certificate; the preparation, however, took place in commercial private schools on which no information whatsoever is available.

In-Service Training of Civil Servants

The only group of civil servants having access to systematic in-service training in Italy are teachers; and even they have only limited opportunities (Giugni, 1974). Over the years, ten national institutes for teaching skills have been created for various levels of instruction. Over a thirty-year period, only 350,000 teachers have been able to participate in courses of these centers, mostly in very large courses of fifty or more. Selection of participants is apparently fairly arbitrary, and very little follow-up occurs. Thus, while up to 20,000 teachers attend in a given year, the impact of this activity is not substantial. A number of these courses take place during vacation periods, so that not all participants can be assumed to have benefited from an educational leave effect. The fairly extensive network of private initiatives in the area of teacher support relies on participants' spare time.

Trade Union Training

Unlike most other European countries, Italy has no legislation providing trade union representatives with a right to attend on company time courses to prepare them for their functions. In view of the importance of such courses to the functioning of the labor market, other means have been found to provide workers' representatives with some form of training. It is impossible, however, to define the scope and nature of these courses precisely. There are two principal avenues of trade union training: courses conducted and financed by the unions themselves, and regular adult education courses. Thus far, there is not evidence that the program of "150 hours" (see discussion later in this chapter) is being used directly for the purpose of trade union training.

The three major unions—CGIL (General Italian Confederation of Labor), GISL (Italian Confederation of Labor Unions), and UIL (Italian Labor Union)—all maintain national training centers to train their members. Since 1974, the federation of the three unions has also been using these centers in rotation. The major unions in the various categories (metalworkers, textile workers, and so forth) also maintain national training centers, and the entire structure is replicated at some regional and local levels. No information is available on the overall scope of these activities, but there are indications that unions in industries that maintain a large in-service training effort tend to have a significant interest in trade union training—the most notable example being the metalworkers' union (FLM).

The founding of these schools (between 1951 and 1966) symbolized an important development in the social and political structure of Italy. Until the late fifties, labor unions had been tied to political parties; labor leaders were selected and trained within the parties on ideological and party lines (Di Gioia and Pontacolone, 1972, p. 97). The founding of the trade union schools represented a break with this tradition and a step toward the unification and political independence of the trade unions that was completed with the creation of the trade union federation in the early 1970s. Whereas the actual number of participants in courses has not been particularly large, their impact has been substantial.

Most labor contracts concluded by the unions in recent years have obliged the employers to "facilitate" participation of trade union representatives in these courses, that is, to make provision for leave without pay. The unions themselves, however, must meet all costs for courses of this kind, including compensation for earnings foregone. This compensation is, as a rule, less than 100 percent of previous take home pay.

In a number of instances private or semiprivate institutions of adult education receiving financial support from the Ministry of Education are in fact devoting the major portion of their resources to the training of trade union members (*Umanitaria* in Milan and FORMEZ in Naples, for example). These grants cover instructional and institutional costs but do not include support payments for participants, who must use direct or indirect trade union resources for this purpose. In practice, a number of possibilities exist: direct payments, the use of released time available for general trade union activities, or the linking of participation to a paid trade union function.

Since most of these courses require only a few hours a week, they can generally still be accommodated within a full work week, at some personal sacrifice but without financial loss. In these courses and in those conducted by the trade unions themselves, the curriculum is composed of topics relating to the role of the participants as trade union representatives: labor law, leadership and negotiating techniques, basics of management, and the history of the trade union movement.

In-Service Training in Industry

Like industry in other countries, Italian industry is engaged in training and retraining its employees, but little information is available on the scope of this activity. According to one estimate, the amount of time available varies from two hours a year for each employee to a maximum of sixteen hours a year for each employee. The average for all industries engaged in such activities is probably not more than three hours a year for each employee.

The most systematic approach to the questions of in-service training has been developed by the complex of state-owned industries in IRI (*Istituto per la Ricostruzione Industriale*), representing 5 percent of the industrial sector. IRI created its own training agencies, ANCIFAP (vocational training) and IFAP (management training). ANCIFAP originally devoted virtually all its effort to initial vocational training, but by 1974, priorities had shifted, so that 70 percent of its resources were being used for the training of those already on the payroll, with about half being trained immediately after hiring.

The courses always have some professionally relevant goal, but over the years they have become shorter, more flexible, and have increasingly tended to cover general psychological and sociological topics. Particularly interesting is the congruence of experience between the industrial training units and the very differently oriented programs of "150 hours" (see below). Both report that very close integration of courses with the place and experiences of work increases their effectiveness. In the last few years, ANCIFAP has developed close relationships with some factories that are particularly active in training and has acted as planning consultant, taking over the entire staffing and administration of these factories' educational activities. Because of the closeness of this relationship, ANCIFAP has made a practice of seeking explicit trade union approval for its more important activities.

The intensity of a particular factory's commitment to inservice training appears not to be clearly linked to particular branches or forms of production but seems to depend on a variety of personal factors, indicating that this form of activity has not yet become an accepted part of industrial operations. Nevertheless, it represents a fairly major undertaking relative to the totality of educational leave effects in Italy.

The "150 Hours"

Since 1974, a program has existed in Italy that substantially meets all the requirements of educational leave under the ILO definition. This program—generally known as the "150 hours"—was introduced through labor market contracts. It derives its name from a distinctive feature of the pioneering contract signed by the metalworkers' union (which includes the automobile industry) in January 1974. Other unions have since followed (see Table 7).

The metalworkers' contract provides that every factory, or every production unit (in the case of very large factories), creates a fund of hours of paid leave for educational purposes at the disposal of its employees. The total number of hours over a three-year period is calculated according to the formula: $H = 10 \times 3 \times N$, where H is the number of available hours and N is the average number of workers over the years (that is, 10 hours per worker per year). The name of the program derives from one of the two major limitations on the use of the collective fund of hours: (1) no worker may use more than 150 hours of this fund over a three-year period. Moreover, he must devote at least an equal number of hours of his free time (evenings, weekends, or vacations) to the educational program for which he is receiving paid leave; (2) not more than 2 percent of the work force of a factory or production unit may be away simultaneously from the place of work under this program.

The name "150 hours" has given rise to misconceptions; excessive focus on the 150 hours provision had led to the notion that the 150 hours program represents a worker's *individual right* (OECD, 1975). One of the key elements in the metalworkers' program is, in fact, that it represents a *collective* right of the workers in a factory.

Since the metalworkers' contract, more than twenty other trade union agreements, involving approximately 4,750,000 workers (or 26 percent of the employed labor force), have been concluded. Only some follow the pattern of the metalworkers' contract. Three basic types have emerged: (1) the *collective* right exemplified by the metalworkers' agreement, with a limitation on the number of hours that an individual may draw from the collective pool; (2) the *individual* right exemplified by the ceramics- and glassworkers, with limitations on the number of hours a worker may use; (3) the *individual* right with no limitation on number of hours but with more rigid mechanisms of consent by unions and employers to individual applications, exemplified by the farm workers. Of these contracts, only the metalworkers' contract has been ex-

Table 7. Educational Leave in Italian Trade Union Contracts

Industry	No. of beneficiaries (in thousands)	Date of contract	Limitations
Metalworkers	1.36	April 19, 1973	Maximum 150 hours per beneficiary over three years, also usable in single year; not more than 2% of the workers of a factory may be absent on leave simultaneously; one hour paid leave for every two hours of course work
Ceramics and abrasives	45	June 17, 1973	Maximum leave per beneficiary of 120 hours annually of which only 40 are paid; not more than 2.5% of the workers of a factory may be absent on leave simultaneously; one hour paid leave for every three hours of leave
Wood and cork	290	June 23, 1973	Maximum leave per beneficiary of 120 hours annually of which only 40 are paid; not more than 2.5% of the workers of a factory may be absent on leave simultaneously
Textiles and garments	700	July 20, 1973	Same as Ceramics contract
Glass	65	January 9, 1974	50 hours of paid leave annually per beneficiary
Publishing	8	January 15, 1974	Same as Metalworkers' contract with an upper limit of 100 hours per beneficiary over a two-year period
Tanneries	25	February 15, 1974	Same as Ceramics contract
Local government	450	March 5, 1974	50 hours annually of unpaid leave

Rubber, plastics, linoleum	210	March 18, 1974	150 hours of leave per beneficiary of which only 50 are paid; not more than 3% of the workers of a factory may be absent on leave simultaneously; one hour paid leave for every three hours of leave
Municipal works and gas	5	April 4, 1974	Same as Glass contract
Dolls, toys, Christmas ornaments	25	May 7, 1974	Same as Ceramics contract
Food retailers	445	June–October 1974	Same as Metalworkers' contract
Farm workers (national contract)	700	July 12, 1974	60 hours unpaid leave for each worker within an indeterminate time period with possibility of additional leave under the provincial contracts
Florists (national contract)	20–30	July 12, 1974	120 hours unpaid leave
Printing	20	January 1, 1975	Same as Glass contract
Municipal waterworks	4	January 31, 1975	Same as Glass contract
Hospital employees (public hospitals)	250		Same as Metalworkers' contract
Sugar	30	December 3, 1974	Same as Metalworkers' contract
Commerce (wholesale)			160 hours paid leave

Source: Dore, 1975, pp. 17–18; Censis, 1975, vol. 1, pp. 15–16.

tensively employed—this because of the strong commitment to
it by the union at all levels. Of all students in the special courses
established for the "150 hours" in January 1974, 77 percent were
metalworkers; public services and textiles provided roughly 5 percent each, and all other sectors accounted for the rest (Censis, 1975,
vol. 2, p. 23, table 7).

To understand the significance of the distinction between
collective and individual contracts requires a more precise understanding of the social and political conditions of the Italian labor
market. In several respects, the Italian situation is most readily
comparable to that of Great Britain. Italian trade unions have consistently refused to consider, let alone promote, plans designed to
assign to them an assured role in the governmental processes and
internal decision making of industry, nor has such a role been
offered. The degree of polarization between the workers and the
property-owning classes continues to be more marked in Italy than
in any other country of the Common Market, and it permeates
many institutions (including schools), affecting the way in which
they are viewed by workers and trade unions. The Italian trade
unions have viewed their primary role as representing workers
in a confrontation in which ideology and class struggle have played
a major part. The relationship of employers and trade union representatives is not characterized by mutual trust.

As has already been mentioned, Italian trade unions were
tied to political parties for the greater part of the postwar period;
their activities were consequently restricted to labor market negotiations in the strictest sense of the term, and trade union membership was often equivalent to party membership. In recent years,
the three trade union movements have federated and cut loose
from identification with particular parties, although they continue
to be closely linked to the parties of the Left (including left-wing
factions of the Christian Democrats) and to be distrustful of those
of the Right (including the larger part of the Christian Democratic
party). For the trade unions, the advocacy of educational leave
was a new venture into social policy, an area they had previously
had to leave to the political party they were affiliated with.

The educational leave program that has developed within the
framework of the trade union negotiations has been decisively

influenced by the development of the trade union movement and by considerations related to its view of the beneficiaries' (workers') role in society. This is a matter not only of rhetoric but also of the program's substance. The terms of the contracts do not provide any guidance concerning the content, emphasis, or implementation of educational leave rights. For these we must turn to a variety of sources: the programmatic statements of the trade unions at national and local levels—the trade unions having been the driving force behind the implementation process; the directives of the Ministry of Education providing courses for beneficiaries of the 150 hours; and the individual contracts with the trade unions at factory level, which provide a number of variations to the basic scheme.

The trade unions do not form a monolithic block in their relationship to the new program. The interests of national and local organizations are quite distinct, as are the attitudes of unions in various industries. The metalworkers are the pacemakers of the program, both at the national and the local level, and are much the most articulate about it. Their industry is also one of the most highly unionized, and the metalworkers are a powerful force in the entire labor movement. To a certain extent one can say that within the framework of an educationally disadvantaged working class, it is the most articulate and powerful who are the first to benefit from the educational leave program.

The national trade union movement took up the cause of education as part of its social program after the student unrest of 1968–69, albeit only in a marginal way, emphasizing that school reform was a matter for local initiative—hardly a very realistic approach to a centralized system of compulsory schooling (see the excerpt from the *Decisions of the Unitary Conference on the Social Struggles*, reprinted in Gurrieri, 1975, pp. 281–287). In our interviews with people from the trade unions and with researchers close to the development of the 150 hours program, there was even some suggestion that the national trade union movement was not prepared for the success of the metalworkers in obtaining the 150 hours or for the energetic manner in which it was subsequently implemented at local levels. In the negotiations on implementation, the national movement has concentrated on relations with the ministry (Dore, 1975; Gurrieri, 1975; Ministero della Pubblica Istruzione, 1974).

Four main issues concern the trade unions: the relationship of the 150 hours to trade union activism in factories, the 150 hours as a means of reforming the schools, the collective use of the 150 hours, and the conditions of work (Dore, 1975, pp. 7–14). The key issue among these is the impact on the existing schools, which are viewed with intense distrust. The national trade unions have set the highest priority on assuring that the courses within the program occur within the framework of the regular educational system. To a certain extent, this reflects a response of a centralized organization that feels easiest in dealing with parallel structures. It is an open question whether the new clientele will have a major reforming impact on the schools or whether the basically conservative nature of the schools will prevail.

At present, the program is staffed predominantly by exceptionally young, committed teachers on short-term contracts. The major demand of the trade unions for 1975–76 is that the teachers in the program be given permanent appointments and be allowed to circulate through the regular secondary schools. This will undoubtedly determine whether or not the schools can be changed by these means. Thus far, there is no evidence of any impact. The programmatic statement is that "the trade union movement is fundamentally opposed to a completely ideological use of the 150 hours, which would lead to a flight into a worker school in contrast to a normal school. This would create a misleading and frustrating response to the workers' demand for the means to a critical understanding of reality (*strumenti critici della realta*), and in practice would mean confining the use of the 150 hours to a ghetto. The result would be an end to any possibility of turning the 150 hours into a new and important factor in the battle for the reform of the school because, insofar as the courses for workers do not have an exemplary character and are not roughly transferable to the normal school once reformed, the possibility arises that a concrete potential for renewal will be dissipated" (Dore, 1975). Certainly this statement is one side of a classic argument concerning reform of institutions from within versus reform from without.

It remains to be seen whether initiatives for adults can change schools as directly as this statement seems to suggest. Whereas the initial program of the national trade union congress placed school reform firmly within the context of a number of interlocking social reforms, the sudden opportunity of the 150 hours is forcing the trade unions to deal with this as an isolated issue at the national level in a virtual one-to-one relationship with the Ministry of Education. The experience of the past two years shows that in terms of national educational policy, the ministry has been successful in channeling the initiative into more or less established lines. The continuing substantial degree of innovation and change can only be perceived at local levels.

Also at the national level, but distinct from the national trade union movement, the metalworkers' union has made a number of key decisions concerning implementation of the program. Compared with the national movement, these decisions appear significantly more pragmatic. The metalworkers have rejected the CRACIS courses as a framework for the 150 hours (see discussion above) because they are considered unsatisfactory. The union has given priority to remedial courses at the lower secondary education level leading to the *licenza media* so as to achieve the recognized minimum level of education for participants. In addition to these courses, priority is to be given to "monographic" courses in the universities, that is, courses dealing with a discrete topic and not part of a degree credit sequence. Wherever possible, workers are to participate in courses jointly with "regular" students (see section on "monographic" university courses later in this chapter). These priorities imply a number of important decisions. While the national union movement still included courses of upper secondary level in their list of priorities (Letter to Minister Malfatti of September 21, 1973, reprinted in Dore, 1975, pp. 86–88; Gurrieri, 1975, pp. 288–291), the metalworkers leave these courses off their list of priorities. In practice, the attitude of the metalworkers prevailed. The so-called worker-students in upper secondary level courses represented the major sector of prior participation in adult education. Leaving these courses off the list of priorities represented an implicit rejection of their vocational, individual orientation and of the private profit-making institutions that dominate this sector of the educational system.

The experience of the 150 hours becomes palpable at re-gional levels. Differences of implementation and emphasis have become apparent, and approaches to student selection, teacher training, pedagogy, and content reveal the impact of the program and its main points of conflict. The regional experience has been documented extensively for various areas, allowing a fairly com-prehensive assessment of the first year of the program in Florence (Gurrieri, 1975), Milan (Pepe, 1975), Lazio (Censis, 1975), and Bologna (Bosi and others, 1974; Barbagli and others, 1974).

The selection of students is the concern of the *Consiglio di Fabbrica*—the works council—which is the most decentralized unit of the trade unions. The council corresponds to the unit of pro-duction, in which the leave credits accrue. In practice, this body has taken on the task of deciding who will go on leave and for how long. The employers, being required to approve leave except in cases where production would be hampered, have generally re-mained passive in this process. The employers receive notifica-tions of enrollment three months in advance and periodic certifi-cates of attendance during the course.

Most regional offices of the trade unions have developed selection guidelines designed to keep the councils aware of the need to have a reasonable representation of all groups in the work force. Trade union membership is, by all accounts, not a critical factor in the selection process, and some effort is made not to favor members of the council, who, in any case, have other leave possi-bilities (see the discussion above). The background of participants has been fully documented. Nearly 92 percent of the students are unskilled or semiskilled workers, with some regional variation (Censis, 1975, vol. 2, p. 27). Almost 70 percent come from large factories with more than 500 employees, and a further 18 percent come from those with 10 to 500 employees (Censis, 1975, vol. 2, p. 25, table 9). Only 15.3 percent are women (Censis, 1975, vol. 2, p. 12, table 1).

In the first year there were generally fewer applications than available leave credits: only in the second year was selection re-quired in some instances as applications mounted. The highly decentralized administration of this aspect of the program has meant that information dissemination has generally been informal, very wide, and quite effective. Graduates of the first year's program have often been used as recruiters for the following year.

Workers in the same factory are expected to attend courses together wherever possible, so that all students in a given course come from the same background. The role of the councils in many instances extends further; they can and do determine what topics should be covered in the courses and have access to the results. Although this is neither a uniform nor a universal practice, the fact that this role is possible at all demonstrates the degree of trade union involvement in the program.

There has been widespread and surprising unanimity over content and didactic approach to the courses, although this consensus has been translated into practice in many different and occasionally contradictory ways. The basic frame of reference is determined by the requirements of the final exam (*licenza media*) and is spelled out in a directive of the Ministry of Education. Students in the course are required to take instruction and pass exams in three subjects: Italian, foreign language, and mathematics. Courses of at least fifteen students each are organized into modules of four, with two (full-time) instructors. This allows a close coordination among the subjects, the assumption being that they will all be taught in relation to an interdisciplinary theme that is in turn related to the individual and collective experience of the participants in the course, the social background, and the work situation. Thus the economics of housing costs can become the topic for the teaching of a variety of general mathematical ideas. Many courses begin with a lengthy period in which the participants narrate, write, and finally synthesize their biographies as a means of harnessing the greater individualism of adults to the common goals of the course. In a later phase, a large number of the courses have undertaken *ricerca:* the systematic application of all the skills being taught to a single topic without a high degree of teacher input.

The overall intent, apart from conveying basic literacy and numeracy, can best be subsumed under the very Italian term *cultura di classe,* a working-class culture. This term describes both the intent and the contradictions of the program. The word *cultura* plays a key role in Italian educational literature, transcending that of *culture* in English-language countries, and is even broader in its implications than is the French word. *Cultura* signifies the essence of articulated existence and has an uncanny way of appearing in key passages of Italian texts at the point at which authors are unable to give explicit meaning to their argument. In connection with the notion of class—the working class in particular—the term refers to an attempt to make workers conscious of all the conditions of their existence and to equip them to cope with its contradictions. In practice this has always meant an analysis of socioeconomic conditions. At the same time, the term *cultura* carries a heavy freight of Italian educational history: the very notion that such a *cultura di classe* exists, distinct but with the attributes of "culture" as understood by educated Italians, highlights, by contrast, the fact that the most articulate arguments on and for the 150 hours are always presented by "cultured" persons, by those who have been educated in the traditional system of education. All the published reports are keenly aware of this fact and make great efforts to allow workers and participants in the courses to describe their experience in their own terms; administration and curriculum are designed to counteract the tendency to dictate from the point of view of a "high" culture. But many participants aspire to the very attributes they are being urged not to acquire because these attributes, even in the trade union movement, have been associated with social and economic success (Battaglia, 1972).

Thus the 150 hours program involves a by now classic paradox, reminiscent of the debate in the United States on black culture and its relationship to remedial education. While the issue of race does not enter here, the social and economic pressures on the participants in these courses are comparable to those that attach easily to race as forms of secondary discrimination. While everybody involved in the program in Italy is aware of these issues in one form or another—probably more than white Americans were in the mid-sixties—the paradox remains, and the evidence is not yet available to prove that the Italian approach can overcome it. The very notion that education is a means of individual and social advancement is part of a very definite cultural heritage.

This problem of relative culture attaches particularly to teachers; teacher training and selection has been the most problematic issue and promises to become the most controversial aspect of the program. Again, it is an issue American education is familiar with in connection with the controversies surrounding the staffing of black studies programs, Head Start programs, and all other remedial programs aimed at groups not belonging to the majority culture. On the critical issue of whether or not such programs are to be staffed by special teachers with a particular affinity to the background of the students or by regular teachers, the Italian trade unions have opted forcefully for the latter; surprisingly, they have been unaware of the choice they were making.

The training of teachers in lower secondary schools in Italy has been lagging behind intended reforms for some years, and teachers have repeatedly proved less adaptable to reform than plans once promulgated envisaged (Fadiga Zanatta, 1972, pp. 125–132). While there is a surplus of teachers in some areas, acute shortages exist in others. All these imperfections are transferred to the new courses, and the more so because the teachers recruited to them are as a rule the youngest or are teacher aspirants, often still in training with little prior teaching experience. Only 13.8 percent of the middle school teachers in the 150 hours program in 1974, for instance, were over 30 years of age and 32.3 percent of them were only 25 years of age or younger (Censis, 1975, vol. 1, p. 92).

It was clear from the start that teachers in the program would need additional training and continuing support throughout the courses, irrespective of their prior experience. Consequently, the work load of teachers was adjusted to allow for four weeks' training before courses began and to make some time available during the period the courses were in progress. Further money to make effective use of the time thus provided was, however, not available; the trade union contract supplied participants with personal support, the Ministry of Education paid the teachers' salaries, regional and local authorities provided space and textbooks, but little money was available for in-service support of teachers, just as such support is essentially unavailable for other teachers. Existing resources, therefore, had to be used, and not all of them were adequate or suitable. This particular problem created one of the major conflicts during the first year of operation in Milan, where the regional authorities wanted to commission a Catholic organization for the task and the metalworkers' union rejected the suggestion. Finally, a special organization was created under the joint sponsorship of the region and the trade unions, with some participation of OPPI. In no instance could a fully funded support effort be mounted.

Examinations have not been a major problem, though there have been arguments with the Ministry of Education. The examinations are based directly on the content of the individual courses and can be taken in groups, although individual ability must be judged at the end. The flexibility of the ministry in this key point is probably in part explained by the fact that the exam has little vocational significance and provides no opportunities for further study other than in selective institutions, so that there is no concern about the putative effects of "too easy" examinations. Nevertheless, in the eyes of participants the significance of a successful examination experience may far outweigh the normative aspects of the examination. In view of the avowedly nonvocational goals of the trade unions, the possibility that these exams may be of a rather different nature from those in the regular school is probably an acceptable risk. At any rate, only a small number of students failed to obtain the *licenza media* at the conclusion of the courses. Of the 13,207 students enrolled in the first year, 11,286 (85.6 percent) took the final exam; of these, 11,198 (99.2 percent) passed (Censis 1975, vol. 1, p. 74, table 10). The attitude of the Ministry of Education to these examinations is perhaps best expressed by the fact that it has thus far refused to consider providing special courses at upper secondary level for beneficiaries of the 150 hours program.

"Monographic" University Courses

In contrast to the lower secondary school courses, which have been extensively documented, virtually no reports exist on the monographic university courses in the 150 hours program (Balbo and others, 1975). The reason lies in the habitual lack of self-criticism and reporting on teaching endemic to most universities and in the fact that formally the university instructors involved in the program are working voluntarily and therefore have no reporting obligation. The list of university courses offered under the 150 hours is not compiled according to a systematic plan; the personal interests and relationships of the university instructors appear, particularly in the case of the trade union, to determine the courses offered. In view of the substantial ability of university instructors to establish their own priorities in courses offered to regular students, it remains a matter of individual practice whether such courses ultimately supplement or replace regular university courses. The courses relate to the situation of the workers only in very general terms.

Contrary to the practice in lower secondary schools, no size limits have been established for the university courses so that some of them are very large (130 students) and require assistantships and fairly extensive support, which has, however, not been available beyond the normal provision for all university faculties.

In spite of the fact that there has been no extensive reporting on the university courses, the growth in numbers and enrollments between 1974–75 and 1975–76 indicates that they do respond to the wishes of some groups of workers. The reports that exist (on the courses in Bologna and Florence) show that while they do represent attempts at flexible and student-oriented programing, they do not represent a major departure from tradition either in terms of course content or of didactic approach—certainly much less than do the courses in lower middle schools. In most instances the faculty members most sympathetic to the trade unions have been involved in this activity. In view of their prior commitment to the cause the courses represent, their colleagues are unlikely to view them other than in the context of continuing relationships within the university.

Current Problems

The 150 hours of the Italian trade unions is remarkable in many respects. Such is the fragmentation of adult education in Europe that the 150 hours represents the most concerted single program of general education for adults; it is the only European program of educational leave that has systematically attempted to make the beneficiaries' situation its point of departure, and in its pedagogy it has put into practice what many theoretical models would consider the most appropriate means. Nevertheless, many problems remain to illustrate how a program that is highly promising in theory can and will be bedeviled by the limits the reality of implementation imposes on it. In many ways these problems are a classic example of how the success or failure of a given program depends less on the perfection of its design than on the conditions at the point of implementation, which is often far from the planning center.

Variations in Union Contracts. At present a number of basic models exist for the granting of educational leave in Italian trade union contracts: the original formula of the metalworkers, the ceramics workers' formula, the hospital workers' formula, and the glassworkers' formula, with variations that incorporate more unpaid leave. Theoretically, each of these would require specially structured courses to accommodate the material to the time available. In practice, courses for the *licenza media* require at least 350 hours—in other words, the majority of the participants under the metalworkers' scheme are contributing at least 200 hours of their own time for course attendance (excluding preparation at home). Under the other schemes, the individual's contribution ranges up to the full 350 hours—an extremely heavy burden in only one year. The ceramics model would seem to imply a two- or three-year course, since it allows 40 hours paid and 80 hours unpaid leave a year. In its present form it obviously favors more specialized, briefer courses such as might be found in connection with vocational training or the monographic university courses.

No information is available on the differential use of educational leave benefits under the various contracts, but a greater conformity of contracts is obviously needed. In practice, many employers are apparently willing to allow an application of all contracts in conformity with the metalworkers' model. Nevertheless, the situation remains unclear and needs to be clarified before the program can be considered to be firmly established.

Status of Teachers. A number of issues related to the status of teachers has already been discussed. The problems associated with the whole complex of issues about teacher status and teacher roles in such a program go even deeper; there is a clear pedagogical requirement for situational flexibility and interdisciplinary facility. But these are certainly not characteristics of the average Italian teacher in lower secondary schools nor are they likely to be achieved by the present training system for these teachers through the upper secondary schools and universities. Beyond any attempt to change the secondary schools, the 150 hours requires a reform of the entire system of schools and teacher training. It is undoubtedly too weak a lever for this purpose, even in the hands of the politically influential trade union movement.

The position of the trade unions on teacher status is emphatic: they want teachers in 150 hours courses to have the same status as teachers in the regular schools. There is an argument, however, for not giving high levels of job security to those active in adult education. This applies with particular force to any program, such as the 150 hours, which has the avowed intention of bridging a cultural gap and reforming the schools. Theoretically, teachers with tenure are supposed to enjoy greater independence; in practice, though they may be individually independent, they still need many forms of assistance and must work in a complex web of institutional relationships if they are to be effective. These can be constraining in many respects, but working outside them is like trying to lift oneself up by one's own bootstraps.

Teacher Support. In recent years it has become almost a commonplace that changing the teaching profession requires a substantial investment in professional support through in-service training and curricular aids. This is unavailable in Italy, and there is no sign that it will be forthcoming in the volume and form required. In the situation teachers in a new program are liable to face, opportunities for continuous, instructed exchange between teachers can prove one of the most important forms of professional support (Pepe, 1975, p. 62).

Inadequate Time. After the rush to innovate in the first two years, there are signs that the time available for the instructional program is insufficient. In Milan, a resolution was adopted that the total number of hours of paid leave and the total hours of instructional time should be raised for analphabetics, since it had proved impossible to develop a satisfactory program within the time available. This special case can probably be taken care of in the next round of negotiations, since everybody concerned is agreed on the desirability of an effective program of alphabetization. Difficulties with such programs, however, may be only the least of problems: 350 hours is an enormous commitment of time, but it may not be enough to break through all the barriers that separate participants in these courses from formal learning experiences, particularly since they continue to hold full-time jobs that are often physically demanding and are probably forced to forego most of their weekends and part of their holidays during the very period of participation. There are already signs that in terms of traditional definitions of subject matter, there is a serious strain on the time available (Pepe, 1975, pp. 50–53). The difficulty is that one cannot avoid having the experience judged by traditional standards (Does the student know how to draw the square root?). The inadequacy of these standards does not obviate the fact that the pressures created run both ways: insofar as the 150 hours constitutes a challenge to the schools, the traditional curriculum of the schools will create pressures for conformity within the 150 hours.

Impact of Monographic Courses. In a program that has generated many volumes of reports and comment within less than two years, the general lack of feedback from the university courses is striking. The only systematic evaluation was a meeting of interested university instructors in Milan early in 1975. The range of topics, students, and settings in the courses is very wide, so that (unlike the courses for the *licenza media*) an assessment of success or failure is almost impossible, even using unconventional standards.

Conflict of Goals. It remains unclear whether the 150 hours is a means to an end or an end in itself. Both views are compatible in theory; in practice they can come into fundamental conflict. The issue of teacher status is only one example of this conflict; major differences also appear in the analysis of results. There is an understandable reluctance on the part of participants in the courses to be drawn directly and personally into the school reform debate. For the participants the meaning of the experience derives from the course itself, and the results should feed back into their place of work rather than into the school reform debate. This difference of approach is visible in the reports and analyses that have been published.

It is also visible in discrepancies in the assessment of reasons for attending the courses. More than 50 percent of the participants said they attended because they wanted to meet other people with similar problems, while only 21 percent of the instructors gave this reason. Conversely, 42.6 percent of the instructors said that participation in trade union and political activities was a motivating factor, while only 9.9 percent of the students gave this reason (Censis, 1975, vol. 1, p. 102, table 14).

Motivations for attending the courses are much more diverse than was expected. Like any other degree provided by institutions of education, the *licenza media* has vocational relevance: it is impossible to obtain any, even menial, public employment without the *licenza media,* and the degree is a prerequisite for a number of vocational courses. Thus a substantial number of students indicated that they were taking the course for essentially vocational reasons. This observation suggests that any course which provides a recognized degree, even if it is a general one, has implicit vocational significance for employees.

Conclusions

In terms of educational leave policies, Italy is a paradox. In most areas it presents at best a fragmentary set of policies, none of which is of great consequence in a comparative sense; at the same time, it offers a particularly interesting example of an educational leave policy in Europe: the 150 hours. This policy highlights a wide variety of issues in the area of remediation and in the relationship of educational leave to the place of work and to the mainstream of the educational system that are not covered by other policies— except in Sweden, under very different circumstances. In regard to the practical experiences, the pedagogy and the difficulties of teacher training, issues of universal concern are being tackled as directly and vigorously as anywhere else in Europe. But the relationship between the rather archaic existing system of education, the weak system of adult education, and the 150 hours is puzzling.

The first years of any new venture are years of hope: difficulties are clearly perceived but counterbalanced by possibilities yet untried. The first enthusiasm and large amounts of volunteer effort carry the program over many of the initial hurdles; participants feel the fishbowl effect: all the world is watching, so we must put forth our best. These are years in which it is possible to study the problems that are to be tackled and the proposed solutions in greater clarity than is possible later, for difficulties have not yet become an accepted burden, possibilities are not exhausted, and the confusion of day-to-day routine has not yet set in. It is impossible to assess reasonably or fairly the prospects of success within a two-year period; but if the 150 hours has even a modicum of success, it will prove to have been an Italian shortcut to an educational leave policy.

8

Austria, Belgium, the Netherlands, Norway, and the United Kingdom

The four principal countries studied in Chapters 4 through 7 are the European countries with the most extensive experience with social, economic, and educational policies having educational leave effects. Their experience illustrates most of the policy issues related to the introduction of educational leave through any of the several available avenues. The experience of these four countries is confirmed in other European countries and, in some details, given further form. Some countries—most notably Norway and the United Kingdom—are remarkable for the scant attention they have given to educational leave policies, though for very different reasons.

In this section we shall discuss the experience of five other European countries. It should be emphasized that these descriptions are based solely on documentary evidence; although an extensive effort was made to collect documentation, the analyses have not been supplemented by visits to the countries involved.

Austria

On October 10, 1974, the Austrian minister of education convened a hearing on educational leave (Bundesministerium für Unterricht und Kunst, 1975). The result was inconclusive, as one suspects it was intended to be. The representative of the trade unions declared that "only after the extension of the basic vacation period [to four weeks] has been achieved can we begin to aspire to a general program of educational leave," thereby setting clear priorities for the trade union movement (ibid., p. 38). One may reasonably assume that under these circumstances, a general educational leave program will not be realized in Austria within the foreseeable future. Nevertheless, a number of programs already exist that achieve educational leave effects, and these may be developed further. The most important is the Law on Labor Market Assistance (*Arbeits-marktförderungsgesetz*, or AMFG) of December 1968, which provides a flexible mechanism of support. In accordance with the availability of this program in the area of vocationally oriented labor market training, the most substantial recorded activities are in industry and continuing vocational education. Most other forms of further education depend on voluntary organizations or the use of participants' free time.

Education and Training in Industry

The kind and level of in-service training and provision for education during working hours in Austrian industry is particularly well documented through a study undertaken in 1974 (Piskaty, 1974). This study is based on a questionnaire and a series of interviews and can be considered representative for all Austrian enterprises (including service industries) with more than a hundred employees. The responding firms employed some 28 percent of the entire work force. Since the survey covered primarily basic industries and commerce, its results are representative for the approximately 50 percent of the work force employed in these areas.

Of the responding enterprises, 40 percent undertook educational activities for their employees during working hours. These firms employ 66 percent of the relevant work force. There is a clear correlation between the size of the enterprise and the ability and willingness to provide education for employees during working hours. Even allowing for an overstatement through the method of the study, the aggregate figures remain impressive. It is probably accurate to assume that close to 50 percent of all employees in commerce and industry have access to some form of education during working hours. A significant number of the enterprises (80 percent) undertake such activities in accordance with a systematic plan. In most instances, this plan is coordinated with projections concerning the employment needs of the firm.

The study shows clearly that industry gives priority to training for skilled workers and middle and upper management. The amount of education available to unskilled workers is negligible. Whereas in-service training and retraining for purposes of the firm are an integral part of the educational program of 75 percent of all firms, a significant proportion are also engaged in imparting general vocational skills or even general or social and economic education. Between 70 and 80 percent of the firms offer courses to allow skilled workers and middle management to specialize within their fields or to allow higher levels of management to develop general management or language skills. Even so, 29 percent of the responding firms indicate that they offer general education courses, and 32 percent mention courses of general social or economic relevance. In the larger firms the percentage of such courses is even greater, reaching as high as 44 percent in both categories for the medium size firms with special education departments.

Most firms offering courses use external agencies as well as internal programs. Information concerning programs is disseminated through the normal channels in all firms. In large enterprises this will probably mean publication in bulletins and dissemination through the management hierarchy. In smaller firms personal relationships will tend to play a greater role.

Perhaps the most striking information provided by the study is that 88 percent of all firms responding to the questionnaire indicated that they provided support for the attendance of their employees in adult education and training programs outside the firm. Moreover, all firms that undertake programs of their own also support participation in outside programs. This form of support of further education is, therefore, complementary to the internal programs. The support generally takes the form of reimbursing course expenses entirely or in part. In addition, approximately 50 percent of all the responding firms indicated that they provided additional paid leave for attendance in further education outside the firm. In most instances courses other than vocationally related ones are also eligible for support, and firms that allow both general and vocational courses do not differentiate sharply between them. Thus it is not accurate to say that the thrust of support for education by Austrian industry is exclusively vocational.

The study gives no indication of the total number of such leaves currently being given or of the approximate cost. It does attempt to make some estimate concerning total expenditure for education by the firms responding to the questionnaire. According to the information supplied, firms with very large payrolls are spending between 0.7 and 2.0 percent of the total payroll on education, whereas firms with smaller payrolls tend to be spending less. This sum reflects only direct expenditure and does not include the cost of leave with pay. Since the cost of continuing an employee's salary represents rather more than 50 percent of the total cost of educational leave programs, it would seem appropriate to assume that large firms are already spending close to or in excess of 2 percent of their payroll sum on education, whereas smaller firms have not yet reached this level. This is a finding which is in striking accord with information available from industry in Germany (Piskaty, 1974, p. 22); it also meshes with the French program of educational leave after 1971, in which the payroll levy on all firms was projected at 2 percent but has thus far reached only 1 percent, with actual expenditures ranging up to 2.4 percent (see discussion in Chapter 4).

The thrust of the educational activity of Austrian firms is much broader than a purely vocational one and reaches a significant proportion of the total work force. There is, however, evidence that a proportion of these activities are already being financed through state subsidies from the labor market assistance program, which is devoted to a substantial degree to supporting persons undergoing training in industry by subsidizing the firms in question (see discussion later in this chapter). Thus there is sure to be a substantial amount of double counting in the information on in-service training in industry and the operation of the AMFG. Figures on the total number of participants in in-service training in industry are, however, not available.

Trade Union Education Programs

Unlike those of most other countries, the Austrian trade unions produce a consolidated annual report on their educational activities, making it relatively easy to develop an overall understanding of their programs without having to put together fragmentary information from the individual union organizations (Österreichischer Gewerkschaftsbund, 1974). Even this material does not allow an exact quantitative analysis of the impact of union education. In 1973, approximately 8,000 persons participated in courses involving at least the equivalent of one week full-time attendance during the year, and between 8,000 and 10,000 participated in weekend or shorter courses. This is equivalent to roughly 0.6 percent of the 2,600,000 employees in the labor force.

In the last few years the scope of trade union activities in Austria has been increasing steadily. The law on the basic rights of the labor market (*Arbeitsmarktverfassungsgesetz,* or AFG) came into effect recently and is rapidly becoming the cornerstone of union training. On the basis of this law there has been a dramatic increase in the number of participants in courses. Under this law, which is comparable to the German law (see discussion in Chapter 5), every member of the works councils has a right to leave with pay to participate in training and educational activities for a total period of two weeks within his or her three-year term of office. These activities must take place in institutions of the unions or employers or institutions recognized by both parties. The subject matter is restricted to material connected with the exercise of the person's function as worker representative on the works councils. In factories with more than two hundred employees the council has the right to delegate one member to participate in training courses for up to one year without pay but with job security.

The latter provision is probably linked to an institution that has existed in Vienna for twenty-five years. Since 1949 the *Sozialakademie der Kammer für Arbeiter und Angestellte für Wien* (Academy of the Chamber of Employees in Vienna) has conducted eight-month and ten-month courses for a total of nine hundred students, all of whom come from working backgrounds. During attendance at the *Akademie* students live in residence and receive compensation for earnings foregone. This institution appears to have served as a major means of recruiting leading functionaries of the trade union movement. The courses are divided into four areas: trade union studies, economic sciences, law, and "auxiliary" sciences encompassing psychology, statistics, rhetoric, and journalism. The fact that a large percentage of graduates appear to have assumed important functions in politics and the union movement does not mean that there is a positive relationship between such courses and later effectiveness. Since participants are nominated by the member unions, mere attendance, in all likelihood, has provided access to positions of greater influence, irrespective of the nature of the courses being taken.

Labor Market Training Programs

Since 1968, Austria has had a flexible law providing support for employed or unemployed persons wishing to receive training to obtain employment, to improve their present position, or to obtain other employment (*Arbeitsmarktsförderungsgesetz*, AMFG 5). All training-related costs can be paid and living expenses provided up to 80 percent of previous income. In practice, not more than 60 percent is normally given unless dependents must be supported. Since the legislation is not tied to professions considered particularly in demand or to unemployed or even potentially unemployed persons, its scope is very wide. Moreover, employers providing such training can be reimbursed by up to 50 percent of their direct expenses, providing a source of support for on-the-job initial training, retraining, or supplementary training during employment, all of which are explicitly included in the law. Only university training leading to a degree or teacher training are excluded, although exceptions can be made in the second instance. Basic training, including apprenticeship, is excluded from this program, except for the particularly needy or the handicapped; thus its effects are focused on the employed.

The overall volume of these activities has been substantial in recent years. In 1974, slightly more than 1 percent of the dependent work force received personal support for participating in retraining activities. A total of 889 firms received support for providing retraining programs.

Summary

Opportunities for continuing one's education in Austria after entry into the labor force can be considered average for a country without an explicit educational leave policy. Labor market assistance programs provide the most flexible form of intervention. No systematic policies for educational leave are likely to be developed in Austria in the near future. Nevertheless, policies at present in operation promise to increase the number of beneficiaries over the next few years to the point where close to 5 percent of the dependent work force will be able to participate in some form of education or training at full pay without loss of status during every year.

All available information indicates that those relatively more educated are the main beneficiaries of existing programs. Insofar as trade union representatives can be considered a privileged group, this is also true of trade union training programs. Correlating information on the training activities of firms with the statistics of the labor market authorities strongly suggests that those who have already completed some form of training are the principal beneficiaries of retraining grants. Unskilled and semiskilled workers have little or no opportunity to improve their educational status unless they are exceptionally active in the trade unions.

The Austrian system of education is highly selective and stratified (OECD, 1975a). Present policies for educational intervention after the period of initial education do not change this basic fact.

Belgium[1]

Law on Credit Hours

On April 10, 1973, the Belgian Parliament adopted a law on credit hours to provide educational leave for vocational purposes to full-time employees under forty years of age. The law is remarkable

[1]Based on OECD, 1975; Moniteur Belge, 21.4.1973, 3.5.1973, 5.5.1973, 17.1.1974 (4613, 4614), 5.5.1973, 18.9.1974, 15.10.1974 (5450, 5451), 24.12.1974, 4.1.1975, 7.3.1975.

for its approach to the problem of educational leave and even more so for its lack of impact. It is one of the simplest educational leave schemes in Europe, couched in the most obscure legal framework. The basic principle of the scheme is that workers attending a vocational training course provided or authorized by the Department of Education obtain the right to be absent from work for a certain number of hours at full pay (up to a maximum of 28,000 francs per month). The number of hours acquired in relation to the number of course hours depends on the number of years of prior training. As of September 1974, the regulations provided for 25 percent of the total class hours as leave during the first year of training, 50 percent of the total class hours as leave after completion of the first year course, and 100 percent of the total class hours as leave after completion of the equivalent of two years' training; in addition, for each day of examination two days of "credit" may be claimed. Through steady extensions of the law in at least eight stages between April 1973 and October 1974, the provisions have been made more generous, and the subject matter has been enlarged to include music, literature, the arts, courses of general education, and university evening courses. Even self-employed persons (politically a very strong group in Belgium) can receive remuneration for earnings foregone according to a scale established by professions.

Insofar as courses take place outside working hours, participants acquire compensatory leave rights that can be used in units of full or half days. No limits have so far been set to the number of beneficiaries or the number of credits per beneficiary, except for the stipulation that the requirements of production must be taken into account—the assumption being that the labor market partners will regulate the matter.

The scheme is financed through a fund based on contributions from the employers of 0.2 percent of the payroll subject to social security tax and a matching contribution from the government, that is, from general tax revenues. Employers maintain the salary of an employee who is utilizing accumulated credits and are subsequently reimbursed from the fund.

This entire complex of legislation would appear to make the Belgian scheme the most comprehensive educational leave policy in Europe. In addition to its broad coverage, it offers the advantage of complete freedom to schedule education to follow, coincide with, or intersperse with work schedules. Even so, after eighteen months only 6,710 workers had exercised their rights under the law: 0.4 percent of the wage-earning population and 0.2 percent of the employed population. Taking into account the limitations and extensions, no more than 1 percent of eligible employees had exercised their rights. As a matter of fact, large numbers of persons actually enrolled in courses who would be eligible simply have not applied for leave.

The reasons for this failure are certainly manifold. Among the most important is legislative and administrative confusion. The law, passed in April 1973, has been amended and augmented by the parliament or by administrative decree so often that it is difficult to keep track of its evolution. Certainly employees will tend to be confused and in all likelihood distrustful. It is virtually impossible to obtain usable information on the scheme from administrators, other than a list of legal references. Thus far, no group has acted as popularizer of the measure. The paper work involved in applying is enormous.

Contradictions in the law also in part explain the failure. The Belgian scheme has a built-in contradiction: while the percentages of creditable time increase with the length of training, the upper limit on the salary is below the wage a person with two complete years of training would expect to receive. Thus the progression is less attractive than it appears to be. At the same time, while the stated objective is to attract persons with low levels of training, the financial incentive is not substantial during the first year. Apparently the law was framed to be open ended while trying to avoid a sudden run on the newly established fund; apparently the latter objective was better served than the former. It must be recognized that provision of 25 percent of salary (and probably even 50 percent) still requires very substantial sacrifices from workers with low incomes, since with decreasing income the marginal utility of earnings foregone increases rapidly.

Another reason for ineffectiveness is exclusive emphasis on long-term programs. The Belgian scheme requires long-term part-time commitments, not only to achieve financial rewards but also to attain educational goals. There is evidence to suggest that such commitments are particularly difficult to make for persons with low levels of education; thus this aspect of the scheme becomes a motivational hurdle.

A final problem is the nature of employer-employee relationships. The credit hour scheme is also intended to finance initial vocational education, irrespective of age. Employees engaging in long-term vocational courses on their own initiative are probably intent on ultimately changing their occupation, and this causes a potential conflict of interest with the employer that would make workers hesitate to divulge their activities. This is particularly so in the case of younger, potentially mobile workers, unless their training is explicitly part of their contract of employment.

It is remarkable how the Belgian law on credit hours has produced results quite different from what might have been expected. The complexity of the law combined with the preexisting social structure have meant that the general scope of the law notwithstanding, its effect is essentially to reinforce the role of existing social groupings, who are capable of interpreting the meaning of the law and counseling its ultimate beneficiaries.

Trade Union Training[2]

In June 1971, employers and unions signed an agreement outlining a joint program of reform along the lines of the French *protocole de Grenelle* (see discussion in Chapter 4). One element of this program was the stipulation that union representatives were to be accorded leave rights for trade union training in the next round of collective bargaining. By the end of 1972, twenty-four such contracts had been signed, giving union representatives (defined differently from one sector to another) only the right to attend courses organized by the unions themselves. Duration, exercise of the right, and financing are also regulated differently from sector to sector, so that no generalizations are possible beyond the statement that union representatives in Belgium have the right to at least the equivalent of one week's paid leave per year to attend union training.

[2]Based on CRISP, 1973.

Taken together, the contract of June 1971 and the law of 1973 would seem to provide an adequate basis for almost any form of educational leave. Inability to shape a cohesive policy out of these elements makes Belgium the prime example of the fact that educational leave policies exist only in the context of the social and political conditions of a country; even the theoretically best of all possible policies cannot be made to work if it does not mesh smoothly with existing institutions—or if existing institutions are not functioning well, an educational leave policy can hardly be expected to function very much better.

The Netherlands

Educational leave has become a topic of discussion in the Netherlands since the ILO adopted its convention in 1974. Perhaps the Netherlands is the country that most clearly reflects the possibilities of stimulating debate through the action in an international body like the ILO. At any rate, the necessity of deciding whether or not to ratify the ILO convention has created a lively debate on educational leave in the Netherlands. A number of ministries and an interministerial commission have taken up the question of appropriate action on the educational leave issue.

The basis on which any further policies in favor of educational leave must be built in the Netherlands is typically a mixed one. Along with areas of notable activity and strength there are other areas in which the Netherlands has surprisingly weak programs by international standards. Not one of these different programs was, however, initially intended for the specific purpose of providing educational leave effects.

Voluntary Adult Education

Voluntary adult education in the Netherlands is strongly integrated with the vocational training and retraining sector, and thus it is extremely difficult to make any comprehensive statements about this area. The most distinctive separate entity is a group of thirteen residential folk high schools that provided, in 1972, education in courses of two days to four weeks' duration to a total of 37,407 participants (Kallen, 1974). The residential folk high schools serve two kinds of clientele: they provide persons who are considering a return to education at a later age with the opportunity of engaging in an initial experience to test their motivation and aptitude, and they provide a setting for educational activities of groups from industry or private associations. In their approach to adult education, the folk high schools derive from a common tradition of adult education in the northern European countries between the two world wars.

In practice, the residential folk high schools provide educational leave effects to the majority of their participants, since forms of cooperation have developed between them and industrial enterprises. A significant number of enterprises allow employees to participate in the courses of the folk high schools without loss of pay during working hours. No quantitative information on the extent of such cooperation is, however, available.

Vocational Adult Education

According to the resources involved and the numbers of the students participating, vocational education and training is the most important part of adult education. Vocational adult education in the Netherlands, however, is spread over a very large number of programs and institutions. A review of available statistical information indicates that by far the most important sector of vocational adult education from the viewpoint of educational leave is training in industry, particularly since the other major sectors (part-time education in evening schools, teacher training, part-time university education, apprenticeship schemes, and correspondence education) all do not take place during working hours and provide no immediate job benefits to the participants.

The figures on training of national and local government employees in Table 8 are derived from an extrapolation based on the figures on vocational training in industry. These in turn are based on an industry survey of 1973 indicating that as many as 23.7 percent to 24.2 percent of employees were enrolled in vocational courses (Lington, 1974). In view of the fact that available evidence covers only major firms with large numbers of employees, one may estimate that approximately 15 percent of all employees are currently participating in employer-funded courses in the Netherlands. It can be assumed that all of these do so without loss of pay

Table 8. Estimates of Total Number of Workers Receiving Vocational Education or Training in the Netherlands in 1971

Type of education	Total	Men	Women
Part-time education (evening schools)	88.440 to 97.750	68.000 to 75.150	20.440 to 22.600
Teacher training	39.880 to 44.070	25.450 to 28.120	14.430 to 15.950
Part-time university education	2.370 to 2.630	1.620 to 1.800	750 to 830
Apprenticeship scheme	68.940 to 76.200	63.110 to 69.750	5.830 to 6.450
Retraining unemployed	2.290 to 2.530	2.290 to 2.530	– to –
Postgraduate education (expected numbers)	19.000 to 21.000	16.360 to 18.080	2.640 to 2.929
Training of national and local government employees	43.700 to 48.300	35.920 to 39.700	7.780 to 8.600
Training in the armed forces	4.800 to 5.300	4.770 to 5.260	30 to 40
Police	351.500 to 388.500	325.380 to 357.420	28.120 to 31.080
Vocational training in industry	227.020 to 250.930	171.590 to 189.680	55.430 to 61.250
TOTAL	853.740 to 943.610	718.200 to 793.780	135.540 to 149.830

Source: Lington, 1974

or position, providing a fairly substantial range of educational leave effects in a fairly narrow field of activity.

Labor Market Programs

A striking feature of the situation in the Netherlands is the restricted scope of labor market training programs. The programs in this area have been slightly extended between 1971 and 1975. At the present time, the government has three major policy instruments in the area of labor market training. First, centers for the occupational training for adults (twenty-five centers with approximately ten thousand participants) provide job-oriented vocational training for adults. Participants in these programs, which are directed mainly toward the metalworking and building sectors, receive compensation for loss of income and travel expenses. Second, the government can contract with industry to repay part of the costs involved in training workers for more highly skilled positions. Third, the government can reimburse direct study costs (but not wages foregone) of courses in approved institutions. The government can support training programs on an industry-wide basis where the public interest is judged to require this (Schop, 1974). The costs for all three programs were projected at only 50,000,000 gulden for 1975, which means that the number of beneficiaries is likely to be very limited.

Trade Union Education

Dutch unions maintain residential centers comparable to the folk high schools. These centers are devoted to the training of the trade union representatives and members of the works councils. They received subsidies from a variety of sources until a new law went into effect in 1974, establishing a fund to support the training of members of works councils. This fund is constituted from a levy of 0.14 percent on the payroll of all firms legally required to have works councils (firms with a hundred or more employees). Present estimates indicate that as many as 10,000 of the total number of 50,000 members of works councils could participate in these courses annually (Schop, 1974, p. 12).

The role of the government in the operation of this training program is extremely limited. Its major function lies in the supervision of relationships between a variety of institutions representing labor and employers that, in turn, have direct supervisory authority over these courses. Consequently, government involvement is significantly less than it is in other educational institutions.

Further Provisions for Educational Leave

Besides the programs described above, there are only negligible opportunities in the Netherlands to participate in education on any basis other than a voluntary one. The laws requiring part-time attendance at educational institutions for those aged fifteen to seventeen who are members of the work force must be considered part of the provision of compulsory first-time education and cannot be counted as educational leave (OECD, 1975, p. 144). While the possibility exists for older groups of young workers to participate in courses after this period of compulsory education, no provision is made for compensation of lost earnings.

A number of central trade union agreements with the employers' organizations include provisions allowing employees to obtain leave to participate in vocational and occupational training. Leave with pay must generally be given for the period of examination (for a maximum of one to five days), but for the rest, leave with pay must only be given when employee and employer agree that the courses are a necessary part of the employee's work. In this case the provisions are indistinguishable from in-service training programs for industry, with the exception that the employee has an explicitly guaranteed right of initiative, without having a legal right to receive approval of his request or even a right to certain procedural safeguards in the processing of this request.

The situation in the Netherlands concerning educational leave is poorly developed. In a country that is conscious of its international image and that tends to maintain a set of social policies consonant with advanced practice in other countries, the ILO convention of 1974 is bound to have a major impact. Obviously, the underdeveloped state of legal and contractual provisions and safeguards of an employee's further training and education will become more evident to policy makers in the Netherlands through the process of deciding whether or not to ratify the ILO convention. One may assume, therefore, that the ILO convention will have a significant impact on further developments in the Netherlands.

Even so, the issue appears to be developing slowly. A recent document on the future structure of the educational system prepared by the Ministry of Education described the entire complex of adult education in terms of an "open school" as a means of conceptualizing and ultimately institutionalizing the presently disparate elements of adult education (Ministerie van het Onderwijs en Wetenschappen, 1975, pp. 81–82). The problem of educational leave was viewed as one of several issues to be discussed at some future date, but no foreseeable solutions were yet being envisaged.

Norway

Educational leave is not a major topic of discussion in Norway. With a firmly established tradition of integrated economic, social, and educational planning at the central level, a relatively specialized segment of the total system such as educational leave does not normally become a topic of discussion; it is seen, rather, as part of a number of other issues: vocational education, labor market intervention, reform of the educational system, financial support for students, and general social policy. There is no inclination to single out educational leave as a special item for discussion.

The Norwegian educational system is characterized by a high degree of centralization and by a steady development toward comprehensiveness in the last few years (OECD, 1975b). Countervailing tendencies toward decentralization exist but have not yet taken firm hold.

The level of general education of the population is still relatively low. Introduction of the nine-year comprehensive compulsory school has only recently been completed, and the greater part of the population has only had elementary schooling. Education has not, however, constituted too powerful a factor in providing social status in a society which still has strong agrarian, egalitarian roots. Consequently, further education has been based on a fairly utilitarian, intrinsic motivation rather than on extrinsic reasons of social class or status. These basic trends and traditions tend to modify the impact of the educational system when compared internationally and also to alter the role and significance of educational leave effects. Norway, like Sweden and Denmark, has a long tradition of adult education through voluntary, populist organizations.

In 1970, employers and unions established a joint Training and Development Fund (*Opplysnings-og utviklingsfond*). The purpose of the fund is to "further the spread of information and education throughout working life" (State Adult Education Council (Norway), 1972, addendum to chapter 2). The fund is financed by contributions of 0.50 kroner per week by the employees and 100 kroner per week per employee by the employers. The proceeds are divided equally among the labor market partners, who are then free to use their share at their own discretion within the general purposes of the fund. In 1974, the available income was 25 million kroner.

In-service Training in Industry

No systematic information is available on the scope of in-service training in Norwegian industry. The funds derived by the employers from the Training and Development Fund are devoted primarily to providing information on mergers and to mitigating their effects and to providing information on available training opportunities. Unions and employers are in agreement that a greater proportion of further vocational education should take place close to the place of work, but no agreement has thus far been achieved concerning the respective roles of the labor market partners in this process.

A number of schools are run within the budgets of the major state industries, all of which deal significantly with in-service training; the Ministry of Consumer Affairs, the railways, post office, television service, customs, job placement service, police, and prisons all have such schools.

Trade Union Education

As in Sweden, the trade union movement has for many years maintained a network of popular schools as part of the overall system of voluntary adult education. The subject matter of these courses covers all aspects relevant to working life and is consequently broader in scope than is specifically trade union-oriented education. More than 35,000 persons participate in these courses annually, or nearly 2 percent of the labor force (NU 1974:10, p. 94). Financing is secured primarily from the Training and Development Fund, which also provides 10,000 scholarships for participants, and from a state subsidy (of 3,550,000 kroner in 1972) toward the training of labor representatives. This sum includes payment of the participants' earnings foregone, since training of labor representatives is considered to be in the public interest (NU 1974:10, p. 94, p. 103).

The basic agreement of 1974 (*Hovedavtalen*) between the national organizations of the union movement and the employers (Landsorganisasjonen i Norge 1974) stipulates that shop stewards "shall not be refused time off without very good reason . . . when attending courses or carrying out other trade union information work" (sec. 7.6) and that full or partial leaves of absence are to be granted for "general education, vocational training, adult education and retraining" if this can be accomplished with only minor inconvenience to the firm (sec. 4.4). These passages do not contain any reference to payment of salary and living expenses, and one assumes the omission is purposeful. Thus only those persons who are entitled to support from the trade unions can apply these rules and obtain educational leave effects.

Voluntary Adult Education

Norway, like the other Scandinavian countries, has a strong tradition of voluntary adult education. Statistics on adult education have long been compiled, but they tend to understate the actual extent of activities, since only those organizations and courses are recorded that have some form of relationship to the Ministry of Education—voluntary associations, municipal or county schools, vocational adult education, and folk high schools. According to these statistics, 333,000 persons enrolled in these adult education courses in 1971–72, corresponding to 11.2 percent of the population fifteen and over, and compared with only 237,845 in 1969–70. Voluntary associations accounted for 305,958 participants; municipal or county schools, for 13,487; vocational adult education courses, for 7,411; and folk high schools, for 7,078. This substantial participation rate on a voluntary basis is bound to affect any discussion concerning educational leave, particularly since by all accounts the groups of participants do not correspond to those already having the most prior education. In this regard, the populist tradition of adult education is important, assuring a wide spectrum of participation and a highly pragmatic solution of the curricular problems that weigh on educational leave discussions. Participation is a value in itself, and the curriculum is held to correspond to the interests of the participants.

In view of the fact that adult education associations are able to provide a major portion of the necessary program, the role of the Ministry of Education has been to subsidize and supplement where necessary. The new reorganization of higher education into regional colleges and the development of vocational secondary schools that are also accessible to adults provide the main focuses of activity (OECD, 1975b). Since participation rates are satisfactory under the present system, there does not seem to be a major need, from a social point of view, to promote participation through financial subsidy. Support is therefore provided only for economic reasons, as in the labor market intervention mechanisms, and where specific effects are desired, as in leave programs for teachers.

Labor Market Programs

In spite of full employment, Norway continues to have pockets of unemployment, particularly in some outlying areas and among young people with minimal levels of education. Since it is firm government policy to try to discourage migration to the more urban centers, detailed intervention becomes necessary. As in Germany, the National Insurance System is used for this purpose, rather than using a full-fledged government agency. Programs in this area have been increasing steadily, but support is still highly selective both in terms of numbers and of forms of support (see Central Bureau of Statistics (Norway), 1974, p. 24, table 10). Only about 0.3 percent of the active labor force involved, and of these only 10 to 15 percent, have received major financial support beyond course costs and personal living expenses. What is notable about this program is that, apart from the heavy concentration of persons under 25, its effects are quite evenly spread in the 25 to 50 age group. These programs of an interventionist character are supplemented by the recognized right of students in advanced general and vocational education to draw stipends and loans on the basis of need, up to the age of 40, provided they are in full-time education. To be eligible for a stipend, training must last at least 3½ months; for a more substantial loan, 7 months are required (NU 1974:10, p. 103). Obviously, this does not provide job security, except on the basis of individual agreements, nor does it represent full or proportional compensation for earnings foregone. Nevertheless, the effect of this program is certainly to facilitate return to full-time study, and some of the regional colleges have developed programs (such as shipping economics or oil-related skills) that clearly assume that participants will retain position and earnings on the basis of personal contracts with their employers.

In-Service Training of Civil Servants

Over the past fifteen years, Norway has been engaged in a continuous program of reform of the educational system. Recognizing that continuing education of teachers is a necessity if any reform is to succeed, the authorities, under prodding from the teachers' unions have provided Norwegian teachers with what may be the most generous program of released time for continuing education in the world (OECD, 1975b). Every teacher in the school system has a right to one week of released time for study and course preparation. Since use of this time is organized by school district, it is in fact fully utilized. Moreover, additional time can be obtained to attend courses and other training events. For this purpose, the Ministry of Education provides local school authorities with funds to pay substitute teachers. In 1972, participation rates in such courses exceeded 100 percent of all teachers. Thus, it can be estimated that Norwegian teachers have close to two full weeks of classroom time at their disposal annually for purposes of continuing their education, without loss of pay and with full reimbursement of costs.

In developing a system of social and educational planning that is fully integrated with the administrative and political process, the Norwegians have gone even further than the Swedes, helped by the fact that communities and political structures remain relatively small. It needs to be remembered that after Luxemburg and Ireland, Norway has the smallest population in Europe, without the political problems of Ireland and, because of its oil resources, without the financial difficulties. At the same time, it has the lowest population density of all European countries. It is interesting that under these circumstances educational leave does not appear to be an issue.

The United Kingdom

The United Kingdom has a long tradition of adult education, particularly adult education for workers. Since well before World War I, first initiatives were developed to make general education available to workers; in the postwar years, the Workers Education Associations (WEA), the principal vehicle for providing workers with further education, experienced rapid growth. The ideas and approaches developed during that period in the United Kingdom have had a seminal influence on adult education worldwide.

The intimate involvement of the institutions of higher education—and of certain of the Oxford colleges in particular—was a distinguishing characteristic of this system. In 1968, the ratio of full-time to part-time students in higher education as a whole was still 7:2, much the highest for any European country (Department of Education and Science, 1973, p. 5 in combination with OECD, 1974b, p. 54, table A). In 1968, slightly more than 2 million persons participated in nonvocational adult education, proportionately less than in Germany or the Scandinavian countries but much more than in any of the other European countries.

In light of the tradition of adult education, the lack of educational leave provisions is all the more striking. The typical policies that have been introduced in most countries of continental Europe in relation to labor market training, trade union training, and the expansion of the availability of adult education have not been adopted in the United Kingdom, with the exception of providing retraining opportunities for the unemployed. Thus educational leave effects are relatively few, widely dispersed, and largely dependent on long-term relationships among government, industry, and the unions rather than on recent conscious policy initiatives.

The most important area of educational leave effects in Britain, as in other countries, is in-service training in industry. This is, however, often indistinguishable in its sources from initial train-

ing, except that the latter has been regulated legislatively through
the creation of Industrial Training Boards under the Industrial
Training Act of 1964. The boards are responsible for training in
particular sectors of industry rather than in geographic regions
and have equal employer and union representation. They are financed by a levy on industry, but most of the training they support
takes place in the enterprises, so that a significant proportion of
the levy is ultimately returned to those enterprises that are most
active in training. There is nothing to indicate that further training has been a priority of the Industrial Training Boards, although
the legislation does assign them responsibility for further, as well
as initial, training.

The initiative for further vocational training has thus lain
with the employers. As the *Education Statistics for the United Kingdom 1972* (1974) indicates, the number of persons who have benefited from daytime release (with or without pay) to take part-
time courses at public sector and assisted institutions is relatively
modest and has declined slightly since 1969—from 726,526 in that
year to 635,617 in 1972. The system is heavily weighted in favor
of the young and the very young, with fewer than 25 percent in
1972 being twenty-one or older, indicating that these releases—
known as "sandwich courses" because of the way in which they are
inserted between work periods—must probably be reckoned an
extension of initial training in the main, largely comparable to the
effect achieved by the "dual" system in Germany.

A recent survey of practice in forty-eight companies in the
United Kingdom indicated a general willingness to grant paid leave
for educational purposes that were reasonably job-related, but the
actual numbers do not appear to be substantial—at least no figures
are available to supplement the persistent omission of further
vocational education from most documents on training and adult
education. Perhaps this involves what may essentially be a record-
ing error: the strength of the traditional adult education system
and its antivocational characteristics have meant that vocational
courses have not been viewed as the legitimate objects of adult education policy. The recent extensive assessment of adult education
by the Russel Committee (Department of Education and Science,
1973) was restricted by its terms of reference to nonvocational

adult education and apparently had no particular difficulty in making the necessary distinctions.

Provision for union training has increased substantially over the last few years, stimulated by the Donovan Report in the late sixties. By 1972, the traditional activities of the Workers Educational Association and of Ruskin College in Oxford had been expanded and supplemented by courses offered at technical colleges to the extent that approximately 20,000 union representatives (or 6.7 percent of the 300,000 representatives in the United Kingdom) were receiving some form of training. Salary support and leave provisions for this kind of activity derive from the Industrial Relations Code of Practice, which came into effect in February 1972 with the authority of Parliament—that is, not as a law, but with force of law (Department of Employment, 1972). Paragraph 118 provides that union representatives shall be enabled to attend courses necessary to the exercise of their duties and that management shall be responsible for the further training of their employees. The relatively weak formulations of the code require more cooperative relations between management and unions than generally exist in the United Kingdom. Moreover, the code is linked to the Industrial Relations Act of 1971, which the unions have consistently sought to undermine, and which is about to be repealed. The same code also stipulates that management is to ensure that any necessary further education and training is provided when there is significant change in the content or level of the job. It should "encourage employees to take advantage of relevant further education and training at all stages of their careers." This particular wording puts the most benign construction on likely employer-employee and employer-union relationships.

In the area of educational leave effects, the United Kingdom has been losing ground in the last few years in comparison to most other European countries in those areas in which it has traditionally been viewed as a pacesetter (full- and part-time adult education, particularly for workers) and has not initiated most of the newer policies that have been developed in continental Europe to supplement these long-standing activities. The major areas of innovation—the Open University and recent alphabetization activities—have not created educational leave effects.

9

Problems in Educational Leave Policies

Educational Leave Effects: Comparative Volume

The experience of several European countries with policies having educational leave effects identifies a number of problems that must be dealt with in the process of formulating policy in any country. Just as interesting as the visible issues, however, are the gaps in our information. Comprehensive adult education statistics covering both vocational and nonvocational further education do not exist in any of these countries; nor do they exist in disaggregated form in the various sources. Indeed, certain aspects of the overall phenomenon, particularly all forms of in-service training in industry and in the civil service, are hardly documented at all. To determine the volume of the activities the available evidence describes and to identify the element of educational leave involved requires an element of clairvoyance.

In several instances, the lack of information stems from the absence of any desire (and to a certain extent need) to develop it. In France, for instance, the budgetary and political purposes are adequately served by the present reporting system; in Italy decentralization has meant that the requirements of national policy for global figures have been reduced. In most enterprises, further vocational training is integrated with other functions, and unless there are tax reasons, as in France, there is no incentive to develop a comprehensive training budget.

In other cases, information is unavailable because it cannot be produced. In Germany, beneficiaries of the educational leave policies of the *Länder* attend the same courses as persons sent by industry or as those attending voluntarily. The educational institutions have no interest in distinguishing between these groups, and neither does industry; the state has no authority to obtain the information. Often the activities of various institutions overlap, with contributions and subsidies coming from a variety of sources, so that double counting is endemic to this sector. Ultimately, the census or large-scale surveys are the only means of obtaining information on the overall order of magnitude of further education; but here the complexity of the system makes it impossible to obtain information on the ways in which further education is being obtained.

The extremes of participation in programs with educational leave effects are supplied by Italy (with less than 5 percent of all employees) and France (which claims 14.1 percent participation in educational leave). But in reality the differences are not nearly so great. Italian information is so unsystematic as to probably understate the actual volume of activities, whereas in France an incentive to overstate exists at all levels of the system; French figures, in fact, contain a large but unidentified portion of the initial training effort. Actual expenditures of government and industry combined were higher in Germany in 1972 (at least 3.6 billion deutsche marks, or 39.6 European Units of Account per employed person in the population) than in France (4.313 billion francs, or 37.6 European Units of Account per employed person in the population), but German figures show only 3.5 percent of the labor force benefiting from this expenditure; it is obvious that comparability is difficult to achieve. In Germany, the figures are based on the entire labor force, including the self-employed, public employees, and employees in small enterprises, whereas the figure of 14.1 percent for France relates only to employees in private enterprises with at least ten employees. Considering the educational leave effects in institutions of voluntary adult education, trade union training, the civil service, and educational leave laws, it is probably accurate to say that a greater proportion of the population benefits from educational leave effects in Germany than in France and that the actual rates of participation lie between 5 percent and 10 percent of the labor force, with probably more than 8 percent involved in each country. Similar figures obtain for Sweden, although a relatively larger proportion of the participating population is handled through voluntary adult education institutions. No more accurate assessment of the orders of magnitude is possible at present.

Educational Leave and the Labor Market

Although the greater portion of material on educational leave in Europe has been written by those involved in educational policy, the vast majority of educational leave effects in Europe today are directly connected with the labor market. Numerically and financially, the two most significant areas of educational leave effects are in-service training of industry and the complex of national programs designed to influence the labor market through retraining, both on the job and during unemployment. The use of periods of training has become an accepted instrument of industrial policy at all levels. Does this mean that it will also provide the major element for educational policy?

The relationship of education to working life is one of the most contentious and difficult issues of educational theory and policy making at the present time. It is generally viewed in a context concerned with the ability of education to prepare persons for practical employment and the effects of education in the distribution of social and economic opportunity. Our consideration of labor market–related training schemes for adults in the context of educational leave reveals that there is an equally complex obverse to this debate: one concerned with the extent to which persons who have once entered employment can perceive educational experiences apart from the pressing day-to-day reality of their work. Can practices acquired on the job rather than through formal education subsequently be changed through the processes of formal education? For many employees the conditions of work is one of the prime determinants of their lives. Work and nonwork are viewed as interlocking, antagonistic elements of one experience. The fact that educational leave allows education or training during working hours without financial or social risk does not change this basic perception. It is therefore important to determine whether educational leave is viewed by participants as work or nonwork. The dilemma is that if educational leave is viewed as work, participants' attitudes will be those they maintain toward work—in many instances a grudging acquiescence rather than the active participation desirable for successful adult education (Freyberg and others, 1975, pp. 124–141); if educational leave is viewed as nonwork, its scope and effectiveness is likely to be limited to areas outside the environment of work. Unquestionably, planners of educational leave policies must make the basic conditions of working life as much a point of departure as are considerations of a more purely educational character.

Work is not a negative experience for all employees, but it is certainly the leading variable in their attitudes toward all other activities, including further education. There is a self-reinforcing relationship between initial education, work, and further education that is almost impossible to alter by educational means alone: persons who have succeeded in initial education have access to more attractive jobs (whether for this or other covariant reasons); they in turn are more willing to participate in further education, and their opportunities to do so are better. Thus educational leave and work appear inextricably linked.

Viewed in isolation, the cycle of education and work that appears to be establishing itself cannot be broken. Education alone is a weak agent for social change, and an impotent one in the face of countervailing tendencies in the labor market and in social policy. As part of a far-reaching, comprehensive policy of change in working life and social conditions, education may provide an instrument to mitigate certain side effects of a technological-industrial society and to assist in moving toward desired change; but the impetus for change comes not from education but from the overall complex process of developing a public consciousness of the pressing issues that need to be tackled. This is essentially the way in which educational leave is to be used in Sweden. Educational leave in this sense should be viewed not as a means of achieving a policy of recurrent education but as part of a number of interlocking social and economic policies, the crux of which must be to change the conditions of work—the leading variable in adult life.

Educational leave in this sense is rare in Europe. Even in

Sweden only a legislative frame of reference exists, and the issues concerning the conditions of work themselves have been dealt with only in the context of programs for industrial democracy and a much-publicized experiment in changed work organization at a new automobile plant. In Italy, the aspirations of the trade unions are in contradiction to most other indicators of social development. In Germany, many of the necessary policies in the labor market and in social policy are still lacking, and educational leave policies have not been dealt with in this context in the legislative process.

The foregoing applies only where educational leave is viewed as an instrument of change, where an attempt is made to straddle the world of work and the more general issues of any broadly educational experience. Where educational leave policies are designed to conform to existing or foreseeable conditions in the labor market or to implement short-term goals in some other area, they can play an important role, as the extensive experience with educational leave effects of this kind in Europe attests.

In view of the fact that the labor market-related programs constitute the largest sector of educational leave effects in all the four countries considered, it is surprising how little is known about the volume of this sector and, more importantly, its effectiveness. The programs of the employers and the labor market authorities cannot be clearly distinguished in terms of their content. All labor market agencies also subcontract a portion of their activities to employers, and all three countries with public labor market programs also provide funds for retraining on the job and for training first-time employees for specific positions—both of which activities are undertaken by industry and duplicated in several of the in-service training programs. The major difference is the element of social desirability of retraining a given group of employees or facilitating their employment for reasons of social policy. In the area of educational leave effects related to labor market interventions, probably the most important criterion concerns the degree of integration of the educational experience with a specific task or place of work.

The number of such programs conducted both by employers on their own initiative and by employers or labor market authorities on the initiative of the latter is very significant. They are interesting from the point of view of education since they offer examples of a kind of integration of educational and work experiences that has often been called for in vocational training. There is every indication that these programs can be effective for their limited purpose: providing specific persons with specific skills in a specific environment. In essence such programs reiterate the distinction between education and training; education is concerned with long-term effects, while training seeks to achieve immediate results. Thus the far-reaching conclusion that closer integration of education and working life would improve the quality of vocational education is not warranted on the basis of this evidence alone. The tasks of in-service training programs are quite different from those assigned to initial vocational education: whereas the former have only a limited purpose, the latter is expected to provide participants with skills for a range of activities over long periods of time.

This raises a further basic issue. Education has always been expected to deal with matters of importance beyond the immediate present; but the evidence suggests that the more immediate the concerns in educational leave, the greater the likelihood of achieving identifiable goals. This may be attributed in part to a testing error. Short-term effects can be tested with existing methods, whereas long-term changes are hardly ascertainable and can never be attributed to given causes. Nevertheless, the difficulties go deeper: the concept of recurrent education implies that there are no long-term goals of education other than the very general one of learning to learn. The underlying image of a person's development is that it is fragmented and that there are probably very few matters of content of long-term significance. This approach to the current problems of education certainly increases the role of adult education while also stripping it of its traditional, cultural, long-term goals. Given the assumption that education will recur periodically, should a student be expected to learn anything that reaches beyond the next anticipated phase of education—particularly since one assumes that all learning will be subject to change? Any such approach would tend to make the conditions of work and the conditions of society as they currently exist or can be foreseen the standard of orientation in the phases of recurrent education. Certainly this is not what proponents of educational leave intended, but, given the powerful relationships between the conditions of work and all other experiences of employed persons, this may ultimately be the effect. Clearly, we need a closer examination of the relationships between education and working life *after* a person has entered employment.

Andragogy

Since the 1920s, the term *andragogy* has existed in European discussions of adult education, particularly in the Netherlands and in Germany, to define a "pedagogy for adults" (Rosenstock-Huessy, 1925; 1970). In what ways do adults differ from children and young people in regard to education? Obviously, this is a critical question in considering the scope and the possibilities of educational leave policies.

When speaking of education we generally assume that persons to be educated have a disposable future that can be changed by educational intervention. In dealing with children and young people this is a reasonable hypothesis; in dealing with adults, it is necessary to accept that there exist increasingly irreversible conditions of age, experience, and social life. At the very least, the input required to achieve change increases when dealing with adults as long as they are employed. The conditions of work are only one such factor.

Again, the critical issue is whether educational leave is conceived of as an instrument of change or simply one of adjustment. European experience to date shows that educational leave effects can indeed be a means of making certain adjustments to changing conditions, most often in relation to changing technology and shifts in employment. The Italian program of 150 hours and the Swedish legislation for recurrent education have relatively far-reaching goals, but thus far there is insufficient evidence to indicate whether they can achieve them even in part.

Andragogy is not only a method of dealing with adults; it also defines questions of content and of teachers: who can teach what to adults? Adult education in Europe was not originally aimed at allowing adults to complete formal educational requirements— which often did not even exist at the time. In the countries with a strong tradition of adult education, this system has been related to democratization and to the building of a more broadly based culture, particularly as part of the process of rebuilding after the two world wars. Remedial and vocational adult education are recent developments that have been grafted on to an established system. While this has brought enormous growth, it has also brought fundamental change. The much more short-term, utilitarian aspects of the newer elements of the adult education system conflict with the more traditional approach. There is a certain danger in the assumption that all adult education is equivalent so long as adults are participating. Not only does the content of adult education differ widely, the adults do also. Initial education is predicated on a certain homogeneity of age as an indicator of homogeneity of experience. But adults can be distinguished by age, marital and occupational status, by whether they have children or grandchildren, as well as by prior education. None of these questions has yet been fully explored in Europe.

The developments of recent years might be described as the "schooling" of adult education—institutionalization and increasing standardization. From the point of view of andragogy this is probably an undesirable effect; certainly the arguments in favor of "deschooled" education have much greater force when applied to adults than to children. Illich (1975) argues that permanent education is an insidious form of extending what he views as the mistakes of the schools to the sector of adult education. The vehement response in France to his comments suggests that Illich touched a sore point with this accusation.

Adult Education: The Market Approach versus the Program Approach

The European situation indicates two possible avenues for developing education for adults. In France a market system has been created, albeit with the employers rather than with the employees/ students as the consumers. In Sweden and in Germany, where a vigorous but uncoordinated adult education sector existed, there has been stronger emphasis on systematizing and supplementing the institutional offerings through regulations and subsidies, and in turn providing students with the means of access—in other words, on a more programmatic approach. Either approach has its own difficulties: if a market mechanism is to be employed, the problem of regulation has rapidly to be faced (as is now the case in France); if a more programmatic approach is adopted, the dangers of "schooling" are particularly acute, since any systematization carries with it the danger of eliminating vital variety.

In all the four countries studied in some detail, adult education—to the extent that it existed—has traditionally been a domain of part-time instructors. This is true even of Germany or Sweden, countries with very large adult education sectors, and the generalization even extends to a surprising degree to residential adult education. While the drawbacks are evident (frequently inadequate preparation and coordination, pedagogic (andragogic) weaknesses, and the lack of subsequent feedback and evaluation), the advantages are much more easily overlooked. Part-time instructors are not simply a matter of lower costs. The pressures on part-time instructors are much the same pressures as their students are experiencing; part-time instructors are, moreover, much more likely to represent a broad range of expertise and experience corresponding more closely to the needs of their students, and they will include a relatively larger proportion of older persons, since one criterion for selection of part-time teachers is that they have shown particular ability in some field *other* than teaching adults. Eliminating any one of these factors is liable to cause serious problems in adult education.

Where educational leave programs have been instituted there is often an increase in the number of full-time instructors, and the beginnings of professionalization are to be expected. By its very definition, professionalization implies a standardization of practice; that is, the elimination of extremes of conduct. Generally this is justified in terms of protecting the consumer. But do adults really require such protection in education, or does it lead to the infantilization of adults?

Almost of necessity, the age structure of new full-time instructors in adult education is unsatisfactory—the instructors are too often younger and less experienced than their students, a situation that can be overcome occasionally but that tends to become the pattern. One of the basic insights of andragogy is that teaching adults requires different and wider experience than teaching children; young instructors have not acquired the necessary experience. The French law of 1971 seeks to counterbalance this danger by providing special rights to persons wishing to take leave to teach adults.

Adult education has come later to the experience of growth that has characterized all other sectors of education, and educational leave policies are probably the most important potential source of growth for the sector. There is, however, nothing to indicate that adult education will weather the experience of growth better than other sectors of education; in fact, at present there is very little discussion in Europe of the risks growth presents to adult education. There is, rather, a tendency to transfer the hopes that have not been fulfilled by the growth of secondary and higher education to the adult education sector.

The Time Frame of Educational Leave

The problems being encountered in Europe in expanding adult education are interlocking, and this makes them particularly intractable. One issue that underlies all others concerns the timing of educational leave: when can it be taken and for how long? The issue of timing education has been of only peripheral importance in the educational debate thus far, since in the initial stages it appears to have been preempted by tradition and inertia. In adult education, timing is a central issue simply because it is one of the manifestations of the potential conflict between education and work. Every country has been trying to find an acceptable compromise between what is educationally necessary, educationally desirable, and economically feasible. Difficulties arise because there are no satisfactory measures either for what is educationally necessary or for what is economically feasible, and at present, the two still appear to be poles apart.

Two basic patterns exist for bridging this gap: provision of regular but limited annual periods of leave with nearly full salary maintenance and provision of occasional lengthy or unlimited periods of leave, generally involving a fairly substantial financial sacrifice on the part of the beneficiary. The former is by far the most widespread form of provision; it is the basic format in France, Germany, and Italy—with national variations—and it is used in labor market programs in Sweden. It appears to be satisfactory for achieving limited ends, such as teaching specific skills, but it is open to serious objections as a means of achieving long-term effects. The Italian program of 150 hours offers an interesting example of this in its success in enabling students to obtain the *licenza media*, albeit with adjustments to the examination procedure.

The Italian program offers the longest time period—normally 350 hours of instruction (equivalent to nearly twelve weeks full-time instruction)—but at the greatest personal sacrifice; the time spent in class is remunerated at the effective equivalent of 40 to 50 percent of normal pay, but overall income is maintained. Programs in other countries range down to a typical leave provision of one week at full pay for labor union training.

In an attempt to confront the problems raised by lack of time, a theory has been developed that educational leave is meant only to provide a "motivational trigger." The idea is that educational leave should attract persons back into the process of education. Rather than provide a substantive educational experience in terms of process and contents, the main initial purpose should be to provide a positive educational experience that will motivate participants to undertake further education in due course. There are elements of this theory in the educational leave policies of all of the countries studied, and it may be said to constitute one of the major considerations in educational leave in Europe at the present time.

The motivational-trigger theory is most visible in policies in Germany and Sweden. Both the special programs of the textile industry and the limited educational leave programs in the *Länder* explicitly state that the purpose of these programs is not so much to provide specific courses in terms of content as to attract those who have been out of the educational system for a long time. In Sweden, the entire organization of the outreach program is directed at creating a network of reinforcing relationships at the place of work that will tend to induce greater participation in education. Again, special courses are being considered for the express purpose of reintegrating those who have for long not had any educational experience.

The theory of the motivational trigger to some extent makes

a virtue of necessity. The time available under the educational leave programs in Germany and under the provisions for outreach education in Sweden is so limited that it is probably impossible to achieve a substantive impact in terms of content without reference to some clearly defined form of application—but this basically would mean replicating courses already being offered in relation to the labor market.

The main difference between the Swedish and the German approaches is that the Swedes are in process not only of offering courses but of creating a major information and support network throughout industry. Experience to date with German courses indicates that this is a minimum requirement. All the available reports on educational leave intervention indicate that positive motivation toward education was either present beforehand or was not created during the course. The main exception is the program of the corset industry, which reports a fairly high level of returnees. Significantly, this program integrates a major element of recreation into the courses from the outset. There are some indications that experiments to date have been overloaded with educational aspirations and burdened with a tendency to parallel adult and compulsory school education.

In Sweden, while the evidence is not yet conclusive, it is clear that the outreach program has indeed drawn persons into education who would not otherwise have participated and that it has succeeded in holding and increasing participation rates over a three-year period. While this must be seen as a remarkable success in view of the great difficulties in attracting persons who have not yet been involved in further education, it must be remembered that the resources devoted to this program have been very substantial indeed and would need to be maintained over long periods of time and large areas if an overall impact is to be achieved. Moreover, the entire effort must be seen in the context of a society with a long tradition of adult education and community activity. It is unclear whether similar successes could be achieved without this background. It will take many years of observation and study before the motivational-trigger theory is proved or disproved, though some impact of its effect should be felt after five years or so. To document any effects would require longitudinal studies of a kind not yet undertaken and that are not planned, as far as we know.

The alternative form of providing educational leave is through occasional entitlements for long periods of absence (sabbaticals, study leaves, and so forth). This is very rare in Europe. The German study support law (*Ausbildungsförderungsgesetz*) effectively provides such opportunities, albeit without job security. The only program that provides long-term leave with job security and financial support is Sweden's, which is pieced together over a period of years through a number of laws. This is too new to be evaluated yet, but it clearly provides great advantages from an educational point of view. It is the educational leave program in Europe in which the educational authorities of the country concerned have been most heavily involved.

Unions and Educational Leave Policies

One of the most striking common features among the countries studied is the role of the trade unions both in initiating and sustaining the debate on educational leave and in the final implementation of policies. It can be stated that in Europe an educational leave policy can be implemented only if the trade unions actively support it. We can say this of no other single group, although we should point out that employers have had, and have taken, the opportunity to implement their own kinds of educational leave policy through in-service training programs. These are not, however, binding on anybody but their own employees.

There are a number of reasons for the special role of the unions in the development of educational leave policies. First, regardless of who provides the legal basis or financing, educational leave policies can be viewed as a fringe benefit and a cost factor in the employment policies of industry. In all such matters, the unions have a major, institutionally secured voice in Europe. Furthermore, the class structure of society remains relatively strong in Europe, and the unions are the only effective spokesmen for those groups that are not at present benefiting from some form of educational leave effects. In other words, educational leave effects have already been achieved through a variety of implicit policies for groups not represented by the unions; consequently, any further policies will involve union constituents. At the same time, the unions offer the most effective means of communication with groups not at present participating in any form of adult education—that is, blue-collar and low-status white-collar workers. Finally, the unions have come to view educational leave as a means of extending their efforts to educate their members to be effective participants in the increasingly complex decision-making processes in industry. After members of works councils have been provided with educational preparation for their tasks during working hours, the extension of this benefit to a larger group of workers appears to be the next logical step.

In all countries, the unions have been the first to raise the issue of educational leave in contract negotiations with the employers. In every instance, the employers have resisted implementing such a proposal, and legislation has been introduced only as a means of resolving fundamental issues that could not be settled at the negotiating table. There are surprising parallels among France, Germany, Sweden, and Italy in this respect—surprising because the policy-making structures and power relationships between unions, employers, and the government are so different in all four countries. In each instance, legislative interventions in favor of educational leave have taken the form of providing guidance and initiative to the negotiating partners, while leaving substantial discretion to the parties concerned. This in itself is an indication of the extent to which educational leave is viewed in the context of labor market and social policy and not primarily as an educational venture: all four countries have strong state-regulated systems of education that would not normally tolerate the degree of leeway in execution allowed in educational leave policies.

The effects of this similar proceeding have differed markedly in the four countries. In Sweden, the position of the trade unions has been significantly strengthened for further negotiations. In France, the national legislation has codified the results of negotiations between labor and employers, which tend to benefit the employers. In Italy no state intervention has occurred, except to provide an increased amount of elementary education for adults at the request of the unions, which obtained educational leave without outside assistance in a straight confrontation with the employers. In Germany, at the federal level, initial plans for educational leave were reduced to providing leave for members of works councils—a provision which fell short of the ambitious aims of the unions but clearly implemented those elements most important to them. Central legislation failed because the character of the ruling coalition government did not allow the resolution of disputed issues between the labor market partners at this level. As a result, educational leave legislation that goes beyond education for members of works councils has been initiated in the various *Länder,* and here again the affinity of the party in power to the unions proves a decisive factor.

The differences in outcome from such similar processes probably reflect differences between the unions in the four countries considered; employers' attitudes are roughly comparable from country to country. German and Swedish unions have participated in formulating economic policy for a long time—in Germany this has occurred even under governments without particularly strong links with the trade union movement. Where Social Democrats are in power—whether in Sweden or at the federal or provincial level in Germany—the unions also have a stronger influence on the development of social and even educational policy. In both countries the union movement speaks with one voice, even when it is subdivided into branch and trade unions. In Italy, unification of the union movement has been difficult and has occurred only fairly recently: it is only now beginning to extend to the development of a joint social policy. Moreover, relations with the Christian Democrats, who have been in office since World War II, have never been particularly cordial. France has three principal unions, none of which has direct links with the government and one of which has been so strongly opposed to any form of cooperation with the present authorities that for several years it refused to accept state subsidies for union training.

The special role of the unions in establishing educational leave policies is also reflected in the process by which the ILO reached its decision on the convention concerning educational leave. Here, too, union representatives were the prime movers.

As a consequence, the first step toward educational leave programs beyond those directly linked to the labor market is often provision for training of trade union officials. In all the above countries, means have been found to subsidize union education, even where, as in Italy, no sanctioning legislation exists. In view of the special role of the unions in this entire area, this is hardly surprising and can to a certain extent be viewed as a necessary preliminary to the development of broader policies of educational leave. In motivating participants, unions play a decisive role. To undertake this task effectively, they will need adequately trained union representatives to educate the beneficiaries of educational leave policies about the availability of these benefits. This view underlies the entire approach to outreach activities in Sweden, where union officials are expected to assume a special role as study organizers for adult education.

Obviously, the heavy involvement of the unions also entails a certain element of risk. The unions are ultimately an interest group, albeit one with a special social role. As employers' organizations like to point out, there exists a possibility that educational leave policies will primarily benefit the interest group of the unions. What is often at issue is the content of courses of an economic or political nature. It is even to some extent desirable that the unions should be strengthened through educational leave programs. The social group that the unions represent includes the majority of all adults who are at present not participating in adult education and not active in the democratic institutions of the countries studied. In keeping with the noticeable trend toward the democratization of industrial processes, a strengthening of the unions can be viewed as desirable—provided that they are representative of the interests of a majority of the workers.

Access to Educational Leave

Our investigation of educational leave effects in Europe has shown that such effects have existed in the labor market in all countries for a surprising length of time and that newer programs just being implemented are probably much more limited in scope than the existing ones oriented toward the labor market. The question arises: Who has access to these labor market programs, and who will have access to the new programs being developed?

Study after study has shown a direct correlation between the length of initial education and the likelihood of participation in adult education. Explanations for this range from individual motivation to an analysis of the subsidiary social and economic benefits of prolonged initial education. It is frequently argued that persons who have experienced success in education will be more likely to return to education at a later stage. Moreover, those with higher levels of education are exposed more directly to the effects of changes in knowledge and technology and will be more easily able to recognize the necessity and benefit of participating in further education as a means of preserving what one has acquired or of improving one's position. Finally, persons with higher levels of education will be in occupations that allow greater flexibility in the disposition of one's time: the right to leave without pay or compensatory time off for extra hours worked is generally not accorded to blue-collar workers or to white-collar workers of low status. This entire complex of reasons makes the finding that persons with more education participate more in adult education highly plausible.

The flaw is that this view is based entirely on the educational aspects of the problem. A careful examination of the available information reveals an even stronger correlation between occupational status and participation in further education. In other words, for persons with short initial education, the higher they rank in the employment hierarchy, the more they tend to participate in further education. Even lengthy initial education seems not to ensure high levels of participation if the employment status is low. Motivation for educational leave thus appears to derive at least as strongly from occupational status as from prior education.

Studies of participants in in-service training in industry in the four principal countries studied clearly indicate that this general observation also holds true for this particular kind of training. Information available shows that persons with higher levels of previous education will participate more often in educational leave activities than will others. The only exception is the very small group of people at the highest occupational levels, who do not participate as heavily in formal educational leave experiences. Only extremely limited possibilities exist for unskilled or semiskilled workers to benefit from the existing in-service training programs of industry in Europe. There exists a sharp difference between semiskilled and skilled workers in participation in further education; skilled workers participate in further education programs, semiskilled do not. This is even true for Italy, where many skilled workers achieve their status with less than the required formal training and without intervening upgrading through formal training, and subsequently engage in various forms of further education, indicating that the leading variable is probably occupational status rather than prior education, although both covary strongly in the countries of northern Europe.

The range of participants is somewhat broader in the labor market programs. The distinction that must be made here is between individual and group participation. In programs that require individual initiative or correspond to the needs of a widely dispersed group of persons, the occupational status and prior education of participants strongly resembled that of participants in in-service training in industry. However, most labor market programs have special provisions for the retraining of members of certain professional groups threatened with redundancy. In this instance, large numbers of unskilled and semiskilled workers with low levels of prior education have also been included in the retraining programs; the best-known example of this program is the German program that took place with the reduction of employment in the coal-mining industry in the late fifties and early sixties. Similar efforts, however, have been undertaken in the other countries at various times, involving industrial groups and, in particular, agricultural groups. Given the goals of existing programs oriented toward the labor market, it is unrealistic to expect a major change in the composition of the groups of beneficiaries in the foreseeable future.

In some countries, especially Germany, civil servants have excellent opportunities of participating in educational leave programs. Participation, however, corresponds roughly to participation rates in industry. In other words, authorization to participate in education during working hours is more readily given in the civil service to higher ranking persons with higher previous levels of education than to others. In all countries, teachers tend to have rather more possibilities of participating in further educational experience than other groups of civil servants, and those in the labor intensive public services—railways, postal services, and public utilities—have less chance of participating.

Finally, union representatives have perhaps the best, most systematic, and least job-oriented opportunities of participating in educational leave programs. This is the only group in which unskilled and semiskilled workers will be represented in significant numbers corresponding to their overall participation in the work force. Given the trend toward greater democratization of industrial decision making, this group of participants probably represents one of the most important in any of the educational leave programs in the countries studied.

All these established programs in favor of educational leave will tend to replicate the prior educational attainments of their participants, with the sole exception of the program for union representatives. In other words, all these programs are designed to provide an adaptation to changing conditions for those groups most visibly affected by changing conditions, namely the better educated and the socially more privileged who are most visibly benefiting from existing conditions.

Given this preexisting structure of educational leave effects, the debate in three of the four countries studied in detail has centered on two issues: (1) whether to create a broad policy framework for this disparate set of educational leave effects and (2) how to reach those groups most obviously failing to benefit from the existing possibilities. The two issues are to some extent divergent: a broad framework would tend to create new opportunities for those who already have opportunities, while attempts to reach groups previously failing to benefit from educational leave opportunities will have to be fragmentary, aimed at specific target populations and designed to exclude those already benefiting most. But obviously these two initiatives can be combined by making special provision for underprivileged groups within the framework of a broad structural policy.

Within the four countries studied, we find examples of the three basic policy possibilities: In Italy, a policy has been developed that is designed to benefit those with the least prior education and the least opportunities for further education; in Germany, a number of *Länder* have developed broad policy frames that will tend to benefit equally all employees within a given region; in Sweden, a number of simultaneous policy initiatives have created both a broad framework for general access to educational leave and a number of specific initiatives directed toward groups previously not participating.

Thus far there is insufficient evidence to indicate whether any of these three approaches is more likely to succeed than the others. In all three instances, local conditions clearly contributed to the formulation of the policy and will contribute equally to success or failure. Given the nature of the German programs, it is, however, unlikely that they will have marked redistributive effects. Both the Italian and the Swedish programs contain elements designed to attract nonparticipants to further education, but in each instance, circumstances of the environment provide the greatest obstacle to success. In Italy the lack of comparable programs and qualified teachers is likely to prove a major stumbling block. Moreover, the Swedish efforts to attract students into further education show that the potential reserve of participants who can be mobilized without a major recruiting effort is not nearly as large as the theoretical demand would indicate; thus one can anticipate that the Italian program will reach its limits of expansion fairly soon unless systematic efforts at recruitment are undertaken. In the Swedish programs, both for immigrants and in outreach education, the problems of course content and didactics have not yet been identified and tackled as clearly as they have in Italy; it may be anticipated that this aspect of the program will pose major problems in the foreseeable future. As German examples show, the lack of suitable teachers and of didactic models for teaching adults with relatively little prior education is a problem that is not restricted to Italy.

To summarize, one can say that the prospects of achieving greater equality of educational opportunity through educational leave policies do not appear to be very promising in countries with highly selective systems of education. The experience of early and decisive selection linked to stratified social hierarchies and relatively low levels of geographic mobility makes it almost impossible to reintroduce persons with low levels of education to the educational process at a later stage.

Financing Educational Leave

Schemes for financing educational leave in Europe are so diverse that no generalization is possible. The extremely complex system of transfers of credits used in France conceals the fact that it differs materially from the deduction of training costs as a normal business expense only insofar as it sets a lower limit to the size of this expense. Thus it is not so radically different from schemes operating in other countries as it may appear at first sight.

In all countries, the state contributes directly or indirectly to the costs of educational leave. In Italy, direct contributions are made through subsidies for transportation costs and textbooks; in Germany, through state support of the labor market schemes and state subsidies to educational institutions; in France, through contributions from general tax revenues to the training fund; and in Sweden, by including educational leave students in the regular education program and through state support of the labor market schemes. In Germany and Sweden, labor market schemes also draw on social security and unemployment contributions paid by the workers, so that an indirect contribution by the workers is made. As a rule, the employers are required to contribute to costs for remuneration of earnings foregone, except in the case of trade union training. In effect, this employers' contribution represents a small shift in the conditions of productivity, insofar as the average number of days worked per year per worker is likely to be reduced. There are some instances in which trade unions have to finance the expense of the attendance of their members at courses that are of educational interest.

In all countries, it has been much easier than expected to expand the educational system to accommodate educational leave by use of available facilities. Only in France has it been necessary to develop additional instructional space and other facilities supported through ministry grants. In all other countries, existing public and private facilities have proved to be underutilized to a sufficient extent to make it possible to accommodate these extra students.

In view of the highly fragmented and disorderly character of educational leave effects in most European countries at the present time, it is also impossible to make any definite statement on the distribution of financial burdens between the three principal parties—the state, the employers, and the employees. Insofar as one can view tax exemption of educational expenses as a state contribution, it is probably accurate to say that more than 50 percent of the funding for educational leave is provided by the state. Employees probably contribute no more than 5 to 10 percent (through travel expenses and earnings foregone), with the remainder coming from the employers.

With a major expense such as that for educational leave programs, it is not ultimately decisive from which source funding is derived. As with education in general, the issues are, rather, who contributes to the revenues of the various sources, in what way, and are these contributions balanced by the benefit from educational leave programs. Industry makes a contribution in real terms only insofar as the costs for educational leave cannot be passed on in the form of higher prices; the state reflects contributions to educational leave only insofar as the revenues of the states may be a distorted charge on the paying power of the citizens. The issue in both instances is not so much the individual institution's ability to pay at a given point in time as the ability of the economy to absorb a redistribution of resources from production to the financing of social policies. The only contribution that cannot be recovered, except under unusual circumstances, is the employee's.

More important than who contributes to the costs of educational leave is the financing mechanism that is chosen. This will have a direct influence on two subsidiary issues: the ease or difficulty of exercising the right to educational leave, and who ultimately decides who will participate in what forms of educational leave. A wide variety of possibilities exist.

The financial requirements for educational leave fall into two major categories: salary maintenance for participants and course costs, each of which requires 40 to 60 percent of the total funding, depending on the formula used. Course costs in turn involve capital investments, teaching and administrative salaries, and direct course expenses (teaching materials and travel and living expenses where applicable). Formulas exist by which the employer, the employee, or the state contributes various amounts to each of these expenditures. As a general rule, employees are unlikely to be asked to contribute to capital expenditures even indirectly; they are likely to be asked to contribute either to salary maintenance or to direct course costs, but rarely to both. The roles of employers and of the state are remarkably interchangeable in regard to all expenditures; in other words, there are no expenditures in educational leave that typically fall to either the employers or to the state.

From the beneficiary's point of view, the critical issue is the amount of nonrecoverable expense or loss of income involved. For the participant it is probably immaterial whether the contribution takes the form of direct expense (as for course costs) or earnings foregone. When a contribution from the participant is required, a contribution of time probably presents the smallest motivational obstacle, although limits probably exist as to the proportion of the necessary time that a participant can be expected to contribute—at some point an educational leave policy comes to resemble a subsidy to voluntary adult education rather than a particularly attractive benefit.

From the employer's point of view, the critical issue is whether he distributes funds directly (to the employee or to the institution offering the course) or whether an intermediary is established. The energetic (and largely successful) opposition of the French employers to making training insurance funds the principal funding vehicle for implementing the law of 1971 reflects this concern. The more direct the form of disbursement, the greater the likelihood that the employer will also be able to influence the utilization of resources.

From the state's point of view, the critical issue is its ability to control, or at least influence, the flow of funds and thereby the priorities of the program.

The particular scheme that is chosen reflects the attempt to balance these three sets of priorities—beneficiary's, employer's, and state's—within the political setting of the various countries.

These priorities are not irreconcilable, at least at the theoretical level, although in practice there are large areas of conflict—about the extent, for instance, to which the unions are to be recognized as fully representative of individual employees' interests. At the heart of the compromise that is ultimately achieved lies the question of who decides who will participate in educational leave. The extent to which this decision can be influenced by legal or financial means is determined by the nature of the work contract.

To be effective, even the best and most balanced of legal contracts requires the goodwill of the contracting partners, and the employment contract is not the most perfect of legal instruments. The individual employee needs to retain the good will of his superiors and employers, while employers need the collective good will of their employees. Even where educational leave is an individual right, therefore, it can be exercised only within the limits of the employer/employee relationship—unless the unions provide purposive intervention. Here again the role of the unions can be recognized as more important than the specific details of the educational leave provision. Given a basically consensual relationship between employer and employee, decisions on educational leave will also be consensual: if there is conflict over other issues, the likelihood is that there will also be conflict over the exercise of educational leave rights.

Within these limits, the rules for granting educational leave can make a difference, particularly in allowing employees to initiate requests at a time of their own choosing for courses of their own choosing, and in admitting nonvocational and longer-term courses as part of the educational leave program. Among the available mechanisms for making these provisions possible, commitment of resources to specific courses and persons is probably the most important.

Relationship to Existing Institutions of Education

Despite the often-expressed hope that recurrent education—and educational leave in particular—will provide impetus for change and the reform of existing educational institutions, there is no evidence to show that this has actually been happening in Europe. To an extent, present curriculum reform in general can be said to provide greater flexibility in terms of teaching skills, but it is questionable whether this general trend toward reform and the liberalization of curricula in Europe can be attributed to theories of recurrent education or the practice of educational leave; these are at best only two of a number of justifications for the reforms being implemented. In all the countries studied, some effort has been made to create constructive relationships between educational leave programs and existing institutions. None of these arrangements seems to have made particular inroads into the existing institutions.

In France, the law of 1971 saw the creation of an entirely new sector of private institutions of further vocational education. These private institutions represented a major departure from the traditional state-controlled system of education and thus constituted an implicit challenge to the existing institutions. In practice, the new private institutions have undertaken tasks that existing institutions could not or would not do; in serving the needs of particular customers in industry, private institutions have flourished notably. They have not, however, provided competition or challenge to existing institutions in areas where this might have been expected. The existing institutions have thus been spared the challenge of taking in new clientele with new demands who might have disturbed their established ways. In areas where existing institutions had an established competence, they have readily expanded to take in adult students.

In Germany, the existing institutions of initial education have not been affected by the development of educational leave programs at all; such programs have been carried out either by institutions oriented toward labor market training or by the adult education institutions, which have in any case mostly been separate from other educational institutions. These traditional institutions of adult education are indeed undergoing a transformation. They are experiencing growth and greater state regulation, and in all probability they will quite soon have to face the fact that they have been changed beyond recognition.

In Sweden, the educational leave programs are designed to integrate students into existing institutions. These new students are expected, however, to conform to the goals of the institutions they enter. Liberalizing access to the universities for those over twenty-five years of age has indeed caused a sharp change in the age composition of the students, but this has not brought significant changes in the ways in which universities operate and in the priorities they have set for themselves. While it is likely (although not documented) that the presence of more adult students in the universities will change the style and level of discourse, the basic relationships and structures of the institutions are not affected.

In Italy, changing the lower secondary schools was an explicit goal of the trade unions in their struggle to achieve contractual recognition of educational leave. If there is any one country in which the introduction of educational leave programs is likely to bring major reform, Italy must be the one. Nevertheless, it remains questionable whether such influence will be exerted on the existing schools through the new programs. If this is to occur at all, it will have to happen over long periods of time and primarily because the program of 150 hours may ultimately become the normal avenue of access to the teaching profession in lower secondary schools. In this case, the experience of teaching adults during one's first years as an active teacher is likely to become an important factor in the overall training and socialization of lower secondary school teachers. All other efforts to change the existing schools through the program of 150 hours have not yet borne fruit, and there are indications that the Ministry of Education is intent on limiting the effects of the program on existing institutions.

The lack of impact on existing educational institutions is hardly surprising in view of the predominance of vocational concerns in most educational leave programs in Europe so far. With the exception of Sweden, vocational education has not been integrated into the institutions of secondary and higher education, which are most often identified with initial education. Thus the impact of educational leave policies has not occurred where one would most often look for it. The major exceptions are the systems of adult education in France and Germany, which are being subjected to change, probably because they are not yet firmly set in structure and procedure in either country.

In assessing the effects of educational leave policies on existing institutions, we must also consider their effects on industry.

Industry is to a certain extent already an educational institution, although opinions differ widely on whether this is beneficial or not. Certainly the impact of the conditions of work on an individual are as important as the impact of education—if not more important. As efforts are made to integrate work and retraining and work and educational leave more closely—a desirable development, as has been seen by the examples of courses in Italy—the place of work could also become the site of education. This has happened only in the narrowest sense: where retraining involves job-induction activities, these have often been conducted at the place of work itself. But the thrust of educational leave is much broader than simply conducting retraining at the place of work; it raises issues about the place of work and its effects on the employee that have thus far been avoided. In this sense, change has occurred no more in industry than in the regular institutions of education, although it must be contemplated as a possible consequence, in some respects even as a necessary condition, of a successful educational leave program.

Is Educational Leave an Educational Policy?

This question is rhetorical in the sense that the answers one gives depend on the definitions one adopts. Nevertheless, it identifies one of the central difficulties in undertaking this study and in formulating and discussing educational leave policies. In the context of the compartmentalized political relationships that characterize virtually all European countries, policy issues dealing with educational leave always have three elements: an educational, a labor market, and a social policy element. Each of these can be, and has been, treated in relative isolation. It is striking that the country with the most integrated system of policy planning—Norway—does not consider educational leave a significant issue for discussion.

The approaches of other countries to the problem of educational leave reflect virtually all possible variations of attitude. However, implemented educational leave effects in Europe have thus far occurred principally in the context of labor market policy and not of educational policy.

Clearly, educational leave policy requires forms of intersectoral planning that do not yet exist in most European countries.

The difficulty lies not only in the coordination of policies but in the reference groups policy makers typically deal with. The labor market partners are represented in the major educational policy-making bodies as well as in those for social and labor market policy. But union representatives on educational matters may have more in common with employer representatives on those policy-making bodies than with the union members directly concerned with labor market and social affairs. The fragmentation of policy making reflects an equal fragmentation of the representative organizations of the major social groupings.

Thus whether or not educational leave policies are educational policies depends on who defines and implements them. Thus far, only very few educational leave policies designed with the typical concerns of the educational system in mind have been implemented. The reasons for the educational systems' relative lack of success in developing viable responses to the challenges they are faced with are manifold. In part they lie within the systems themselves, in part they are external. A contributing factor to the lack of success is the distaste for the messy business of industry and labor. This distaste is reflected in the unwillingness of many persons in education to recognize that all forms of in-service training are also forms of education and that work itself can have a profoundly educative effect—in both a positive and a negative sense.

Educational leave policies offer the prospect of involving educational authorities in the labor market and in social policies. The authorities are ill-equipped for the kinds of relationships now expected of them. The aggressive marketing approach of some private institutions in France is not in the style of traditional institutions of education in which process is as important as product. In Germany, there is a tendency in the large industries to do as much of their own in-service training themselves as possible because it is felt that external institutions—even private ones—are not sufficiently efficient. From the educational point of view, there is a clear danger in this development, but it is a danger inherent in the concept of educational leave: while you may be able to provide an employee with the right to leave, as long as you provide job security you cannot remove him from the continuing influence of his employment.

Educational institutions have never been forced into this kind of a relationship with other social institutions before. While it has become a truism to point out that educational institutions have important social functions in establishing criteria for the distribution of benefits, they never do so in what is potentially a confrontational situation. In response to this difficulty, several educational writers, particularly in Germany and to a lesser degree in Sweden, have tried to extend the traditional principle of the autonomy of educational processes to educational leave by attempting to define it in purely educational terms. Given the present distribution of power in social and labor market policy, they are unlikely to succeed. Educational leave policies are of necessity also social and labor market policies, and until educational authorities learn the necessary skills of negotiation, compromise, and political maneuver, educational leave policy will remain primarily an instrument of social and labor market, rather than educational, policy. The question is, of course, whether acquiring the necessary skills may in the end compromise the original functions of the educational system.

Disseminating Information on Educational Leave

Since World War II, Europe has undertaken a remarkable simultaneous expansion of its political institutions and of its social policies; citizens of all the countries studied now possess an unprecedented number of rights and a multitude of possibilities of exercising them and of expressing their opinions. The very multiplicity of rights now poses a problem: as rights have become more numerous, they have also become more difficult to identify and to exercise; they involve more and more special groups, and it requires a great effort not to duplicate them. This development places a burden on the information systems and creates a critical problem in developing a new policy: how information can be provided when and where it is needed, while simultaneously avoiding an information overload that can defeat the purpose.

Our analysis of educational leave effects has demonstrated the complexities of the systems of provision in all countries—overlapping provisions and a multiplicity of agents are endemic in this field. It is, therefore, hardly surprising that individual beneficiaries are unable to exercise their rights except as a member of some group: as an employee of a specific firm or as a member of a union, a club, or an association. Even where educational leave is an individual right, the complexities of the societies involved make collective organization a precondition to exercise of that right. The flow of information thus becomes a process of at least two stages: the individual deals with a group, the group with an intermediary organization which ultimately leads to direct contact with the source of information. Seen in this light, the distinction between educational leave as an individual right as opposed to a collective one becomes much less important than one might assume: with few exceptions, the exercise of the individual right requires some form of collective support.

The flow of information itself is also usually a two-step process: first it is necessary to inform people that information exists; then it is necessary to provide counseling to assist in obtaining and interpreting this information. The provision of counseling alone is probably not sufficient. The four countries studied in detail reflect a wide variety of approaches to the critical issue of information dissemination. It is probable that efforts using informal channels of communication trusted by the workers and designed to reach as close as possible to the place of work offer greatest promise of success. Methods currently in use range from the totally unsystematic in Germany to the highly financed, systematic effort being mounted in Sweden; approaches in France and Italy would be ranked between these two.

In those *Länder* of Germany that at present have educational leave legislation, no major effort has been undertaken to inform beneficiaries of their rights. Thus it is left largely to the initiative of local union groups to motivate their members to participate or not. The unions also see to it that members of works councils attend courses. For labor market programs, the labor market authorities have until recently undertaken active recruitment. As of the summer of 1975, this has been reduced because the large number of unemployed have strained resources. In the present situation, it is primarily unemployed persons who are counseled concerning their right to training when they claim unemployment benefits; but private institutions of education offering courses eligible for support by the labor market authorities have also begun to engage in public advertising of their courses on a commercial basis. Since, however, the entire information system in Germany is not coordinated or directed toward specific audiences, the response tends to be somewhat arbitrary.

In France, the new policies to promote educational leave were an important item of social legislation and were consequently subjected to intense public debate both before and after passage. The government has undertaken a major effort to publicize the availability of educational leave and has produced posters and pamphlets informing employees of their rights. This has been primarily a government activity or one carried out by semigovernment agencies. As such, its successes in achieving broad penetration have been substantial. An overwhelming majority of people are aware of the legislation and of their rights under it. Nevertheless, the government initiative appears not to be a factor motivating participation in educational leave. Moreover, the actual distribution of authority is such that the employers have the decisive vote in attributing leave. As a result, the internal hierarchies of the firms and initiatives of the employers in informing employees of their rights remain a major, if not the major, vehicle of information on the law of 1971. In general, it can be said that the unions have remained relatively inactive and have not been an important source of information or motivation.

In Italy, in contrast, the unions have been the only source of information for the beneficiaries. The unions in turn relied heavily on their most decentralized organizations and on informal networks of contacts to develop participation. No national program of study organizers has been developed; but in all regions, and more particularly in subdivisions of regions, local organizations have developed information and have increased the motivation of employees to participate. In general, this effort has been quite successful in drawing persons who have been out of the educational system for a long time back into it through the courses offered. To some extent the Italian unions have made a virtue of necessity, since no large-scale information program could be developed. The successes indicate, however, that the approach that was adopted actually provided as good a means of recruiting as any other that might be developed in another country.

By far the most systematic approach to the problems of recruitment has been developed in Sweden. After a period of experiment, regulations have been adopted that give the unions responsibility for disseminating information about educational leave and for recruiting participants at the factory level. These so-called study organizers are financed through government grants and are specially trained for their tasks. The evidence of several years of experiment shows that this systematic approach to recruitment can even overcome such problems as shift working or the difficulties experienced by employed women in participating in educational leave programs because of their responsibilities outside their regular employment.

With the exception of Sweden, no studies have thus far been undertaken on the effectiveness of the systems being employed to provide beneficiaries with information about their rights. In France, survey research has shown a high degree of penetration by the public information campaign (see Table 5), but there is no indication of the extent to which this has been leading to participation. Certainly, the figures on participation give no indication that the generalized information campaign has had effects in the particular instances where employees are receiving no assistance from their employer, from their union, or from any other group.

Conclusion

When we started our analysis of educational leave in Europe, we found that no clear definition of educational leave exists, and we were therefore forced to use a theoretical construct—educational leave effects—to achieve an understanding of the situation. The analysis has shown that the absence of an accepted definition corresponds to the absence of educational leave policies, and that even within the context of the theoretical frame of reference we developed there remain many practical and fundamental problems to be resolved; with the single exception of the developing situation in Sweden, it is certainly premature to speak of educational leave policies in Europe.

It is difficult indeed to arrive at an overall assessment of so complex and, in many respects, so nebulous a phenomenon as educational leave effects. What is quite evident, however, is that in a large number of countries and by many different means, all groups interested in the question of educational leave have been steadily expanding the importance attached to education and training that is directly interfaced with work. There has been an expansion of all phases of education for adults, and the interest therein far transcends individual advantage or benefit. There is a consensus that this represents a vital social, societal concern. Perhaps more by such action than by express formulation, the parties concerned have, at least in Europe, declared their commitment to policies giving rise to educational leave effects.

The further prospects for educational leave depend heavily on the overall economic situation and specifically the availability of resources for an extension of education. In view of the uncertainties surrounding the future economic development in the late seventies, it would be rash to venture any prediction of the future development of educational leave in Europe. Nevertheless, it is worth spelling out in greater detail the possibilities that educational leave policies offer. Clearly no further progress toward the realization of educational leave policies is to be expected, unless the potential of educational leave as a means of purposive change to the benefit of participants and society has been made clear both to the decision makers and the potential participants in such programs. The diverse European experiences with elements of educational leave to date may serve to provide a frame of reference for future debate in this area.

The usefulness and effectiveness of educational leave measures in relation to the labor market is by now beyond question. At issue is the most effective means of achieving results that are known to be possible. In the initial stage, such measures oriented toward the labor market were largely passive and reactive, trying to provide assistance to those most affected by technological change and economic fluctuation. The scope for individual initiative was generally restricted to choosing one of a few alternative training schemes for vocational skills that corresponded to present or future bottlenecks determined or assumed by labor market authorities. This basic situation has not changed much in the second stage of such policies, where preventive measures have been substantially reinforced on the basis of much more elaborate prognostic efforts.

By now the well-informed employee does not have to wait until he is laid off or dismissed; he can take the initiative for retraining, provided his professional choice lies within certain priority areas determined on the basis of general economic and social policy. The question is how such a pragmatic policy could be integrated into a more comprehensive educational leave policy covering curative or preventive labor market considerations.

A desirable educational leave policy should rest on two indispensable premises: (1) it must be oriented toward the diverse needs and the condition of adult students and should rely on their voluntary cooperation in the educational process; and (2) it must not only serve fairly short-term economic and social purposes but also contain elements which are clearly educational in the sense that they transcend the individual, the immediate, and the specific to include questions relating to the character and future of our society and its history and means of expression and achieving change. Although these goals do not need to be in conflict with one another, in practice they often are. Every country has its own means of expressing the element we have called "educational": The terms culture, civilization, general education, civics, and emancipation have all been used in one context or another.

The future development of educational leave policies clearly hinges on the clarification of the difficult questions connected with this "educational" element of such policies. We are confronted with the apparently unbridled development of modern societies and the increasing inability of individuals to experience themselves as effective members of these societies. One can even speak of an extension of the social impotence of childhood into adult life. These are clearly issues education must address itself to, and the context for such a venture could very well be educational leave. In this sense, educational leave policies have an important contribution to make to the further development of Western democratic societies. They could contribute to the development of what might be termed "nonmarketable qualifications." Nonmarketable qualifications refer to an increased awareness and understanding of the present conditioning socioeconomic factors and the capacity to act on them through existing or even new channels of active participation in decision finding. Such qualifications would lead to a more active and determined involvement in the problem areas of political and economic life; they would result in active citizenship.

These issues have long been at the heart of debates about adult education in general. Why do we now need educational leave policies to cope with them, even in countries like Sweden and Germany, where there is a long tradition of voluntary adult education? The stress and contradictions of the various roles of adult life and their growing habituation over time make it almost impossible or at least very unlikely for an adult to stand back and reexamine the multiple aspects of these roles. The irrevocability of some of the roles (for example, age, parental obligations, livelihood), the fragmentary, often alienating, character of the work role in particular, and the dependence on mass media and popular myths for orientation or comfort all lead to an almost casual, at best perfunctory, perception of the social process and the individual's functioning in it. Through the ascendency of technology and industrial economy, the organizing principles of specialization and division of labor have received almost universal application. One does not need Marxist analysis to accept that the problems of alienation associated with these principles have thus become universal in our societies. There are few institutions still capable of providing an embracing view of our societies. In spite of their dedication to specialization, educational institutions still have this possibility, particularly when dealing with adult populations. But participants must be removed from the continuing pressures of adult life if they are to be receptive to what education still has to offer them. Only a leave of absence can allow the adult to step back and take a fresh look at his position in life and to review some of the otherwise suppressed difficulties.

Adults have, on the other hand, accumulated a wealth of experience, both positive and negative, that is hardly ever tapped for educational purposes or for policy formation. Normally, a wide gap separates political and economic decision makers from those who must live with the consequences of their decisions. The average citizen is dangerously near to political illiteracy, leaving important issues to professionals and bureaucracies. Particularly in Europe, the possibilities for informal political expression still remain relatively limited; the importance of citizen participation and of citizens' action groups have been widely reorganized only recently.

How could educational leave be instrumental in breaking up the compartmentalization of public life? Certainly it would be overstating the case to pretend that educational leave presents a panacea to the shortcomings of contemporary society. But if individuals with their preoccupations and their awareness are the building stones of society, increasing their consciousness on a broader scale could contribute to the process of social reform conducive to a saner society. Perhaps educational leave could add to this prospect by giving individuals an opportunity to overcome the critical threshold of indifference so they could, as a first step, pause and step back and reflect on the daily existence and its conditioning factors, articulate suppressed needs and desires, and explore feasible avenues of expression, with the intention of finding ways to have social reforms taken into account in the economic and political processes.

This development is easier described than achieved, especially since many adults have never acquired the capacity to translate personal experience into broadly social and political terms or to analyze the context in which they exist. To realize this objective, however, a structured educational experience is required. Such a goal could not be achieved within a week or two of educational leave because in most cases it is not realized even in years of initial schooling. The educational situation of adults offers greater opportunities for providing the necessary stimulus for insight and continued learning—adults have already gained the basis of experience that youth are lacking. In fact, the ultimate goal cannot and will not be achieved in a conclusive manner, since in itself it is a lifelong process that could be abridged only in favor of ideological shortcuts, which definitely are not the purpose of educational leave. A safeguard against such shortcuts lies in the practical orientation of most adults and their insistence on their own experience as a valid standard of judgment.

As the Swedish and Italian approaches to educational leave indicate, such a pragmatic yet problem-oriented policy of educational leave must be centered on the place of work as a starting point. Experience and theoretical reflection show that the work role is the pivotal factor for the self-perception, attitudes, and behavior of adults. What is important is that the experience offered through educational leave ultimately transcends the confines of this work role. In this respect, the Italian program of 150 hours perhaps provides the most instructive example of the possibilities and difficulties of using education to change the conditions of adults. So far as these considerations will enter into the further development of educational leave policy, clearly this would have to lead to a new round of intensive rethinking and reform throughout the educational system.

References

Amt für Berufs-und Weiterbildung (Office for Vocational and Further (Adult) Education). *1001-mal lernen (Learning 1001 Times)*. Verzeichnis der genehmigten Bildungsurlaubsveranstaltungen, Stand 5. März 1975 (List of Authorized Course Offerings for Educational Leave, as of March 5, 1975). Hamburg: Behörde für Schule, Jugend und Sport (Authority for Schools, Youth and Sport), 1975.

Avveduto, S. "Il punto sul 'nuvo verbo': L'educazione permanente" ("The 'New Word': Permanent Education"). *International Review of Community Development*, nos. 29–30, Summer 1973, pp. 61–70.

Baethge, M., Gerstenberger, F., Kern, H., Schumann, M., Stein, H. W., and Wienemann, E. *Produktion und Qualifikation: Eine Vorstudie zur Untersuchung von Planungsprozessen im System der beruflichen Bildung (Production and Qualification: A Pilot Study for the Investigation of Planning Processes within the System of Vocational Training)*. Göttingen: Soziologisches Forschungsinstitut (Sociological Research Institute), 1973.

Balbo, L., Capecchi, V., and Facchini, C. "Università e le 150 ore" ("The University and the 150 Hours"). *Inchiesta (Inquiry)*, April–June 1975, 5 (19), pp. 39–54.

Barbagli, M., and others. "Le 150 ore all' Università di Bologna" ("The 150 Hours at the University of Bologna"). *Inchiesta (Inquiry)*, Oct.–Dec. 1974, 4 (6), pp. 68–70.

Battaglia, F. "Profilo dei gruppi dirigenti confederali" ("Profile of Trade Union Leaders"). *Rassegna Sindacale (Union Review)*. Quaderni (Revista della CGIL) (*Notebooks* (Journal of the CGIL)), July–Aug. 1972, 10 (37), pp. 29–55.

Bechelloni, G. "Educazione permanente e azione culturale" ("Permanent Education and Cultural Action"). *International Review of Community Development*, nos. 29–30, Summer 1973, pp. 71–94.

Belorgey, J. M. "La formation professionnelle continue et la promotion sociale en France" ("Continuing Vocational Training and Social Advancement in France"). *Notes et Etudes Documentaires (Documentary Notes and Studies)*, 3864–3865. Paris: La Documentation Française, March 3, 1972a.

Belorgey, J. M. "Le financement de la formation professionnelle continue" ("The Financing of Continuing Vocational Training"). *Education Permanente*, July, Aug., Sept., 1972b, (15), pp. 5–36.

Belorgey, J. M., Boubli, B., and Pochard, M. *Apprentissage-Orientation-Formation Professionnelle (Apprenticeship-Orientation-Vocational Training)*. Préface de N. Catala. Paris: Librairie de la Cour de Cassation (Library of the Supreme Court of Appeals), 1974.

Bengtsson, J., and Bengtsson, M. *Recurrent Education: Some Observations and a Bibliography*. UKÄ-rapport 1975:8. Stockholm: Research and Development Unit at the Office of the Chancellor of the Swedish Universities, 1975.

Blumenthal, V. von. "Zur Diskussion über den Zusammenhang von Arbeitsplatzstruktur, Qualifikationsbedarf und Qualifikationsvermittlung in Italien" ("On the Discussion About the Relation Between Work Organization, Qualification Needs, and Provision of Qualifications in Italy"). In Marburger Forschungsstelle für vergleichende Erziehungswissenschaft (Marburg Research Unit for Comparative Educational Science) (Ed.), *Texte, Dokumente, Berichte zum Bildungswesen ausgewählter Industriestaaten (Texts, Documents, and Reports on the Educational Systems of Selected Industrial Nations)*, no. 6. Marburg, 1973, pp. 1–55.

Bosi, P., and others. "Corso 150 ore Università Bologna: Introduzione ai meccanismi di una economia capitalista" ("The 150-Hour Course at Bologna University: Introduction into the Mechanisms of a Capitalist Economy"). *Inchiesta (Inquiry)*, Oct.–Dec. 1974, 4 (6), pp. 12–48.

Bundesanstalt für Arbeit (Federal Labor Agency). "Arbeitsstatistik 1974–Jahreszahlen" ("Labor Statistics 1974–Annual Figures"). *Amtliche Nachrichten der Bundesanstalt für Arbeit (Official Communications of the Federal Labor Agency)*, 23. Jg. Sondernummer (Special Issue), May 30, 1975.

Bundesministerium für Unterricht und Kunst (Ministry of Instruction and Art). *Enquête Bildungsfreistellung (Hearings on Educational Leave of Absence)*. Erwachsenenbildung in Österreich, Sonderheft (Adult Education in Austria, Special Number). Vienna: Austrian Ministry of Education, 1975.

Bund-Länder Kommission für Bildungsplanung (Joint Commission for Educational Planning). *Bildungsgesamtplan (Comprehensive Plan for Education)*. Stuttgart: Verlag, 1973.

Castello, P. "Un caso di politica culturale della Stato: Appunti sui Centri di servici sulturali del Mezzogiorno" ("An Example of State Cultural Policy: Remarks on the Centers for Cultural Services of the Mezzogiorno [South]"). In G. Bechelloni, *Politica Culturale? Studi, materiali, ipotesi (Cultural Policy? Studies, Materials, Hypotheses)*. Florence: Guaraldi, 1970, pp. 208–223.

Censis (Centro Studi Investimenti Sociali). "La situazione educativa del paese" ("The Educational Situation of the Country"). *Quindicinale di note e commenti (Quindicinale of Notes and Comments)*, Oct. 1974 (211–212), pp. 943–1108.

Censis. *Indagine sui corsi sperimentali di scuola media per lavoratori (150 ore) (Study of Experimental Middle School Courses for Workers (150 Hours))*. 4 vols. Roma, 1975.

Central Bureau of Statistics (Norway). *Educational Statistics: Adult Education and Popular Education, 1972/73*. Oslo: Statistisk Sentralbyrå, 1974.

Centre de Recherche et d'Information Socio-Politiques (CRISP) (Center of Sociopolitical Research and Information, Belgium). "Le crédit d'heures de formation syndicale" ("Hours of Credit for Trade Union Training"). *Courrier Hebdomadaire (Weekly Courier)*, March 16, 1973 (596), pp. 2–24.

CFDT. *See* Confédération Française Démocratique du Travail.

CGT. *See* Confédération Générale du Travail.

Charnley, A. *Paid Educational Leave. A Report of Practice in France, Germany, and Sweden*. London: Hart-Davis Educational, 1975.

Cheramy, R. "La formation professionnelle continue" ("Continuous Vocational Training"). *Journal Officiel du Conseil Economique et Social (Bulletin of the Economic and Social Council)*, no. 20. Paris, 1976.

CME. *See* Conference of European Ministers of Education.

CNEL. *See* Consiglio Nazionale dell' Economia e del Lavoro.

Commission sur l'Avenir de la Formation (Commission on the Future of Vocational Education). *L'Avenir de la Formation (The Future of Vocational Education)*. Rapport de la Commission instituée par le Secrétaire d'Etat auprès du Premier Ministre chargé de la Formation Professionnelle (Report of the Commission established by the Secretary of State for Vocational Training in the Office of the Prime Minister). Paris, July 1975.

Commission of the European Communities. "For a Community Policy on Education" (Janne Report). *Bulletin of the European Communities*, Supplement 10/1973, Brussels, 1973.

Commission des Finances, de l'Economie Générale, et du Plan de l'Assemblée Nationale (Commission of Finance, General Economy, and Planning of the National Assembly). *Formation professionnelle et promotion sociale (Vocational Training and Social Advancement)*. Rapport d'information par Monsieur Ribadeau Dumas, no. 1625 (Informative report by Mr. Ribadeau Dumas, no. 1625). Assemblée Nationale, Seconde session ordinaire 1974/75 (National Assembly, Second Ordinary Session, 1974/75). Annexe au procès-verbal de la séance du 7 mai 1975 (Appendix to the Minutes of the Session of May 7, 1975). Paris: Assemblée Nationale, 1975.

Confédération Française Démocratique du Travail (CFDT) (French Democratic Labor Confederation). *Le Congé Education (Educational Leave)*. Typescript. Paris, 1974.

Confédération Française Démocratique du Travail (CFDT) (French Democratic Labor Confederation). "La formation professionnelle et l'éducation permanente" ("Vocational Training and Permanent Education"). *Formation (Training)*, numéro spécial (Special Edition), no. 96. Paris: Cahiers nos. 1–5, Sept.–Oct. 1972. (CFDT Formation 1972).

Confédération Générale du Travail (CGT) (General Confederation of Labor). *Un tremplin pour nos luttes: Les textes contractuels et légaux sur la formation professionnelle (A Platform for Our Struggle: The Contractual and Legal Texts on Vocational Training)*. Les commentaires de la CGT (Commentaries of the CGT). Paris, May 1972.

Conference of European Ministers of Education (CME). *Recurrent Education: Trends and Issues*. Analytical report presented by the Secretariat of the Council of Europe. CME/IX, 3 (75). Strasbourg, 1975a.

Conference of European Ministers of Education (CME). *Permanent Education, A Framework for Recurrent Education: Theory and Practice*. Analytical report presented by the Secretariat of the Council of Europe. CME/IX, 4 (75). Strasbourg, 1975b.

Consiglio Nazionale dell' Economia e del Lavoro (National Economic and Labor Council). *Rapporto sulla situazione sociale del paese (Report on the Social Condition of the Country)*. Rome, 1968.

Council of Europe. *Educational Leave: A Key Factor of Permanent Education and Social Advancement*. Strasbourg: Council for Cultural Cooperation, 1969.

Council of Europe. *Permanent Education*. Strasbourg: Council for Cultural Cooperation, 1970.

CRISP. *See* Centre de Recherche et d'Information socio-politiques.

Department of Education and Science (U.K.). *Adult Education: A Plan for Develop-ment.* Russell Committee Report. London: Her Majesty's Stationery Office, 1973.

Department of Employment (U.K.). *Industrial Relations: Code of Practice.* London: Her Majesty's Stationery Office, 1972.

Deutsche Presse Agentur (German Press Agency). *dpa Hintergrund, Bildungsurlaub: Chancengleichheit für Arbeitnehmer (DPA Background Report, Educational Leave: Equality of Opportunity for Employees).* Typescript. Hamburg: dpa Archiv, 1974.

Deutscher Bildungsrat (German Education Council). *Strukturplan für das Bildungs-wesen: Empfehlungen der Bildungskommission (Fundamental Plan for the Educational System: Recommendations of the Education Commission).* Stuttgart: Ernst Klett Verlag, 1970.

Deutscher Bildungsrat (German Education Council). *Bildungsurlaub als Teil der Weiterbildung: Gutachten und Studien der Bildungskommission (Educational Leave as an Element of Continuing Education: Briefs and Studies of the Education Commission),* no. 28. Stuttgart: Ernst Klett Verlag, 1973.

Deutscher Bundestag (German Federal Parliament). *Bericht der Bundesregierung nach Paragraph 239 des Arbeitsförderungsgesetzes (Arbeitsförderungsbericht) (Report of the Federal Government in Accordance with Section 239 of the Labor Promotion Act (Labor Promotion Report)).* Drucksache 7/403 (Document 7/403). Bonn: Verlag Dr. H. Heger, 1973.

Deutscher Bundestag (German Federal Parliament). *Kosten und Finanzierung der ausserschulischen beruflichen Bildung (Abschlussbericht) (Cost and Financing of Non-institutional Vocational Training (Final Report)).* Drucksache 7/1811 (Document 7/1811). Bonn: Verlag Dr. H. Heger, 1974.

Deutscher Volkshochschulverband (German Association of Folk High Schools). *Statistische Mitteilungen: Arbeitsjahr 1973 (Statistical Surveys: Academic Year 1973).* Frankfurt: Pädagogische Arbeitsstelle des DVV (Pedagogic Working Unit of the German Assoociation of Folk High Schools), 1974.

Di Gioia, A., and Pontacolone, C. "La scuola CGIL di Ariccia negli anni '60" ("The CGIL School of Ariccia in the Sixties"). *Rassegna Sindacale (Union Review). Quad-erni* (Revista della CGIL) (*Notebooks* (Journal of the CGIL)), July–Aug. 1972 (37), pp. 95–113.

Document Annexe (Appended Document). "Formation Professionnelle et Pro-motion Sociale" ("Vocational Training and Social Advancement"). In *Projet de Loi de Finances pour 1975 (Budget Proposal for 1975).* Paris: Imprimere Nationale (Government Printing Office), 1974.

Dore, L. *Fabbrica e scuola: Le 150 ore (Factory and School: The 150 Hours).* Collana di attualità sindacale (Collection of Union News). Rome: Edizione Sindacale Ital-iana (Italian New Union Editions), 1975.

EBAE. *See* European Bureau of Adult Education.

Economist, 256 (6891), pp. 46–51.

Education Statistics for the United Kingdom 1972. London: Her Majesty's Stationery Office, 1974.

Eliasson, T., and Höglund, B. *Vuxenutbildning i Sverige (Adult Education in Sweden).* En strukturell översikt. Rapport från pedagogiska institutionen vid lärarhög-skolan i Stockholm, no. 54 (A Structural Survey. Report of the Institute of Ped-agogy at the Teachers College in Stockholm, no. 54). Stockholm: Utbildnings-departementet (Ministry of Education), 1971.

European Bureau of Adult Education (EBAE). *Adult Education Legislation in 10 Coun-tries of Europe.* Amersfoort: European Bureau of Adult Education, 1975.

Eurostat. *Statistiques de Base de la Communauté 1973/74 (Basic Statistics of the European Economic Community 1973/74)*. Luxembourg: Statistical Office of the European Communities, 1974.

Fadiga Zanatta, A. L. *Il sistema scolastico Italiano: Studi e ricerche dell'Istituto "Carlo Cattaneo,"* no. 2 (*The Italian School System: Studies and Analyses of the Carlo Cattaneo Institute*, no. 2). Bologna: Il Mulino, 1972.

Federazione Lavoratori Metalmeccanici (FLM) (Metalworkers Labor Federation). "I Metalmeccanici e il diritto allo studio" ("The Metalworkers and the Right to Education"). *FLM Notizie (FLM Notes)*, Jan. 8, 1975 (76), pp. 3–72.

Federazione Regionale CGIL-CISL-UIL, Lombardia (Regional Federation of Unions CGIL-CISL-UIL, Lombardia). *Introduzione al convegno regionale 150 ore (Introduction to the Regional Convention on the 150 Hours)*. Typescript. Milan, June 23, 1975.

FLM. *See* Federazione Lavoratori Metalmeccanici (Metalworkers Labor Federation).

Fondazione Giovanni Agnelli (Giovanni Agnelli Foundation). *La Formazione professionale in Italia*. Ricerca condotta dal Censis (*Vocational Training in Italy*. Research Conducted by Censis). 2 vols. Bologna: Il Mulino, 1972.

Freyberg, T. v., Jaerisch, U., Kirchlechner, B., and Kramer, H. *Bildungsurlaub: Bericht über ein Experimentalprogramm (Educational Leave: Report on an Experimental Program)*. Typescript. Frankfurt am Main: Institut für Sozialforschung an der Johann Wolfgang Goethe-Universität (Institute for Social Research of the Johann Wolfgang Goethe University), 1975.

Giori, D., and Pepe, G. R. "150 ore per una cultura di classe" ("150 Hours for a Class Culture"). *Classe (Class)*, Nov. 1974 (9), pp. 67–120.

Giugni, G. "L'aggiornamento degli insegnanti in Italia" ("Continuing Education for Teachers in Italy"). *Quaderni della Regione Lombardia: Istruzione, Studi e Documenti*, no. 23 (*Notebooks of the Lombardy Region: Instruction, Studies, and Documents*, no. 23), Milan, Apr. 1974.

Görs, D. "Bildungsurlaub als Teilelement der Bildungsreform" ("Educational Leave as an Element of Educational Reform"). *Gewerkschaftliche Bildungspolitik (Unionist Educational Policy)*, 1974 (7/8).

Gurrieri, G. *Tornare a scuola da protagonisti: L'esperienza delle 150 ore (Return to the School of the Activists: The Experience of the 150 Hours)*. Politica Culturale, no. 5 (Cultural Policy, no. 5). Collana della Regione Toscana (Papers of the Toscana Region). Dipartimento Istruzione e Cultura (Department of Instruction and Culture). Florence: Guaraldi, 1975.

Hein, R. "Zum Stand der Auseinandersetzungen um den Bildungsurlaub in Frankreich" ("On the Present State of Discussion about Educational Leave in France"). In Marburger Forschungsstelle für vergleichende Erziehungswissenschaft (Ed). (Marburg Research Unit for Comparative Educational Science (Ed.)), *Texte, Dokumente, Berichte, zum Bildungswesen ausgewählter Industriestaaten*, no. 1 (*Texts, Documents, and Reports on the Educational Systems of Selected Industrial Nations*, no. 1). Weiterbildung-Bildungsurlaub (Continuing Education-Educational Leave). Zur Diskussion in Frankreich und Schweden (On the Discussion in France and Sweden). Marburg, 1973, pp. 5 ff.

Hordern, F. *Histoire de la formation professionnelle en France (History of Vocational Training in France)*. Aix-en-Provence-Université d'Aix-Marseille II. UER-ITRES. Institut Régional du Travail (Regional Institute of Labor), 1973.

Illich, I., and Verne, I. "Le piège de l'école à vie" ("The Trap of Lifetime Schooling"). *Le Monde de l'Education (The World of Education)*, January 1975 (1), pp. 11–14.

ILO. *See* International Labor Organization.

Intergroupe Formation, Commissariat Général au Plan (Vocational Training Coordinating Group, General Commissioner of the Plan). *Préparation du VIème Plan (1971–1975) (Preparation of the Sixth Plan (1971–1975))*. Rapport de l'Intergroupe "Formation, Qualifications Professionnelles" (Report of the Coordinating Group on Vocational Training and Qualifications). Paris, 1971.

International Labor Organization. *Paid Educational Leave.* International Labor Conference, 58th Session, Report VI (1). Geneva, 1972.

International Labor Organization. *Paid Educational Leave.* International Labor Conference, 58th Session, Report VI (2). Geneva, 1973.

International Labor Organization. *Paid Educational Leave.* International Labor Conference, 59th Session, Report IV (1). Geneva, 1973a.

International Labor Organization. *Paid Educational Leave.* International Labor Conference, 59th Session. Report IV (2). Geneva, 1974.

International Labor Organization. *International Labor Conference, Provisional Record,* 59th Session, 17, 17A, 17B, 32. Geneva, 1974a.

ISTAT. *See* Istituto centrale di statistica.

Istituto centrale di statistica (Central Institute for Statistics). "Distribuzione per età degli alumpi delle scuole elementari e media nell'anno scolastico 1966/67" ("Distribution by age of graduates of elementary schools in 1966/67"). In *Note e Relazioni (Notes and Reports)* 38, November 1968.

Jäschke, R. *Die Berufsförderung der Bundeswehr im Rahmen der Soldatenversorgung— Organisation, Aufgaben, Probleme (Vocational Advancement in the Armed Forces in the Framework of Support Services—Organization, Functions, Problems).* (Magisterzwischenprüfungsarbeit). Unpublished master's thesis. Aachen: Institut für Erziehungswissenschaft (Institute for Educational Science), 1975.

Johannson, B. *Government-Subsidized Adult Education in Sweden.* Stockholm: The Swedish Institute, 1973.

Johannson, R. *Studiecircel 1970: Social bakgrund, begåvning, personlighet (Study Circles, 1970: Social Background, Behavior, Personality).* Uppsala: Uppsala Universitet, Institutionen för pedagogik, 1973.

Kallen, D. *Holländisches Fallbeispiel: Heimvolkschochschule in den Niederlanden (Dutch Case Study: Residential Folk High School in the Netherlands).* Typescript. Herzberg ob Aarau: Swiss Coordination Center for Research in Education, 1974.

Kern, H., and Schumann, M. *Industriearbeit und Arbeiterbewusstsein (Industrial Work and Worker Consciousness).* Frankfurt am Main: Europäische Verlagsanstalt, 1970.

Kornadt, H.-J. *Lehrziele, Schulleistung, und Leistungsbeurteilung (Teaching Objectives, School Achievement, and Performance Assessment).* Düsseldorf: Pädagogischer Verlag Schwann, 1974.

Landsorganisasjonen i Norge (LO) (Main Norwegian Labor Union). *Basic Agreement of 1974 (Hovedavtalen).* Oslo, 1974.

Lington, H. *Adult Education and Training in the Netherlands: An Estimate of the Volume and Costs of All Forms of Adult Education.* Typescript prepared for the OECD. Amsterdam: Kohnstamm Institute for Educational Research, 1974.

Luttringer, J. M. *Les institutions de la formation permanente et leur rôle (The Institutions of Permanent Education and their Role).* CNIPE formathèque. Paris: Armand Colin, 1974.

Luttringer, J. M. "La difficile naissance du droit au congé de formation" ("The Difficult Birth of the Right to Educational Leave"). *Droit social (Social Law),* Jan. 1975, pp. 33–39.

Marten. H. R. *Synopse: Gesetze und Gesetzesentwürfe zur Erwachsenenbildung/Weiter-*

bildung (*Synopsis of Laws and Bills Concerning Continuing Education*). Hanover: Evangelische Erwachsenenbildung (Protestant Adult Education Organization), 1974.

Meister, J. J. *Erwachsenenbildung in Bayern* (*Adult Education in Bavaria*). Stuttgart: Ernst Klett Verlag, 1971.

Ministerie van Onderwijs en Wetenschappen (Netherlands) (Ministry of Education and Science). *Contouren van een toekomstig onderwijsbestel: Discussienota* (*Outline of a Future Educational System: Discussion Notes*). Tweede Kamer der Staten-General, Zitting 1974–75, 13459, nos. 1–2. (Second Chamber of the Dutch Parliament, 1974–75 Session, 13459, nos. 1–2.) The Hague: Staatsuitgeverij (Government Printing Office), 1975.

Ministero della Pubblica Istruzione (Italia), Direzione Generale dell'Istruzione Secondaria di primo grado (Ministry of Public Education (Italy), Director General for Lower Secondary Education). *Corsi sperimentali di scuola media per lavoratori* (*Experimental Courses of the Middle School for Workers*). Vols. 2–4. Rome, Apr. 1974.

Ministero della Pubblica Istruzione (Italia), Direzione Generale dell'Educazione Popolare (Ministry of Public Education (Italy), Director General for Popular Adult Education). *Educazione degli adulti: Repertorio delle Istituzioni operanti in Italia* (*Adult Education: Catalogue of Institutions Operating in Italy*). Rome: Istituto Poligrafico dello Stato (Government Printing Office), 1975.

Moniteur Belge (Bulletin of the Belgian Government). Brussels.

N. N. "I.L.O.-Conferentie voor betaald studieverlof" ("ILO Conference on Paid Educational Leave"). *De Werkgever* (*The Employer*), Aug. 1, 1974 (15).

Nordisk Utredningsserie (NU) (Nordic Series of Public Surveys). "Voksenopplaering i de nordiske land: En kartlegging" ("Adult Education in the Nordic Countries: A Survey"). *Nordisk Utredningsserie 1974:10* (*Nordic Series of Public Surveys*). Ed. by Secretariat for Nordic Cultural Cooperation of the Nordic Council. NU. 1974:10. See Nordisk Utredningsserie.

Nytt om högskolan (*News of Higher Education*). Fortbildningsmaterial om högskola, studiestöd och arbetsmarknad i serien Studieval und Arbetsmarknad (Further Education Materials on Higher Education, Study Support, and the Labor Market, in the series. Choice of Studies and Labor Market). Ed. by UKÄ, SÖ, CSN, AMS (Swedish Administrations). Stockholm: Umeå, 1975.

OECD. See Organization for Economic Cooperation and Development.

Organization for Economic Cooperation and Development (OECD). *Interdisciplinarity: Problems and Research in Universities*. Paris, 1972.

Organization for Economic Cooperation and Development. *The Measurement of Scientific and Technical Activities*. (Frascati Manual.) (rev. ed.) Paris, 1972a.

Organization for Economic Cooperation and Development. *Recurrent Education: A Strategy for Lifelong Learning*. Paris, 1973.

Organization for Economic Cooperation and Development. *Toward Mass Higher Education*, Paris, 1974a.

Organization for Economic Cooperation and Development. *Toward Mass Higher Education: Issues and Dilemmas*. Paris, 1974b.

Organization for Economic Cooperation and Development. *The Developments and Implications of Educational Leave of Absence*. Doc. C.E.R.I./R.E./75 (01). Paris, 1975.

Organization for Economic Cooperation and Development. *Reviews of National Policies for Education. Austria.* Paris, 1969. *Germany.* Paris, 1972. *Austria.* Paris, 1975a. *Norway.* Paris, 1975b.

Österreichischer Gewerkschaftsbund (ÖGB) (Austrian Federation of Trade Unions).

Schulung, Kultur und Weiterbildung (Schooling, Culture, and Continuing Education). Vienna: Österreichischer Gewerkschaftsbund, 1975.

Pepe, G. R. La scuola delle 150 ore: Esperienze, documenti e verifiche (The School of the 150 Hours: Experiences, Documents, and Testimony). Milan: Franco Angeli, 1975.

Piskaty, G., and Jedina-Palombini, A. Betriebliche Bildungsarbeit in Österreich (Educational Activities of Austrian Enterprises). Ein Beitrag zu Fragen der Erwachsenenbildung (A Contribution to Questions of Adult Education). Ed. by the Wirtschaftsförderungsinstitut der Bundeskammer der Gewerblichen Wirtschaft (Federal Chamber for Nonmanufacturing Industry). Vienna: Sparkassenverlag 1975.

Prop. 23:75. Regeringens proposition no. 23 ar 1975 om vidgat vuxenutbildning samt studiestöd till vuxna m.m. Feb. 27, 1975. (Swedish Government Proposition No. 23 (February 27, 1975) on Widened Adult Education Including Study Support for Adults). Riksdagen (Swedish Parliament) 1975. 1 saml. no. 23 (Collection of Documents no. 23), Stockholm, 1975.

Regione Lombardia, Assessorato all' Istruzione (Region of Lombardy, Division of Education). "Progetto di piano regionale dei corsi di formazione professionale per l'anno 1972–73" ("Project of a Regional Plan for Vocational Training Courses for the 1972–73 Year"). Quaderni della Regione Lombardia: Istruzione, Studi e Documenti, no. 11 (Notebooks of the Lombardy Region: Instructions, Studies, and Documents, no. 11). Milan, Mar. 1973, pp. 52–93.

Regione Lombardia, Assessorato allo Studio (Region of Lombardy, Division of Studies). Aggiornamento degli insegnanti (The Further Training of Teachers). 2 vols. Istruzione, Studi e Documenti, nos. 23–24 (Instructions, Studies, and Documents, nos. 23–24). Milan, Assessorato Istruzione (Division of Education), 1973a.

Regione Lombardia, Assessorato all'Istruzione (Region of Lombardy, Division of Instruction). "La formazione professionale in Lombardia: Rapporto sul primo anno di gestione regionale" ("Vocational Training in Lombardy: Report on the First Year Under Regional Authority"). Quaderni della Regione Lombardia: Istruzione, Studi e Documenti, no. 20 (Notebooks of the Lombardy Region: Instructions, Studies, and Documents, no. 20). Milan, Feb. 1974, pp. 7–59.

Regione Lombardia, Assessorato all'Istruzione (Region of Lombardy, Division of Education). "Piano dei corsi di formazione professionale per l'anno 1973–74" ("Plan for Vocational Training Courses for the 1973–74 Year"). Quaderni della Regione Lombardia. Istruzione, Studi e Documenti, no. 25. (Notebooks of the Lombardy Region. Instructions, Studies, and Documents, no. 25). Milan, Sept. 1974a, pp. 65-228.

Regione Lombardia, Assessorato all'Istruzione (Region of Lombardy, Division of Education). Le 150 ore: Prima valutazione sui corsi organizzati dalla regione Lombardia (The 150 Hours: First Evaluation of Courses Organized by the Lombardy Region). Documenti di Lavoro, no. 2 (Documents of Work, no. 2). Milan, Regione Lombardia, 1975.

Renaix, J. P. La promotion sociale. Vol. 1: Le Bilan: les lois de 1959 (Social Advancement. Vol. 1: A Balance: The Laws of 1959). Paris: Peuple et Culture, 1967.

Renaix, J. P. Education populaire et promotion sociale. Vol. 2: Le Bilan de la loi de 1966 (Popular Education and Social Advancement. Vol. 2: A Balance of the Law of 1966). Paris: Peuple et Culture, 1968.

Ribadeau Dumas. See Commission des Finances.

Rosenstock-Huessy, E. "Andragogik" ("Andragogy"). Archiv für Erwachsenenbildung (Archives of Adult Education), 1925 (1), pp. 248–276.

Rosenstock-Huessy, E. "Teaching Too Late, Learning Too Early." In I Am an Im-

pure Thinker. Norwich: Argo, 1970, pp. 91–114.

Sasse, J., Segenberger, W., and Weltz, F. *Weiterbildung und betriebliche Arbeitskräfte-politik: Eine industriesoziologische Analyse (Further Education and Manpower Policies of the Enterprise: A Sociological Analysis of Industrial Relations).* Arbeiten des Instituts für Sozialwissenschaftliche Forschung, München (Studies of the Institute for Social Science Research, Munich). Cologne, Frankfurt am Main: Europäische Verlagsanstalt, 1974.

SCB. *See* Statistiska Centralbyrån (Sweden).

Schop, J. J. *Educational Leave in the Netherlands: An Inventory of Views and Provisions.* Typescript prepared for the OECD, 1974.

Schwartz, B. *Permanent Education.* Plan Europe 2000. Project no. 1, vol. 8. The Hague: Martinus Nijhoff, 1974.

Scuola di Barbiana (School of Barbiana). *Lettera a una professoressa (Letters to a Lady Professor).* Florence: Libreria editrice fiorentina, n.d.

SFS. *See* Svensk författningssamling.

Siebert, H. (Ed.) *Bildungsurlaub: Eine Zwischenbilanz (Educational Leave: A Provisional Record).* Düsseldorf: Bertelsmann Universitätsverlag, 1972.

Simpson, J. A. *Today and Tomorrow in European Adult Education: A Study of the Present Situation and Future Developments.* Strasbourg: Council of Europe, 1972.

SÖ *National Board of Education* (Sweden). Internal mimeographed report on recent results of study circle activities. SÖ Dnr V 75: 6 474. Stockholm: National Board of Education, 1975 (SÖ, 1975).

SOU. *See* Statens Offentliga Utredningar (Swedish Government Social Surveys).

State Adult Education Council (Norway). *Structure and Organization of Adult Education in Norway.* Oslo: Universitetsforlaget, 1972.

Statens Offentliga Utredningar: SOU 1974:29. Arbetsmarknadsdepartementet (Swedish Government Social Surveys: SOU 1974:29. Ministry of the Labor Market). *Att utvärdera arbetsmarknadspolitik (Assessing Labor Market Policy).* Betänkande avgivet av Expertgruppen för utredningsverksamhet i arbetsmarknadsfrågor (Report of the Expert Group for the Investigation of Labor Market Problems). Stockholm: EFA report, 1974.

Statens Offentliga Utredningar: SOU 1974:54. Utbildningsdepartementet (Swedish Government Social Surveys: SOU 1974:54. Ministry of Education). *Vidgad vuxenutbildning (Widened Adult Education).* Uppsökande verksamhet och studiecirklar, Erfarenheter och förslag (Outreach Activity and Study Circles, Experiences and Proposals). Huvudbetänkande av kommittén för försöksverksamhet med vuxenutbildning (Final Report of the Committee for Experimental Programs in Adult Education). Stockholm: FÖVUX report 1974. (Summary in English available.)

Statens Offentliga Utredningar: SOU 1974:62. Utbildningsdepartementet (Swedish Government Social Surveys: SOU 1974:62. Ministry of Education). *Studiestöd åt vuxna (Study Support for Adults).* Betänkande av kommittén för studiestöd åt vuxna (Report of the Committee for Study Support for Adults). Stockholm: SVUX report, 1974.

Statens Offentliga Utredningar: SOU 1974:79. Arbetsmarknadsdepartementet (Swedish Government Social Surveys: SOU 1974:79. Ministry of the Labor Market). *Utbildning för arbete (Training for Work).* Betänkande av kommittén för översyn av arbetsmarknadsutbildningen (Report of the Committee for the Examination of Labor Market Training). Stockholm: KAMU Report, 1974.

Statistiska Centralbryån (SCB) (Central Statistical Office, Sweden). "Kommunal Vuxenutbildning samt deltidskurser inom företagsskolor och enskilda yrkesskolor" ("Municipal Adult Education, Including Part-Time Courses of Inservice Training and Private Vocational Schools)". *Statistika Meddelanden (Statistical Reports)*. SCB Nr. U 1974:42. Stockholm: SCB, 1974.

Statistiska Centralbryån (SCB) (Central Statistical Office, Sweden). "Statlig Vuxenutbildning" ("The State Schools for Adult Education: Students, Participants and Achieved Qualifications in the Spring Semester 1974"). *Statistiska Meddelanden (Statistical Reports)*. SCB Nr. U 1974:54. Stockholm: SCB, 1974.

Stein-Ruegenberg, L. "Urlaub für Bildung: Ein wenig genutztes Privileg des öffentlichen Dienstes" ("Leave of Absence for Education: A Rarely Used Privilege of the Civil Service"). *Deutsche Zeitung (German Journal)*, July 18, 1975.

Stiftung zur Förderung von Bildung und Erholung der Arbeitnehmer der Miederindustrie (Foundation for the Promotion of Education and Recreation of Employees of the Corset Industry). *Grundsätze, Informationen, Ausblicke (Principles, Information, Prospects)*. Düsseldorf: Stiftung Miederindustrie, 1974 (2).

Svensk författningssamling (SFS) (Serial publications of Swedish Laws).

Trivellato, U., and Bernardi, L. *La scuola delle tute blu: Scuola, formazione professionale e mercato del lavoro (The Blue-Collar School: Vocational Training and the Labor Market)*. Ricerche economiche e sociologiche, no. 10 (Economic and Sociological Research, no. 10). Venice/Padua: Marsilio, 1974.

Trivellato, U. *Adult Education in Italy: A Preliminary Assessment of Its Structure, Volume and Costs*. Paris: OECD, 1975.

United Nations Educational, Scientific and Cultural Organization (UNESCO). *International Standard Classification of Education (ISCED): Three Stage Classification System*. Paris: UNESCO, 1972.

Urbach, D., and Winterhager, W. D. *Bildungsurlaub: Gesetze, Pläne, Kontroversen (Educational Leave: Laws, Projects, Controversies)*. Berlin: Walter de Gruyter, 1975.

Vaudiaux, J. *La formation permanente, enjeu politique (Permanent Education, A Political Issue)*. Paris: Armand Colin, 1974.

Vinzier, L. "L'expérience Lip" ("The Experience of Lip"). *Esprit*, 1974, (10), pp. 470–480.

Weizsäcker, C. V. "Die permanente Berufsausbildung in der heutigen Gesellschaft" ("Permanent Vocational Training in Contemporary Society"). *Universitas*, 1968, (12), pp. 1249 ff.

Weber, H. "Zur Anhebung des Qualifikationsniveaus in Italien: Vorschläge und Massnahmen" ("On the Improvement of the Qualification Level in Italy: Proposals and Measures"). In Marburger Forschungsstelle für vergleichende Erziehungswissenschaft (Ed.) (In Marburg Research Unit for Comparative Educational Science (Ed.)), *Texte, Dokumente, Berichte zum Bildungswesen ausgewählter Industriestaaten*, no. 6. (*Texts, Documents, and Reports on the Educational Systems of Selected Industrialized Nations*, no. 6.). Marburg, 1974, pp. 56–73.

Wema Institut KG. *Strukturanalyse der beruflichen Erwachsenenbildung (Structural Analysis of Vocational Education)*. Typescript. Cologne, 1974.

Wirtschafts-und Sozialwissenschaftliches Institut des Deutschen Gewerkschaftsbundes (DGB) (Economic and Social Science Research Institute of the German Federation of Trade Unions). *Tarifvertragliche Vereinbarungen über Bildungsurlaub (Educational Leave in Labor Contracts)*. Gesamtübersicht, Stand 31. 12. 73 (General Survey as of December 12, 1973). Typescript. Düsseldorf: DGB, 1974.

WSI. *See* Wirtschafts-und Sozialwissenschaftliches Institut des Deutschen Gewerkschaftsbundes (DGB).

Zekorn, K. "Der Bildungsurlaub" ("Educational Leave"). *Bundesarbeitsblatt (Federal Labor Journal)*, 1967, p. 201.

Index

V

VHS (folk high schools, Germany), 108–109

Vocational Support Service, 106

Vocational training: centers for, 44; as crisis management, 44; decided against by Italian trade unions, 20; financed under Law of 1971, 59; in Italy generally, 163–166; in Norway, 206–208; status of, relative to general education, 5, 21, 22, 57; "stepchild" of French educational system, 37; supported by outside study, 193–194

Vocational Training and Social Advancement Fund, 45–46, 63, 65

Vocational Training Law of 1966, 47, 49, 50

Voluntary adult education organizations: Dutch, 201–204; German, 92–93; Norwegian, 208–209

W

Women: in conversion and prevention programs, 69; in FPC, 79; French unemployment measures intended to favor, 61; subject of outreach in Sweden, 147

Work conditions: as permitting only limited increase of technological knowledge, 31; as starting point for educational leave policy formulation, 22, 185, 216–220, 240, 248–249

Workers' Educational Association (ABF), 122, 123, 125, 146, 148, 156

Workers' Educational Association (UK), 211, 213

Working-class culture, 181–182

Working group, as research design, 1

Working Life and Training (ALU), 139

Work councils, 59, 83, 100, 114, 180, 181, 204, 227